MARINERS,

RENEGADES &

CASTAWAYS

REENCOUNTERS WITH COLONIALISM:
NEW PERSPECTIVES ON THE AMERICAS

Dartmouth College Series Editors
Marysa Navarro
Donald E. Pease
Ivy Schweitzer
Silvia Spitta

For the complete list of books that are available in this series,
please see www.upne.com

———————

MARINERS,
RENEGADES &
CASTAWAYS

*The Story of Herman Melville
and the World We Live In*

C. L. R. James

THE COMPLETE TEXT

WITH AN INTRODUCTION BY DONALD E. PEASE

Dartmouth College Press
Hanover, New Hampshire

PUBLISHED BY UNIVERSITY PRESS OF NEW ENGLAND
HANOVER AND LONDON

DARTMOUTH COLLEGE PRESS
Published by University Press of New England,
One Court Street, Lebanon, NH 03766
www.upne.com

© 1953, 1978 by C.L.R. James
Introduction © 2001 by Donald E. Pease
Originally published by C.L.R. James, New York, 1953.
Second, revised edition by Bewick, Detroit, 1978.
Allison and Busby, London and New York, 1985.

Printed in the United States of America 5 4
ISBN-13: 978-1-58465-094-2

LIBRARY OF CONGRESS CATALOGING-IN-PUBLICATION DATA

James, C. L. R. (Cyril Lionel Robert), 1901–
  Mariners, renegades, and castaways : the story of Herman Melville and the world we live in / C.L.R. James, the complete text ; with an introduction by Donald E. Pease.
    p. cm. — (Reencounters with colonialism—new perspectives on the Americas)
  "Originally published by C. L. R. James, New York, 1953."
  Includes bibliographical references and index.
  ISBN 1-58465-093-1 (alk. paper) — ISBN 1-58465-094-X (pbk. : alk. paper)
    1. Melville, Herman, 1819-1891—Political and social views.
  2. Literature and society—United States—History—19th century.
  3. Melville, Herman, 1819-1891. Moby Dick. 4. Alienation (Social psychology) in literature. 5. Social problems in literature.
  6. Working class in literature. I. Title. II. Series.
    PS2388.P6 J36 2001
    813'.3—dc21   2001001237

CONTENTS

C. L. R. JAMES'S *Mariners, Renegades and Castaways*

AND THE WORLD WE LIVE IN

Donald E. Pease

"So I sat down and wrote the book on Melville, and it was published just-about '52. And today everybody accepts it as one of the books on Melville that matter. But Publishers don't publish it."[1]

C.L.R. JAMES was born into a lower-middle-class family in Tunupuna, Trinidad, in 1901 and was educated at Queen's Royal College, the British colonial university. After graduation, he published short fiction in the literary journal *Trinidad*, which he helped to found, wrote biographical studies of local political leaders in the West Indies, and reported on cricket for the *Port of Spain Gazette*. When James's literary ambitions aroused the desire to travel to England so that his writings might reach a wider audience, it was his knowledge of cricket that provided him with the visa and the funds he required to make the trip.

James travelled to Great Britain with the Trinidadian cricket star Learie Constantine in 1932. During his six-year stay in England, he worked as the cricket correspondent for the *Manchester Guardian* and formed lifelong friendships with George Padmore, Harold Moody, Paul Robeson, and other black intellectuals in the Pan-African movement. The members of this circle were like James in that each had became increasingly persuaded as to the pertinence of the Marxist dialectic to their common struggle to overthrow colonial domination. James adopted Marxian categories and modes of analysis in *The Black Jacobins: Toussaint L'Ouverture and the San Domingo Revolution*, his magisterial analysis of the role Toussaint L'Ouverture played in the San Domingo uprising of 1791. The publication of this book in 1936 marked a turning point in James's career.

James entered metropolitan London as a colonial immigrant. *The Black Jacobins* established for him a reputation as one of the principal intellectuals in the metropole that he entered. He wrote *The Black Jacobins* as part of an effort to close the cultural and political gap between Caribbean black history and European history. The book examined the French Revolution, whose history had formerly been monopolized by the metropolitan historians, from the perspective of the resistance led by former slaves. It thereby promoted the belief James's experiences in Trinidad had fostered, namely that the African people in the western hemisphere had been at the center of its most important social and political transformations.

In England, James became immersed in political activities surrounding the Trotskyist movement. But James's project would remain rooted within the Marxist philosophy only so long as the imperatives of that philosophy did not throw up roadblocks to his commitments throughout the world. His writing, as Edward Said has remarked, "was an adjunct to his engagement with and commitment to African and West Indian political struggle, a commitment that took him to England, to the United States, to Africa (where his lifelong friendship with George Padmore and a mature association with Nkrumah were crucial to the formation of politics in Ghana, as is clear from his highly critical study *Nkrumah and the Ghana Revolution*), then to the West Indies again, and finally to England."[2] These involvements led him to doubt the contentions of the vanguard party that world revolution would originate in the metropolitan countries of Europe rather than in the underdeveloped peripheries.

The works he wrote to establish his credentials in Marxist circles included his 1937 publication of the first history of the Trotskyist movement, *World Revolution 1917–1936: The Rise and Fall of the Communist International.* The *History of the Negro Revolt,* an historical account of the pan-African movement, which James published that same year, was designed to protect that movement from the Stalinism of Moscow and its British counterpart, the Communist Party. In 1938, James travelled to the United States at the behest of Leon Trotsky, who had become the focus of his opposition to Stalinism. Trotsky had challenged James to turn his historical understanding into the basis for organizing black workers.

Upon arriving in the United States in 1938, James admonished Trotsky for his failure to criticize the Soviet Union's bureaucratization of the workers' state. Under the pseudonym J. R. Johnson, James, along with Trotsky's former secretary Raya Dunayevskaya (a.k.a. Freddie Forest) and the Chinese American Grace Lee Boggs (a.k.a. R. Stone), formed what they called the Forest-Johnson tendency. While the group was small in size, the Johnsonites' ambitions were global in scale, calling for the mobilization of the proletariat against a world system administered through state structures.

The Johnsonites characterized all efforts to centralize the labor force as forms of state capitalism, for which they would substitute the modes of organization that workers spontaneously invented. James in particular was convinced that the collective's primary role was not to direct the workers' struggles, as a vanguard party would, but to provide workers with the means to deploy the creativity that was already evident in their work. As a consequence of these beliefs, the members of the Johnson-Forest tendency differentiated themselves from the two extant Trotskyist organizations—the Socialist Workers' Party and the Workers' Party—with the formulation of the following three doctrines: the rejection of the Soviet Union's bureaucracy as a form of state capitalism, the rejection of the vanguard party, and the insistence on the relative autonomy of spontaneous social movements.

In the books that he published with the Johnson-Forest group— *The Invading Socialist Society* and *State Capitalism and World Revolution*— C. L. R. James had articulated his opposition to state capitalism. He distinguished capitalist formations in the United States from what he called the state capitalism of the Soviet Union in that the former operated as a contradictory bloc of rival structures while the latter was under the unitary control of the USSR's bureaucratic apparatus. But no matter whether it was under the unitary control of the USSR's bureaucratic structures or extended across separate competitive parts, the exploitation of workers remained the invariant feature in both forms of state capitalism.

When he began writing *American Civilization: The Struggle for Happiness* in 1950, James consolidated his Trotskyite and Johnsonite beliefs to an array of new concerns. The book reiterated James's promotion of the importance of collective action and his rejection of political elitism. But it also advanced the argument that various sectors—the family, the political community, the civil sphere—of American civilization were in crisis along a racial division that could only be resolved through the development of a mass revolutionary movement that would reorganize American culture on an egalitarian and participatory basis.

In the fourteen-year interim between entering the United States in 1938 and his deportation in 1953, James wrote on the movies, pulp fiction, television soap operas, black Marxism, the history of American civilization, and the novels of Herman Melville. Sylvia Wynter has spelled out the many polarities implicit in this brief account of James's life with the following succinct itinerary:

> James was a Negro yet British, a colonial native yet culturally a part of the public school code, attached to the cause of the proletariat yet a member of the middle class, a Marxian yet a Puritan, an intellectual who plays cricket, of African descent yet Western, a Trotskyist and Pan-Africanist, a Marxist yet a supporter of black studies, a West-Indian majority black yet an American minority black.[3]

While the pluralized dimensions of C. L. R. James's career received little notice while James was alive, they have become the subject of growing scholarly interest. During his lifetime, most of James's books were published with the help of friends who distributed them privately, and the majority of his works went out of print. But as a consequence of the spectacular renewal of interest in his work, the Jamesian corpus is gradually being restored.

Scholarly attention has not been restricted to *Beyond a Boundary* and *The Black Jacobins,* which had already been published by reputable presses, but has been extended to include the previously unpublished manuscript of *American Civilization,* brought out by Blackwell's in 1993, and the *C. L. R. James Reader,* which collected selections from *Notes on Dialectics, Facing Reality, The Future in the Present, At the Rendezvous of Victory,* and other of James's writings including his letters to Constance Webb. Over the last decade, more than three dozen volumes covering various aspects—political, literary, historical, cultural, biographical, theoretical—of James's project have been published in the United States.

The numerous biographies, monographs, dissertations, and anthologies of essays on James that have appeared since his death in 1989 have received widespread notice from scholars in the emergent academic fields of Cultural Studies, African-American Studies, and Postcolonial Studies. Major Afro-Caribbean scholars such as Stuart

Hall, Sylvia Wynter, Derek Walcott, and Hazel Carby have singled out James's scholarship for the clarity with which he articulated what is now referred to as postcolonial criticism and favorably compared the analytic dimension of James's anticolonialist project with those of Frantz Fanon and Aimé Césaire.[4] The formation of a C. L. R. James Institute for which Jim Murray ably serves as the New York director, and the guide to the C. L. R. James archive which Murray edits, offer ample proof of the scholarly vitality of the James enterprise—as do the C. L. R. James Society and the *C. L. R. James Journal*, and the planning for what will become the C. L. R. James Collection.

The variety of genres that James mastered—short story, novel, drama, the memoir, manifesto, historical narrative, newspaper column, journal, letter, philosophical treatise—and the multiple publics to which he addressed them reveal the range and depth of James's commitments. Discrepant aspects of his intellectual estate have precipitated arguments over its proper reception that have aroused the interest of a number of potential heirs inside the academy as well as within the various political and social movements with which James was associated.

The dramatic change in the intellectual standing of James's project might be explained in part by its compatibility with a range of academic disciplines. James's various affiliations have challenged his academic and nonacademic supporters to engage multiple and often contradictory interpretive strategies in their efforts to endow his career with meaning and coherence. James's ability to participate in and thereafter to reflect upon ideological and cultural change has enabled contemporary interpreters of his work to argue the pertinence of those reflections to theories of political struggle and cultural resistance in the established disciplines of history, political science, and literature as well as in the emergent fields of postcolonial and cultural studies.

But if James has permitted his exponents to firm up the institutional authority for these emergent fields of knowledge, his work has also led to the critical interrogation of the divisions of academic knowledge. The incompatibility of James's various political involvements has also raised questions as to how the contradictory aspects of his project might be combined in a meaningful sequence.

Scholars who have attempted to conceptualize James's intellectual trajectory within the terms of the available master narratives—

Marxism, black emancipation, anticolonialism—have inevitably encountered aspects of his thinking that undermine the generalizable
patterns on which those narratives ground their explanations. As we
have seen, James made raids upon the Marxian narrative in particular
as a justificatory masterplot for his political causes. Because James also
challenged the leftist assumptions concerning the applicability of
Marxist analysis to anticolonial struggles, however, Marxism will only
incompletely illuminate the significance of James's network of interests. Indeed James's complicated means of accomplishing his at times
antagonistic political aims defy efforts to emplot them as a meaningful
sequence of events.

Perhaps because it appeals to James's contradictory political and
cultural commitments as its principle of composition, *Beyond a Boundary* has recently been significanly re-evaluated. Once considered only
as the book in which James consolidated his lifelong meditations
about the sport of cricket, *Beyond a Boundary* has undergone a redefini-
tion: More than merely a book about cricket, it is viewed as establishing the invariant space that grounds James's lifelong project. As a consequence of such wholesale redescription, *Beyond a Boundary* is now
reputed to be James's most important contribution to the discourse of
postcolonialism as well as the locus of the key metaphors and organizational schemes that inform James's other writings and can therefore
serve to adjudicate the conflicting academic claims to the Jamesian
legacy.[5]

But if *Beyond the Boundary* has enabled James's exponents to redefine
the entire Jamesian corpus, the work that has provided James's heirs
with the greatest problem of inheritance is the commentary on the
Melville canon that he wrote while interned on Ellis Island in 1952.
James entitled his study *Mariners, Renegades and Castaways: The Story of
Herman Melville and the World We Live In.* The writing practice that
James fashioned in it enabled him to turn relatively discrete questions
concerning the interpretation of Melville's novels into reflections on
much more significant matters of social change and transformation.
While this practice constituted the prototype for the mode of compo-
sition James would refine in *Beyond the Boundary, Mariners, Renegades and
Castaways* has proven recalcitrant to the postcolonial and Marxist
interpretations to which the later work has yielded more easily.

Mariners was first published privately by James's associates in the
Johnsonite movement after his deportation in 1953. Of the twenty

thousand copies published, all but two thousand were reclaimed by the publisher for nonpayment.[6] Despite its potential significance for historians of the Cold War as well as for scholars in the fields of American Studies, African-American Studies, and Postcolonial theory, however, the book has never been republished in its complete form. The account of his internment on Ellis Island that James appended as the book's last chapter has proven the greatest impediment to full republication. The version of *Mariners* that Martin Glaberman and George Rawick brought out as a Detroit Bewick edition in 1978 lacked the final chapter, and the Allison and Busby 1985 edition broke that chapter off before James made his plea that the book be taken by the reading public as proof of his competence for U.S. citizenship.

James began writing the book on June 10, 1952, after officials from the Immigration and Naturalization Services removed him to Ellis Island, where he was detained for the next six months. While awaiting appeal on the claim that this change of venue had denied him due process, James continued writing the interpretive study of Melville's literary works that he had begun in *American Civilization,* particularly of *Moby Dick,* a novel that Americanist critics had recently elevated to the rank of national classic.

In linking his experience with the I.N.S. authorities on Ellis Island to his reading of an exemplary national classic, James fashioned a writing practice that was in one of its aspects an interpretive exercise and in another a juridical appeal. He worked these discrepant facets into a personal memoir through which he came to literary terms with the ordeal he underwent there.

The interpretation of *Moby Dick* that James advanced in *Mariners, Renegades and Castaways* radically challenged the conventional understanding of Melville's work. Americanist scholars of the standing of F. O. Matthiessen and Richard Chase had elevated *Moby Dick* into the foundational fiction of the Cold War state.[7] Both Chase and Matthiessen fostered an allegorical understanding of *Moby Dick* that posited Ahab's monomania as the symbol of the totalitarian Other in opposition to which Ishmael's Americanness was defined, elaborated upon, and defended. While subsequent interpreters of the novel would introduce at times ingenious variations upon this theme, the essentialized opposition between Ishmael and Ahab would dominate readings of the novel in the field of American literary studies for the next fifty years.

James believed that Americanist interpretations of *Moby Dick* like Chase's corroborated the emergency powers of the national security state whose hegemony the field of American literary studies had indirectly legitimated. Engaging himself in the work of constructing a counter-hegemony, James confirmed the prevailing understanding of Ahab as a "totalitarian type." But after arguing that the security state had put into place the totalitarian rule it purported to oppose, he also generalized this type to include Ishmael, whom he described as "an intellectual Ahab,"[8] as well as the members of the McCarran committee and the administrators of the national security state. As justification for this extension of the applicability of the type, James cited the administrators' individual and collective failure to repeal the state's emergency powers as signs of their complicity with Ahab's totalitarian rule.

In his efforts to question the legality of the state's emergency powers, James discriminated the people the McCarran legislation presumed to represent, whom he correlated with Ahab's officers, from those who, like Ahab's crew, were its potential victims. James associated the emergency powers of the state with Ahab's transgression of his duly constituted authority and offered the following contrary proposition as the theme the book allegorized: "how the society of free individualism would give birth to totalitarianism and be unable to defend itself against it" (*Mariners*, 54).

Perhaps because the I.N.S. had cited the volume as an example of the "subversive activities" for which they were deporting James, Melville scholars said little about *Mariners, Renegades and Castaways* when it appeared in 1953, and it has continued to be absent from nearly all of the bibliographies and critical studies devoted to Melville. In the following genealogy James has underscored the relationship of the earlier work to the production of his later work: "It took more than ten years, but by 1952 I once more felt on solid ground, and in consequence, I planned a series of three books. The first was published in 1953, a critical study of Herman Melville as a mirror for our age, and the second is this book of cricket."[9]

Mariners, Renegades and Castaways employed a vernacular style of writing that selected certain elements from *Moby Dick* whose significance for American culture had already been articulated by the Americanist literary establishment. When James then recoded them as forms of emancipatory struggle, he contradicted the received

interpretation of the novel. By reinterpreting this Americanist masterwork from the standpoint of the crew, James had extended into the
largest metropolitan nation of the mid-twentieth century a practice of
social resistance that he had learned on the colonial cricket field.

In the remainder of this introduction to the book's republication, I
hope to demonstrate the importance of *Mariners, Renegades and Castaways* to the Jamesian corpus as well as to the field of American Studies. My efforts to accomplish those interrelated tasks require that we
consider the rationales for its having been refused inclusion within
those domains by two of the prominent executors of James's intellectual estate.

William Cain and Paul Buhle have been in the vanguard of the
James renaissance. They have nevertheless found related if opposed
reasons for excluding the book from the two traditions—the field of
American literature and the history of American radicalism—
wherein it should have been hospitably received. Upon analyzing the
book according to interpretive criteria developed within American literary studies, Cain placed James outside of its precincts because of
what Cain called its promotion of a world revolutionary agenda. But
in writing about James from the perspective of the American left,
Buhle found that James was involved in writing a quasi-apologia for
American capitalism.

Cain's analysis deserves careful attention because its publication
marks the first occasion in which an established Americanist critic
carefully evaluated the significance of James's *Mariners, Renegades and
Castaways: The Story of Herman Melville and the World We Live In.* Cain represented the essay he contributed to the 1995 volume *C.L.R. James: His
Intellectual Legacies*—"The Triumph of the Will and the Failure of Resistance: C. L. R. James's Readings of *Moby-Dick* and *Othello*"[10]—as in
part an effort to redress Melville scholars' history of neglect of James's
Mariners. He documented this neglect in the following footnote:

> Stanley T. Williams, in *Eight American Authors*, an important refer-
> ence book published in 1956, dismisses James's book in three
> sentences (235). Incredibly, it is nowhere cited in John Bryant's
> nine-hundred-page *Companion to Melville Studies.* Nor is it cited by
> Kerry McSweeney or Martin Bickman ("Introduction"), both
> of whom provide overviews of the novel and its place in modern
> criticism. It is also absent from all the anthologies of criticism

devoted to Melville in general and to *Moby Dick* in particular.
Richard Brodhead mentions it in passing ("Introduction" 19),
but inappropriately links it to D. H. Lawrence's chapter on Melville in *Studies in Classic American Literature* (1923) and Charles
Olson's *Call Me Ishmael* (1947). Lawrence's and Olson's commen-
taries have been widely read and have informed scholarship on
Moby Dick. Melville specialists as well as historians of American
literature and criticism, either have not known about, or have
ignored, James's work. (270–271)

Now, in the wake of such observations, Cain might have been expected to provide an account of the difference James's project would
make to the received understanding of the Melville archive. But in
place of integrating it, Cain supplied a compelling argument for the
book's exclusion. Cain's elaboration of the book's irredeemable flaws
turned on James's interpretation of the crew. According to Cain,
James had substituted a narration of the crew as a collective movement that aspired to social change in place of Melville's representation of them as wholly subordinated to Ahab's will.

Cain's dispute with James originated with a question that James
asked of Melville's novel and that Cain believed violated the novel's
aesthetic integrity: "Why, in Melville's *Moby Dick*, don't the crew members aboard the *Pequod* rebel against their diabolical captain?" (260).
Cain states that, in answering this question, James championed "the
creativity of the masses and the resolve and resourcefulness of workers." This interpretive tack resulted in James's "over-honoring the
men and dissociating them from Ahab." James has not carefully read
Melville's novel, Cain concluded, but bent it into conformity with his
own ideology, and thereafter recreated it to make it "serve his own social, political and historical purposes and affirm his goals" (270).

But in lodging the critique that James had replaced the novel Melville had written with his "reimagination" of *Moby Dick*, Cain has
failed to consider the passage in Melville's text from which James had
derived the authority for his reading:

> If, then, to meanest mariners, and renegades and castaways, I
> shall hereafter ascribe high qualities though dark; weave round
> them tragic graces; if even the most mournful, perchance the
> most abased, among them shall at times lift to the most exalted

mounts; if I shall touch that workman's arm with some ethereal
light; if I shall spread a rainbow over his disastrous set of sun;
then against all mortal critics bear me out in it, thou just Spirit
of Equality, which has spread one royal mantle of humanity
over all my kind! (Quoted in *Mariners*, 17)

Rather than continuing the narrated action, this scene represents
the site from within which the narrator construes himself as still in the
process of composing *Moby Dick*. The passage opens onto a scene that
involves the narrator in a deliberation over the means of its narration
as if this scene were locatable within the narrative proper. As the representation of a scene of writing in which the narrating "I" is still de-
liberating over how to do narrative justice to his book's actions, characters, and events, this scene intends an eventfulness that has not yet
settled into Melville's narratives. In the here and now of the moment
of narrative decision about the fate of the crew, their narrating "I" remains caught up in the process of deciding how to narrate the crew's
relation to the action. Its "If I shall" clauses constitute quasi-promises
whose primary addressee is the "Spirit of Equality." But they are sec-
ondarily addressed to the members of the crew concerning the possible outcomes of their narratives. The promises involve the narration
of the ship's mariners, castaways, and renegades' heroic deeds as the
condition of their accomplishment.

In stating that it is clear "that Melville intends to make the crew the
real heroes of his book, but he is afraid of criticism" (*Mariners*, 18);
James has not merely provided this scene with an interpretive gloss.
He has arrived at a decision as to Melville's intention and provided a
rationale—"but he is afraid of criticism"—for Melville's having failed
to realize it. The question of justice has linked the scene that James
interprets with the scene upon which he conducts his interpretation.
Melville's scene of writing includes the site upon which James interprets it as one of the possible referents for the clause "I shall hereafter
ascribe."

With the enunciation of this statement, James has split himself into
an interpreter of "the story of Herman Melville" as well as a
narrator-mariner whose story of his experiences on Ellis Island consti-
tutes one of the possible narratives that Melville intended to write. As
Melville deliberates over how to do narrative justice to the crew;
James attempts to do interpretive justice to Melville's story.

If James's *Mariners* was in one of its aspects an interpretation of *Moby Dick,* in another it was a juridical appeal of the state's decision to deport him. It is by way of his identification of his political condition with that of Ahab's crew that he advocates to the American people the crew's right to revolt in *Moby Dick.* In addressing this heroic narration that Melville was afraid to write to the American people, James intends that the American people understand the condition they share in common with the Pequod's crew. In relation to the emergency powers of the national security state, the American people enjoy no more freedom than James's fellow mariners on Ellis Island. James thereafter shifted the register of his commentary from that of interpreting a secondary theme within an Americanist masterwork to that of acting upon the social injustice he found within the state.

Upon remarking the parallel between Ahab's illegal change of the contract and the emergency powers claimed by the Cold War state, James replaced the Ishmael-Ahab opposition, which establishment Americanists had proposed as the narrative's thematic center, with the unacknowledged knowledge that the "meanest mariners, renegades and castaways" constituted alternatives to both forms of totalitarian rule. In writing as one of the persons the state has included within the category "mariners, renegades and castaways," James derives his interpretive authority from his having lived the experience of their narratives. In drawing upon this subaltern knowledge to focus his reading, James also disclosed the state's interest in its disqualification.

The temporality that James's writing might be understood to enact in the relationship he adduces between the crew's past and his own present is neither the past definite that historians deploy to keep track of completed past actions nor the present perfect, the what has been of who I now am, of the literary memoirist. It is more properly understood as the future anterior tense. The future anterior links a past event with a possible future upon which the past event depends for its significance.

The future anterior tense provided James with a mode of conjectural reading with which to challenge McCarran's usage. As we have seen, the McCarran bill proposed to have represented a public will that it produced retroactively. The action that James has employed the future anterior in order to produce "will have repealed" McCarran legislation, retroactively. In *Mariners, Renegades and Castaways: The Story of Herman Melville and the World We Live In,* James correlates a past event—the collective revolt that did not take place in the past—as dependent on a future event—the repeal of the McCarran bill—by which the crew's revolt will have accomplished it. When he links the revolt that had not taken place on the *Pequod* with the possible future repeal of the McCarran legislation, the future repeal returns to the past to transform this virtual revolt into what will have been its legal precedent.[11]

James has not "reimagined" Melville's novel, *pace* William Cain. He has instead continued the narrative Melville intended to write but "was afraid of criticism." Cain focused his criticisms of the book on James's representations of his Ellis Island experiences in the book's final chapter. Cain expressed particular concern over the fact that the reprinted edition of *Mariners, Renegades and Castaways,* from which he has drawn his quotations, still includes the "disconcerting" seventh chapter from the 1953 edition. What Cain found especially offensive about the reprinted chapter is that in it James had engaged "in forms of special pleadings, laced with warnings against Communist subversion, to which he does not stoop in his other writings" (271).

Paul Buhle, who is perhaps the most respected historian of American radical movements, has written an influential biography of James, *The Artist as Revolutionary,* in which he has built Cain's complaints about James's special pleading into the basis for the following allegation concerning the import of the "bizarre conclusion to the original edition": "In this condemnation of an individual, and defence of American society against such individuals, he [James] more nearly approached an apologia for social life under capitalism than at any other time before or since."[12]

While Buhle never explained how James might be understood to have embraced American capitalism, his accusation draws upon the following descriptions of Ellis Island Communists from the book's final chapter:

> The Department of Immigration knew my attitude to Communists. . . . The first thing that happened was that within an hour of my arrival, I was placed in a special room for political prisoners, the only occupants of which were five Communists. The reader of this book knows what I think of Communists. But this was more serious than my mere thoughts. Though I had expressed

radical ideas, and in fact was in trouble because of that, the
Communists knew me as their open and avowed enemy. I had
written or translated books against them, which had been published in England and France and the United States. They knew
me well and knew all about me, or if they didn't, they soon
would know. I also knew all about them. I knew their long
record of murders of political enemies. . . . I was not so stupid as
to think would murder me. But if they wanted to, they could
make my life miserable. And in my case the reader of this book
will not need to be told how deep in me is the revulsion from
everything they stand for. (*Mariners*, 126)

Throughout this passage, James has turned to the State
Department's official policy of offering asylum to political refugees as
the backdrop necessary to explain his indignation over their decision
to house him with his political enemies. But the opposition to the
Communist Party to which James gives expression here has merely reiterated the position he first developed in England fifteen years earlier
when he condemned the British Communist Party for having failed to
support revolutionary campaigns against imperial aggression in Abys-
sinia, the West Indies, and Africa.

In this passage as well as the others to which Buhle has alluded,
James was not engaged in an ideological dispute with his Communist
cellmates. James had articulated his differences with the American
Communist Party in the books he published with the Forest-Johnson
group, in which he had famously described the Russian Workers'
State as a form of state capitalism. James was instead intent upon
bringing a complaint against the government on the very good
grounds that it had misrepresented his political views and had failed
to grant him a hearing in which he could represent this complaint.

James makes clear the target as well as the juridical grounds for his
dispute in the following sentence that Buhle does not quote: "But the
people really responsible are those who put me in with them, and
whose conduct of affairs would have pushed me into their arms were
it not for my knowledge of them" (*Mariners*, 133–134). In objecting to
the government's having placed him in the cell reserved for Communist detainees, James makes clear in this passage that his dispute was
with the government officials whose decision had done more than
simply misrepresent his political imperatives.

In the following passages, however, if James has not, as Buhle asserts he has, exactly condemned the person he calls M, he does express his strong suspicions concerning M's apparently benevolent motives:

> I did not learn in Melville that Communists were men of purpose. But Melville made me understand how all-embracing was this purpose, its depth, its range, its flexibility, its deep historical roots, the feebleness of all opposition to it which is not animated by feelings as sure and as strong. I thought I now understood this well. I was mistaken. In the course of the next few weeks, I saw one of those Communists in particular acting as the defender and champion of the people on Ellis Island against the cruelties and inhumanity of the administration. (*Mariners*, 127–128)

> You needed a long and well-based experience of Communism and Communists to know that M in reality was a man as mad as Ahab, in all that he was doing pursuing his own purpose with the flexibilty, assurance and courage that are born of conviction. (*Mariners*, 132)

> M was writing articles against the injustice on Ellis Island for the Communist press. . . . Whether the Department of Justice was feeling the repercussions of M's articles in the foreign press, or for whatever reason, a man from the F.B.I. had come to see M and asked him to prepare a report on conditions on the Island. (*Mariners*, 131)

The vehemence of James's reaction against M's advocacy had primary reference to the fact that the state had chosen M to represent the Ellis Islanders' views. In doing so, the government had done more than deny to James and to the other detainees the right of self-representation. When linked with the I.N.S.'s decision to place him in the Communist jail cell, the selection of M as James's representative constituted an act of political categorization with disastrous implications for James's deportation hearings. In placing James in the Communist cell and in endowing the Communist "M" with the authority to represent his political demands, the I.N.S. had in effect produced conclusive state's evidence of the F.B.I.'s accusation that James's radical political activities were indistinguishable from Communism. And the state's production of this evidence effectively had disqualified the grounds for his appeal.

In this section of his narrative, James demonstrated as well the use to which the government had put Communism: it was a way to classify all forms of opposition to capitalism. When Buhle cites James's at times aggressive insistence that he is *not* a Communist as evidence of his defense of capitalism, however, he would appear to have constructed a similarly reductive taxonomy. Whereas the state's classification of James as a Communist justified his extradition on July 3, 1953, Buhle's characterization of *Mariners* as coming closer than any of James's other published works to "an apologia for society under capitalism" has authorized the segregation of this book from the American radical tradition.

In spite of its lack of supporting evidence, Buhle's accusation has acquired a truth value of its own. In his 1997 book *At Home in the World: Cosmopolitanism Now,* Timothy Brennan filled in the contours of the quasi-apologia Buhle had accused James of writing by adding content to that empty category. "It is not that James was in the least naïve" about the fact that in America democracy was a strictly "nominal" rather than material value, Brennan begins this explanation, but since James possessed "little faith in the character of the United States' Cold War enemy, the only logical option was to exaggerate the power of the nominal democracy." Without acknowledging the fact that James's Johnsonite movement had proffered socialist rather than "logical" options, Brennan charged that in writing *American Civilization,* James also looked forward to *Mariners* as an opportunity to link American exceptionalism with "the country's immunities to the Red Threat. . . ." Following the description of *Mariners'* final chapter ("A Natural but Necessary Conclusion") as a very embittered tirade against the Communist Party, Brennan concluded that "it was so fiercely drawn, in fact, that it was suppressed in later editions by his own friends and associates."[13]

Brennan's descriptions of James's work could easily be refuted as blatant misrepresentations.[14] But Brennan makes such refutation unnecessary when he proceeds to expose these "logical options" as themselves figments of the interpretive exigencies his reading of James has demanded. In the footnote that was supposed to verify the suppression of the final chapter as a matter of fact, Brennan has himself acknowledged: "That this was a 'suppression' is my interpretation, not his admission." Brennan then attempts to justify his manufacturing of evidence with the phrase "although the interpretation is neither unique nor unfair" (343).

This interpretation of the historical record may not be unique. But it is, I think, quite unfair. Martin Glaberman, a fellow member of the Johnsonite movement who oversaw the publication in Detroit of the 1978 Bewick edition, would not verify what Brennan had represented as a matter of fact (343). Its "facts" were produced out of Brennan's misrepresentations of James's final chapter. And they would appear to have been invented by Brennan to corroborate Buhle's earlier allegation that James's final chapter constituted a quasi-defense of capitalist society.

What it is true to say is that the book James wrote in 1953 has never been reprinted in its entirety. The version that Allison and Busby republished in 1985 concluded before James's declaration of his book's intention: "I publish the protest [against the government's denial of his rights] with the book on Melville because as I have shown, the book as written is a part of my experience. It is also a claim before the American people, the best claim I can put forward that my desire to become a citizen is not a selfish or frivolous one" (*Mariners*, 166).

While recovering the radical dimension of their historical practices, Buhle and Brennan have repositioned the book within the oppositional logic that it was written to discredit. But exactly how Buhle originally justified the accusation (that, in his concluding chapter, James "more nearly approached an apologia for social life under capitalism than at any other time before or since") that Brennan has subsequently elaborated to explain why the final chapter has been suppressed (and apparently should not be republished) requires some further reflection.

Buhle's commentary on *Mariners* begins with a tendentious reading of James's interpretation of Ishmael. Without citing textual evidence that might substantiate this construal, Buhle proposes that James understood Ishmael as the rebellious son of the middle class who had thereafter "launched upon his own personal avant-garde adventure— like so many real Marxist intellectuals of the twentieth century," concluding that Ishmael had become for James a "proto-totalitarian of a generic kind—both Nazi and Stalinist" (109).

When Buhle moves next to a psychoanalytic reading of his interpretation of James's description of Ishmael, it is to find that James had projected onto Melville's Ishmael a condition of intellectual alienation that was in fact more applicable to James himself. "From a day-to-day standpoint," Buhle continues his diagnosis, "Trotskyism and the small group activity permitted him to live the American revolution for the most part vicariously, without contacting any but the smallest fraction of the activists. He had a clear but almost impersonal, artistic view of socialism and American life" (109).

While Buhle concedes that James, "the very private Bolshevik," may have had great trouble with his legal standing—"he suffered continual harassment from the FBI in the last months before his confinement to Ellis Island"—the "level of unpleasantness" James was made to undergo did not approach the suffering experienced by American Communists who were "driven from jobs, spotlighted in the press and called before Congressional Hearings" (109).

Buhle's mention of the congressional committees before which American Communists were likely to be brought does not simply constitute one more instance of the persecution American Communists were made to suffer throughout the red-baiting campaigns of the McCarthy era. This scene should also be understood as the affective backdrop for Buhle's harsh judgment of James's Ellis Island testimony. The memory of political persecution conveyed by the scenario in which American citizens were subjected to a congressional inquisition gives Buhle the emotional authority required to find James guilty of having failed to give expression to feeling of solidarity with these fellow prisoners of the Cold War state.

But it is when Buhle then elevates the distinction he has adduced— between the "suffering" undergone by American Communists and James's feelings of comparatively minor "unpleasantness"—into the determination that James's experience of the left was un-American that his account should give us pause. Upon declaring that members of the American left had "suffered humiliation in American society akin in character if not quality to the humiliation of Afro-Americans," Buhle decides that James had never himself become "'Black' in the American cultural sense . . . nor anything like an American intellectual" (109). Having thus disallowed James the identification of himself as either an American black or an "American intellectual," Buhle pronounced the judgment that the society to which James might be understood to belong was more proximate to American capitalism than to the society of the American left, which was united in its opposition to society under capitalism.

Throughout his account Buhle has silently transposed James's negative characterizations of American Communists on Ellis Island into the affective equivalent of James's having testified against them before the aforementioned congressional committees. As we have seen, Buhle found evidence of such testimony in the passages from the book's concluding chapter, wherein James complained that Immigration and Naturalization officials had placed him in the same cell with five Communists, and in related passages in James that condemn the I.N.S. authorities for having designated a Communist as the representative through whom James was required to articulate his requests for hospital care for an ulcerated stomach. "James implies that this man, by his apparently benevolent acts, demonstrates the dangers of Communism," as Buhle explains the matter, "and the inability of time-serving American government officials to combat it. A part of James's appeal for freedom and citizenship is based upon his grasp of this significance" (110).

Pace Buhle, James's insistence on the distinction between his politics and M's has not disallowed him solidarity with M's opposition to capitalism. Nor has James denied M or his other Communist cellmates inclusion within the political category out of which he has organized an alternative to the I.N.S. social order. James's efforts to undermine the misrepresentations that he has found inherent to the state's system of classification have led him to extend the category "mariners, renegades and castaways" to cover all of his fellow detainees on Ellis Island.

What Buhle fails to acknowledge throughout this commentary is that James's juridical position differed dramatically from that of American radicals whom the state brought before congressional committees. When the government agents cited the McCarran Act as warrant for having interrupted his writing the Melville book, they also placed James in an untenable legal position. Their reclassification of James as an illegal alien and the transporting of him to Ellis Island had removed from James the power to speak in his own name. The state's pronouncement that he was a foreign subversive had disallowed the possibility that James would ever be brought to give testimony before a congressional committee. The testifying phrases of an alien subversive were defined by the state as void of truth-value. As a consequence of this classification, James was denied the legal rights of due process and habeas corpus.

James explains how officials from the Immigration and Naturalization Services removed from him the rights and liberties that Buhle's
reading has presupposed in the scene which opens the book's final
chapter:

> I had lectured on Melville for three seasons, in many parts of the
> United States, to audiences of all kinds, putting forward many of
> the ideas contained here. What stood out was the readiness of
> every type of audience to discuss him and sometimes very heat-
> edly as if he were a contemporary writer. I had long contem-
> plated a book on Melville, had decided to write it in the summer
> of 1952, and was busy negotiating with publishers. What form it
> might have taken had I written it according to my original plans I
> do not know. But what matters is that I am not an American citi-
> zen, and just as I was about to write, I was arrested by the United
> States government and sent to Ellis Island to be deported.
>
> My case had been up for nearly five years. It had now
> reached the courts, and there would be some period before a
> final decision was arrived at. I therefore actually began the writ-
> ing of this book on the Island, some of it was written there,
> what I did not write there was conceived and worked over in my
> mind there. And in the end I finally came to the conclusion that
> my experiences there have not only shaped the book but are the
> most realistic commentary I could give on the validity of
> Melville's ideas today. (*Mariners*, 125)

As their warrant for James's internment, the state agents cited the
McCarran-Walter Act, which, despite the fact that it was passed two
years after James had completed the examinations qualifying him for
citizenship, would nevertheless ultimately become the juridical instrument invoked by the state to justify James's detainment.[15] Although
the state had kept James under scrutiny from the time of his formal
application to become a legal resident in 1938, the McCarran Act's
designation of him as a subversive brought about a drastic change in
James's juridical relationship to the category of U.S. citizenship.

The McCarran bill authorized I.N.S. officials to apply different
combinations of rules and norms for the purpose of sorting immigrants into economic and political classifications. After the state pronounced James a security threat, James's legal subjectivity underwent

demotion to the status of "you." As its secondary addressee, James was subject to the law's powers of enforcement but he was no longer recognized as the subject of its norms. James's loss of the power to speak as "I" also deauthorized the testifying phrases through which he could convey his claims before a court and invalidated his interlocutory privileges within the civil society. The state's restriction of his pronominal identifications to the "you" who must obey the law had also disallowed James membership in the "we" of "we the people" whose sovereign will the state was understood to represent. "You" could never become "we" because "you" named the subversive with whom the state had refused the rights of dialogue as an "I."[16]

The phrases whereby the bill distinguished immigrants (whom the state could exclude on political grounds) from migrants (whose labor it could exploit) included, for the former, "any alien who has engaged or has had purpose to engage in activities 'prejudicial to the public interest' or 'subversive to the national security.'"[17] In addition to granting the state the right to expel subversives, the bill also called for a careful screening of persons seeking to reside in the United States and installed cultural literacy as one of the criteria whereby the state might determine whether or not "they" were adaptable to the American way of life.

Because the damage for which James sought legal remedy originated with the legislation whose rules the courts were required to render applicable to their decisions, the judgment James sought exceeded the appellate courts' juridical authority. James could not appeal the state's ruling without calling for the repeal of the McCarran bill. But he could neither organize nor participate in a movement calling for the repeal of the McCarran bill without providing the state with an example of the activity for which he was accused. Moreover, any United States citizen who came to James's defense was liable to prosecution for collaborating with a subversive.

It was in an effort to supply a rule of judgment the courts lacked that James produced his interpretation of *Moby Dick*. James's commentary was underwritten by a juridical standard by which he intended to define the illegality of the McCarran legislation and to represent as well the wrong against him that the state had perpetrated on McCarran's authority.

Overall *Mariners, Renegades and Castaways* put into place a multilayered strategy. It produced a frame of intelligibility that supplied

James with the categories and themes required to challenge the find-
ings of the McCarran legislation, with the pronominal rights of an
interpreting "I," and with an interpretive object through which he
could express his grievances against the state. As the continuation of
the activity James had undertaken at the time of the state's forcible re-
settlement, the book was construable both as the proximate cause for
the state's action and as documentation of the violence the state had
exerted against his person. James's interpretation of Melville brought
this example of his activities before the court of public opinion and
invited its readers to decide about the justice of the state's actions.

In his reading of *Moby Dick*, James produced a fictive retroactivity
whereby he represented the experiences he underwent on Ellis Island
as having "realized" in historical time one of the national futures
Melville had imagined a century earlier. James transformed this temporality into a writing practice that joined slightly different orienta-
tions toward U.S. citizenship: at once not quite a citizen but also not
yet not one, James characteristically split the difference between these
dis-positions into the desire for forms of citizenship that, while incom-
patible with I.N.S. categories, were consistent with the relationships
that pertained among the mariners, renegades, and castaways.

The participants in a transnational social movement, "mariners,
renegades and castaways" did not belong to a national community.
The irreducible differences and inequivalent cultural features charac-
terizing the "mariners, castaways and renegades" would not conform
to a state's monocultural taxonomy and could not be integrated
within a nationalizing telos.

Thus far I have argued the importance of the book's final chapter
to James's commentary on *Moby Dick*, and I have indicated some of
differences between James's commentary and the interpretive norms
that have regulated the reading of the Melville archive. But I cannot
conclude this introduction to the book's republication without some
brief account of the differences the inclusion of James's book would
entail for the field of American Studies.

Moby Dick was not, for scholars of American Studies, merely an object of analysis. It provided the field itself with a frame narrative that
included the norms and assumptions out of which the field was organized. The action that *Moby Dick* narrated was made to predict the
world-scale antagonism of the Cold War. The narrative provided the
state with an image of itself as overcoming the totalitarian Other to

which it defined itself as opposed, and it supplied the literary sphere with an image of itself as exempt from the incursions of the state. Overall this frame narrative assisted in structuring the constitutive understanding of the society it purported to represent.

This frame narrative accumulated its cultural capital as a result of the readings of Melville's novel that scholars produced throughout the era of the Cold War. These readings, whether they were produced by scholars who embraced liberal causes, as did F. O. Matthiessen, or by those with conservative agendas, such as Richard Chase, represented the ideological imperatives of the Cold War state. Their literary protocols were tied to cultural axioms and interpretive norms that lay sedimented within this frame narrative.

The disciplines within the field of American Studies intersected with the United States as a geopolitical area whose boundaries field specialists were assigned the task of at once naturalizing and policing. Previous interpreters of *Moby Dick* had accommodated its themes to the national mythology through which they had demarcated and policed the national border. Rather than corroborating the nationalist imperatives organizing the field of American Studies, James questioned the dominant discourses and assumptions within the field.

The vast majority of scholars in the field of American Studies would have understood their work to be far removed from the Immigration and Naturalization Services' deportation policies. Through the juxtaposition of his reading of *Moby Dick* and his transactions with the I.N.S.'s bureaucratic apparatus, however, James materialized concrete and specific linkages between the two orders. The I.N.S. officers applied the rules and classifications that determined the conditions of national belonging. But the coordinated rationalities of U.S. history and literature supplied the standards, norms, and explanations that naturalized the I.N.S.'s taxonomy.

The I.N.S. had resettled James on the Island so as to segregate him from the nation's civic and public spaces. But James's interpretation of *Moby Dick* from the mariners' perspective also, in effect, minoritized the classic. His interpretation produced knowledges about *Moby Dick* that turned it into a cultural process that could not be confined by a national telos. It brought the discrepant places and temporalities assembled on Ellis Island into critical relation with the American Studies field whose spatial boundaries were reflective of the binarized relations that pertained between the U.S. and other nation-states.

Mariners, Renegades and Castaways: The Story of Herman Melville and the World We Live In transported James beyond the U.S. borders. In it James explored configurations of race and nationality in a transnational frame. In linking his experiences there with the floating culture on board the Pequod, James transformed Ellis Island into a mobile landscape whose geographically indeterminate space transgressed the national boundaries. After James extracted from *Moby Dick* these extraterritorial properties, he rendered it impossible to determine to whose national culture it now belonged. The practices of aesthetic self-enactment that he generated out of it produced a multiple identity that avoided the state's categorical obsessions and challenged its belief that cultural identity is based on a national patrimony.

James thereby accomplished a transference of spatial and temporal properties that empowered him to redescribe a possible model of American Studies as, like Ellis Island, a site where becoming American would become indistinguishable from becoming "mariners, renegades and castaways." James reimagined the field as a postnational space that engendered multiple collective identifications and organizational loyalties.

As James imagined it on Ellis Island, Transnational Americas Studies presupposed a global analytic model that would no longer move from the U.S. center. It would entail hemispheric coverage by way of an analytic approach informed by several disciplines that would offer multicultural perspectives on the peoples and cultures of the Americas. James distinguishes transnational from national and international formations by their relatively greater unmooring from national contexts.

Transnational Americas Studies does not merely refer to the movement but also to the objects taken up for analysis and the means of analyzing them. The complex strategies required to discern the disjunctures and to articulate the linkages among these levels would undermine the synthesizing powers of any single category—no matter whether the nation-state or the identitarian community—and displace as well the centrality of the United States as the organizational matrix of transnational studies.

The emergence in James's work of acts of narration capable of bringing about transnational and international relations of a kind then excluded from the field of American Studies turns this work from the historical past toward a future that has emerged within our historical present. The book's republication might enable a transition from American Studies to Transnational Americas Studies.[18]

Notes

1. Stuart Hall, "A Conversation with C. L. R. James," in *Rethinking CLR James*, ed. Grant Farred (Oxford: Blackwell, 1996), p. 35.

2. Edward Said, *Culture and Imperialism* (New York: Alfred Knopf, 1993), p. 253.

3. Sylvia Wynter, "Beyond the Categories of the Master Conception: The Counterdoctrine of the Jamesian Poesis," in *C. L. R. James's Caribbean*, ed. Paget Henry and Paul Buhle (Durham: Duke University Press, 1992), p. 69.

4. Stuart Hall's "C. L. R. James: A Portrait" and Sylvia Wynter's "Beyond the Categories of the Master Conception: The Counterdoctrine of the Jamesian Poesis" can be found in *C. L. R. James's Caribbean*, ed. Henry and Buhle. Hazel V. Carby's "Proletarian or Revolutionary Literature: C. L. R. James and the Politics of the Trinidadian Renaissance" appeared in the *South Atlantic Quarterly* 87, no. 1 (1988). Derek Walcott's "A Tribute to C. L. R. James" was first printed in *C. L. R. James: His Intellectual Legacies*, ed. Selwyn R. Cudjoe and William E. Cain (Amherst: University of Massachusetts Press, 1995).

5. Grant Farred offers an excellent account of the competing claims to the Jamesian legacy in his introduction to *Rethinking CLR James*, p. vii–xvi.

6. See Kent Worcester's *C. L. R. James: A Political Biography* (Albany: State University of New York Press, 1997), p. 112.

7. Francis Otto Matthiessen, *American Renaissance: Art and Expression in the Age of Emerson and Whitman* (Oxford: Oxford University Press, 1941). Richard Chase, *Herman Melville* (New York: Alfred Knopf, 1949). At a time in which the legal apparatus for surveillance had been put into place to purge universities of politically heterodox activities, Richard Chase's *Herman Melville* continued the state's policing measures by other means. He described the book's purpose as an effort "to ransom liberalism from the ruinous sell-outs, failures, and defeats of the thirties. . . . It must present a vision of life capable . . . of avoiding the old mistakes: the facile ideas of progress and 'social realism' . . . the idea that literature should participate directly in the economic liberation of the masses . . . the equivocal relationship to communist totalitarianism and power politics" (vii).

8. C. L. R. James, *Mariners, Renegades and Castaways: The Story of Herman Melville and the World We Live In* (New York, privately printed, 1953). (Subsequent page references to this edition are included in the body of the text, identified as *Mariners.*)

9. C. L. R. James, *Beyond a Boundary* (London: Stanley Hall/Hutchinson, 1963), p. 29.

10. William E. Cain, "The Triumph of the Will and the Failure of Resistance: C. L. R. James's Readings of *Moby-Dick* and *Othello*," in *C. L. R. James: His Intellectual Legacies,* ed. Cudjoe and Cain, pp. 260–273. (Subsequent page references are included in the body of the text.)

11. For further discussion of these points, see Donald E. Pease, "Doing Justice to C. L. R. James's *Mariners, Renegades and Castaways, boundary 2* 27, no. 2 (summer 2000): 1–20.

12. Paul Buhle, *The Artist as Revolutionary* (London: Verso, 1988), p. 110. (Subsequent page references are included in the body of the text.)

13. Timothy Brennan, *At Home in the World: Cosmopolitanism Now* (Cambridge: Harvard University Press, 1997), p. 224. (Subsequent page references are included in the body of the text.)

14. The decision not to reprint the final chapter in the 1978 edition was more probably financial rather than political. In his biography of James, *C. L. R. James: A Political Biography* (Albany: State University of New York Press, 1997), Kent Worcester has cited Martin Glaberman's discovery that publishing and distributing the original *Mariners, Renegades and Castaways* was an extremely expensive enterprise as having informed his decisions as the publisher of the Bewick edition. These resentments over the "financial burden" also "helped to fuel the fight between the Dunayevskaya camp and the group loyal to James' legacy" (112).

15. According to the itinerary James provided in *Mariners, Renegades and Castaways: The Story of Herman Melville and the World We Live In,* his examination was concluded on August 16, 1950, under the Act of 1918. The Internal Security Act was passed on September 23, 1950, and the Attorney General's decision was handed down on October 31, 1950.

16. Jean-Francois Lyotard has observed that a just society is one that recognizes and allows all participants to have a voice, to narrate from their own perspective. It is desirable "to extend interlocution to any human individual whatsoever, regardless of national or natural idiom." Jean-Francois Lyotard, "The Other's Rights," in *On Human Rights: The Oxford Amnesty Lectures,* ed. S. Chute and S. Hurley (New York: Basic Books, 1993), p. 139.

17. Cited by Lisa Lowe, *Immigration Acts: On Asian American Cultural Politics* (Durham: Duke University Press, 1996), p. 9.

18. I elaborate on this reading in "C. L. R. James, *Moby Dick* and the Emergence of Transnational Americas Studies" in a forthcoming issue of *Arizona Quarterly*.

MARINERS,

RENEGADES &

CASTAWAYS

FOR MY SON, NOB,

WHO WILL BE 21 YEARS OLD

IN 1970

BY WHICH TIME I HOPE

HE AND HIS GENERATION

WILL HAVE LEFT BEHIND THEM FOREVER

ALL THE PROBLEMS OF NATIONALITY.

INTRODUCTION

THE MIRACLE of Herman Melville is this: that a hundred years ago in two novels, *Moby-Dick* and *Pierre,* and two or three stories, he painted a picture of the world in which we live, which is to this day unsurpassed.

The totalitarian madness which swept the world first as Nazism and now as Soviet Communism; the great mass labor movements and colonial revolts; intellectuals drowning in the incestuous dreams of psychoanalysis—this is the world the masses of men strive to make sense of. This is what Melville coordinates—but not as industry, science, politics, economics or psychology, but as a world of human personalities, living as the vast majority of human beings live, not by ideas, but by their emotions, seeking to avoid pain and misery and struggling for happiness.

In the course of lecturing upon Melville in many parts of the United States, I have discovered that, once the veil of bookishness is torn away, his characters are instantly recognizable by us who have lived through the last twenty years and particularly the last ten.

I have written all that I wanted to write. Yet the book has been written in such a way that a reader can read it from beginning to end and understand it without having read a single page of Melville's books. I believe that this is in the spirit of what Melville had to say.

A great part of this book was written on Ellis Island while I was being detained by the Department of Immigration. The Island, like Melville's Pequod, is a miniature of all the nations of the world and all sections of society. My experience of it and the circumstances attending my stay there have so deepened my understanding of Melville and so profoundly influenced the form the book has taken, that an account of this has seemed to me not only a natural but necessary conclusion. This is to be found in Chapter VII.

November 28, 1952   C.L.R.J.

3

"There is something in the contemplation of the mode in which America has been settled, that, in a noble breast, should forever extinguish the prejudices of national dislikes.

"Settled by the people of all nations, all nations may claim her for their own. You can not spill a drop of American blood without spilling the blood of the whole world. Be he Englishman, Frenchman, German, Dane, or Scot; the European who scoffs at an American, calls his own brother *Raca,* and stands in danger of the judgment. We are not a narrow tribe of men. . . . No: our blood is as the flood of the Amazon, made up of a thousand noble currents all pouring into one. We are not a nation, so much as a world. . . ."

       —MELVILLE, in *Redburn*

"Those whom books will hurt will not be proof against events. Events, not books, should be forbid."

       — MELVILLE, in *Las Encantadas*

Chapter I

THE CAPTAIN AND THE CREW

One evening over a hundred years ago, an American whaling-vessel is out at sea on its way to the whaling-grounds, when suddenly its one-legged captain, Ahab, asks Starbuck, the first mate, to send everybody aft. There he tells the crew that the real purpose of the voyage is to hunt down a White Whale well-known among whaling men for its peculiar color, its size and its ferocity. This is the whale, he says, which took off his leg and he will chase it round perdition's fires. His passion and his tactical skill win them to excited agreement.

For Starbuck, the mate, people hunt whales to get money and anything else is madness. He protests violently. For money he is ready to do anything, "'for the jaws of Death too, Captain Ahab, if it fairly comes in the way of the business we follow; but I came here to hunt whales, not my commander's vengeance. How many barrels will thy vengeance yield thee even if thou gettest it, Captain Ahab? it will not fetch thee much in our Nantucket market.'"

Ahab now utters words which strike at the very foundation of American civilization. He says, in effect, to hell with business and money.

"'Nantucket market! Hoot! . . . If money's to be the measurer, man, and the accountants have computed their great counting-house the globe, by girdling it with guineas, one to every three parts of an inch; then, let me tell thee, that my vengeance will fetch a great premium *here!*'"

And he smites his chest.

That free enterprise should produce goods for sale, that by working for as much money as possible men helped themselves and made their country great, that it was every man's duty to do this, these were the unchallenged foundations of American civilization in 1851 and are still its official doctrines. But here was a man who trampled upon these sacred principles, derided them, and set up instead his own feelings as a human being.

Captain Ahab has a similarly profound scorn for other pillars of Americanism.

One day oil is leaking from the vessel and Ahab, intent on his pursuit of Moby Dick, refuses to stop to repair the leak. Starbuck, as usual, protests: "'What will the owners say, sir?'"

Ahab consigns the rights of owners to perdition.

"'Let the owners stand on Nantucket Beach and outyell the Typhoons. What cares Ahab? Owners, owners? Thou art always prating to me, Starbuck, about those miserly owners, as if owners were my conscience. But look ye, the only real owner of anything is its commander . . .'"

It is obvious that whatever *Moby-Dick* is, it is no mere adventure story. If even it was such, it is no longer so. If Captain Ahab were to express these opinions today, he would not only be blackballed from any kind of job by every employer in the country, but he would be rigorously investigated by the F.B.I.

Who is this extraordinary character? We can today, after our experiences of the last twenty years, reconstruct his biography and understand him far better than the people for whom the book was written.

His ancestors are among those who founded the United States. He was born about 1790 in New England. He therefore grew up in the period of expanding freedom after the War of Independence. America was the freest country in the world, and above all, in freedom of opportunity.

When still a boy Ahab chose whaling as his profession and at eighteen he struck his first whale. Nantucket, his birthplace, was one of the great whaling centers of the day, and whaling was on the way to become one of the greatest industries of the United States. Ahab was a part of this striking growth of material progress, of trade and of money. By his energy, his skill and his devotion to his work, he becomes captain of his own vessel like so many other gifted and energetic young men. In fact, he is a master of his difficult craft.

But having become a captain, Ahab finds himself in continual revolt against his work, his personal life, and the opinions of the people around him. He is not a man of peculiar personality. It is the life that he lives that makes him what he becomes.

One of the first things we are told about Ahab is how he eats his meals. Ahab eats in his cabin with his officers. But eating for a man who commands a vessel is no longer merely a meal. It has become a part of the means by which the captain maintains discipline over his men. At sea the captain presides over this table like a Czar. First mate, second mate, third mate enter in order, they are served in order, and leave in reverse order. Flask, the third mate, must come in last, is served last and must leave when Starbuck, the first mate, rises. Flask complains that, on account of this, he can never get enough to eat and since he has become an officer, he is starving. The cabin meals are eaten in such awful silence that it is a relief when a rat makes a sudden racket in the hold below.

The meals are the symbol of Ahab's isolation from the men with whom he works, an isolation forced upon him by his position of command. Nobody stayed in that cabin one minute longer than he had to. "In the cabin was no companionship; socially, Ahab was inaccessible. Though nominally included in the census of Christendom, he was still an alien to it. He lived in the world as the last of the Grisly Bears lived in settled Missouri." Even Ahab himself could not stand it. "'It feels like going down to one's tomb,' he would mutter to himself," as he descended the scuttle to his berth. And often when the watches of the night were set, he would leave his lonely berth to visit the night-cloaked deck.

The gospel of America has been, first, above all things, devotion to work. Ahab, a man of Quaker upbringing, has followed it. In forty years he has spent only three ashore. The drive to work kept him from marrying until late in life and has separated him from his wife and son. So now we can understand his heart-felt cry as toward the very end of his long search for the White Whale he reviews his life. He has done what everyone said a man should do, and it has turned to dust and ashes in his mouth. "'Oh, Starbuck! it is a mild, mild wind, and a mild looking sky. On such a day—very much such a sweetness as this—I struck my first whale—a boy-harpooner of eighteen! Forty—forty—forty years ago!—ago! Forty years of continual whaling! forty years of privation, and peril, and storm-time! forty years on the pitiless sea! for forty years has Ahab forsaken the peaceful land, for forty years to make war on the horrors of the deep! Aye and yes, Starbuck, out of those forty years I have not spent three ashore.'"

He now recognizes what the isolation of being in command has done to him.

"'When I think of this life I have led; the desolation of solitude it has been; the masoned, walled-town of a Captain's exclusiveness, which admits but small entrance to any sympathy from the green country without—oh, weariness! heaviness! Guinea-coast slavery of solitary command!—when I think of all this; only half-suspected, not so keenly known to me before—and how for forty years I have fed upon dry salted fare—fit emblem of the dry nourishment of my soul—when the poorest landsman has had fresh fruit to his daily hand, and broken the world's fresh bread to my mouldy crusts—away, whole oceans away, from that young girl-wife I wedded past fifty, and sailed for Cape Horn the next day, leaving but one dent in my marriage pillow—wife? wife?—rather a widow with her husband alive! Aye, I widowed that poor girl when I married her, Starbuck; and then, the madness, the frenzy, the boiling blood and the smoking brow, with which, for a thousand lowerings old Ahab has furiously, foamingly chased his prey—more a demon than a man!—aye, aye! what a forty years' fool—fool—old fool, has old Ahab been! Why this strife of the chase? why weary, and palsy the arm at the oar, and the iron, and the lance? how the richer or better is Ahab now?'"

These words, coming where they do, are among the strangest words in the book.

"'What a forty years' fool—fool—old fool, has old Ahab been!'" And then he adds: "'I feel deadly faint, bowed, and humped, as though I were Adam, staggering beneath the piled centuries since Paradise.'"

The average American worker of today does not see management in this way. Industry has changed, and the man who today bears this burden is the foreman. But Melville here is dealing with essentials, and though the form changes the basic type remains. Ahab knows what is wrong but he is helpless. Habit, necessity, discipline, all permit him as captain to do no work. He can stay in his cabin for days—the work on board goes on. The dash at the whales, the conversion of the ship into a factory where the blubber is extracted, the varied and incessant activity, he has no part in it. For two hundred pages we shall see the men at work, and either Ahab does not come in at all, or when he does, he is concerned only with what life has done to him and his monomaniac revenge.

Let us stop for a moment and with the vast knowledge that we have gained during the last twenty years place Ahab in some perspective.

He is the most dangerous and destructive social type that has ever appeared in Western Civilization.

For generations people believed that the men opposed to rights of ownership, production for the market, domination of money, etc. were socialists, communists, radicals of some sort united by the fact that they all thought in terms of the reorganization of society by the workers, the great majority of the oppressed, the exploited, the disinherited. Some there were, of course, who believed that the experiment, if made, was bound to result in tyranny. Nobody, not a single soul, thought that in the managers, the superintendents, the executives, the administrators would arise such loathing and bitterness against the society of free enterprise, the market and democracy, that they would try to reorganize it to suit themselves and, if need be, destroy civilization in the process. There are a number of writers, chiefly German, who have shown that they more or less understand the type. But there is not one ruler, foreign minister, state department representative or member of parliament, who, despite all the preparations for war yesterday against Nazism and today against Soviet imperialism, shows the slightest sign that he understands the enemy against whom he is preparing. It is the unique and solitary greatness of Melville that he saw and understood the type to the last degree and the relation to it of all other social types. How he was able to do this a hundred years ago, we shall also show but the first point is to understand the totalitarian type itself.

Ahab is no common man. He has a fine brain and has had some education. He is a man of splendid physique, great courage, and a passionate, sincere temperament. He is a Quaker, and in his early days so hated the Catholic Church that he spat into one of the sacred vessels of a cathedral. In short, he is a man who wants to live fully and completely according to his beliefs. That precisely is the cause of his undoing.

He has dropped Quakerism. His basic religion for years has been the religion of his age—material progress. Of this, the symbol in *Moby-Dick*, as it has been all through the ages, is the worship of fire. Melville here went back to a symbolism as old as history itself. The old Sanskrit word for fire-bringer is *pramantha*. Prometheus was the name the Greeks gave to the god who introduced fire into the world. For giving this knowledge to man Prometheus was thrown out of heaven, nailed to a rock and made to suffer for thirty thousand years. But he refused to beg for pardon. His story is perhaps the most famous of all the Greek legends. Every real advance in the arts and sciences means a crisis. The crisis of Ahab is that of a civilization which has recognized that it is on the way to complete mastery of the arts and sciences of civilization. Ahab, a true son of nineteenth century America, worshipped fire but he was struck by it (probably lightning) and was marked from head to foot.

Living all his life away from civilization, hunting whales in remotest seas, looking up at the stars at night, and thinking his own thoughts, he gradually began to discard the ideas of his times and to think independently. This is what he arrived at.

Fire, power, the civilization of material progress, was a mighty creative force. But its creativity was mechanical. Mechanical is a word he will use many times. It is this which is destroying his life as a human being. And he will fight it. As he will say one evening when the thunder and lightning of a frightful storm are flashing around his ship and magnetic lights are burning on the masts:

"'In the midst of the personified impersonal, a personality stands here. Though but a point at best; whencesoe'er I came; wheresoe'er I go; yet while I earthly live, the queenly personality lives in me, and feels her royal rights. But war is pain, and hate is woe. Come in thy lowest form of love, and I will kneel and kiss thee; but at thy highest, come as mere supernal power, and though thou launchest navies of full-freighted worlds, there's that in here that still remains indifferent. Oh, thou clear spirit, of thy fire thou madest me, and like a true child of fire, I breathe it back to thee.'"

Somewhere behind this mighty impersonal force was something that was truly creative in the human sense of the word. He does not know what it is. Fire, power, mechanical creativeness, he does not reject. He knows that they have made him what he is. He rejoices in that. But as long as it means an inhuman existence such as he has lived, he will defy it.

He has now reached the stage where he sees the problem philosophically, as a problem of world civilization. How to reconcile the undoubted advantages of an industrial civilization with what that very civilization is doing to him as a human being. Ahab here has formulated the question which his countrymen would begin to ask only many, many years later. But there is a fatal flaw in his misery and his challenge and defiance. Never for a single moment does it cross his mind to question his relations with the people he works with. Those relations he accepts. *His* personality is suffering. *He* will defy his tormentor. *He* will find a way out. He has been trained in the school of individualism and an individualist he remains to the end.

So far tens of millions of Americans can understand Ahab. They have worked under such men. A smaller but not insignificant number have gone through his experiences. The Diesel engine and now atomic energy face the vast majority with the same problem that he faced: the obvious, the immense, the fearful mechanical power of an industrial civilization which is now advancing by incredible leaps and bringing at the same time the mechanization and destruction of human personality.

Men who are thinking like that, classes of people in a nation who are thinking such thoughts, are being steadily prepared for desperate action. If now there descends upon them a violent catastrophe that ruins them and convinces them that the life that they have been living is intolerable and the grave doubts that have previously tormented them are justified, then they are going to throw aside all the traditional restraints of civilization. They are going to seek a new theory of society and a program of action, and, on the basis of this theory and this program, they are going to act. This is what happens to Ahab when a whale bites off his leg. The whale is Moby Dick.

To get the full effect of this catastrophe we must understand not only the history of Ahab but the history of Moby Dick. Moby Dick is an extraordinarily large and powerful whale. What is striking about him is that he does not rush away from ships and whale-boats, but wherever they appear, chases and fights them. He fights with such ferocity and cunning that he has become a terror of the seas. In time the cunning of his attacks seems to the superstitious sailors to be the result of some inscrutable malignant intelligence. In all this the White Whale was unusual but he was not by any means unique. Such whales were known to the industry, some even by names. And bold captains had set out on voyages with the express purpose of hunting down these monsters and ridding the fishery of them. So that Ahab's pursuit of Moby Dick was in itself, while a little strange, nothing to surprise anybody. It had happened before and would happen again.

But Ahab was the man we have seen him to be. This loss of his leg was for him final proof of the absolute unreasonableness of the world. And in the long hours of pain and suffering which followed, Ahab's doubts and difficulties and frustrations about the world in which he lived came to a head. In Moby Dick, he decided, was the solution of his problems. If he killed Moby Dick it would solve all that was troubling him.

"The White Whale swam before him as the monomaniac incarnation of all those malicious agencies which some deep men feel eating in them, till they are left living on with half a heart and half a lung. . . .All that most maddens and torments; all that stirs up the lees of things; all truth with malice in it; all that cracks the sinews and cakes the brain; all the subtle demonisms of life and thought; all evil, to crazy Ahab, were visibly personified and made practically assailable in Moby Dick. He piled upon the whale's white hump the sum of all the general rage and hate felt by his whole race from Adam down; and then, as if his chest had been a mortar, he burst his hot heart's shell upon it."

Mad he undoubtedly was by now, but that which was madness in a book one hundred years ago, today is the living madness of the age in which we live. It has cost our contemporary civilization untold blood and treasure. We shall conquer it or it will destroy us. Before we go further with Ahab, let us take a look at ourselves.

Out of the very heart of Western Civilization, there emerged in 1933 the Hitler regime as master of Germany. To this day people resist accepting the fundamental fact about the Nazis. The Nazis said that world civilization was disintegrating and they had a solution—the creation of a master race. This was their program. It involved not merely Anti-Semitism, but the destruction of tens of millions of Poles, Slavs and other races they deemed inferior. They said that this was the solution to the problems of Europe. They would carry it through, and if they failed, they would bring down Europe in ruins. And every single thing they did, to their last-minute attempt to destroy Germany, was subordinate to this program. People today still talk about Nazi imperialism, dictatorship, lust for power, living space, etc. They cannot believe that all these were merely instruments for the achievement of the purpose. And they could not face Hitler yesterday with a clear mind and good conscience (as they cannot face Stalin today) because the madness of both was born and nourished in the very deepest soil of Western Civilization.

The political organization of Modern Europe has been based upon the creation and consolidation of national states. And the national state, every single national state, had and still has a racial doctrine. This doctrine is that the national race, the national stock, the national blood, is superior to all other national races, national stocks and national bloods. This doctrine was sometimes stated, often hidden, but it was and is there, and over the last twenty years has grown stronger in every country in the world. Who doubts this has only to read the McCarran Immigration Bill of 1952, which is permeated with the doctrine of racial superiority.

Western Europe in 1914–1918 had given itself the blows from which it would never recover. Wounded and stricken beyond all others, the national state of Germany sought a theory of society and a program. Amid the ruins it could now see the foundations, the theory of the superiority of the national race. The Nazis fastened on to this and discarding all half-truths, decided to carry it to its logical conclusions. The national state *was* the one god without any hypocrisies or pretenses. The national race *was* the master race. By this they would solve everything or ruin Europe finally, and this they have done. They have solved nothing, but they have left behind a Europe shattered beyond repair.

That this is how masses of men would sooner or later behave is what Melville was pointing out in 1851. Being a creative artist, he had seen it in terms of human personality and human relations, and therefore could only present it that way. The house in which Ahab had lived, and this house was American civilization of the nineteenth century, this house had fallen into ruins about him. And searching desperately for some purpose and some program, he found it in what was always implicit in the whaling industry but which he now dragged out into the open, the pursuit of whales, in his case symbolized by one whale, irrespective of all other considerations, of civilization, humanity, religion or anything else.

The whole point is the intimate, the close, the logical relation of the madness, to what the world has hitherto accepted as sane, reasonable, the values by which all good men have lived. At the same time that he was writing *Moby-Dick,* Melville wrote an article in which speaking of another famous literary character, King Lear, who also went mad, he says: "Tormented into desperation the mad king tears off the mask and speaks the sane madness of vital truth."

Hitler was no sooner destroyed than Stalin threatened to overwhelm not only Europe but the whole of the world. The type is the same. If the political basis of the national state was the racial superiority of the national stock, its strictly economic basis was the development of the resources of the national state. In Russia by 1928, from a revolution, exhausted and desperate, and seeing in the world around it no gleam of hope, arose the same social type as the Nazis—administrators, executives, organizers, labor leaders, intellectuals. Their primary aim is not world revolution. They wish to build factories and power stations larger than all others which have been built. They aim to connect rivers, to remove mountains, to plant from the air, and to achieve these they will waste human and material resources on an unprecedented scale. Their primary aim is not war. It is not dictatorship. It is the Plan. In pursuit of what they call planning the economy, they have depopulated Russia of tens of millions of workers, peasants, and officials so that it seems as if some pestilence sweeps periodically across the country. In pursuit of their plan, they have placed and intend to keep millions in concentration camps.

Their purpose is to plan. And they will carry out their plan or, like the Nazis, bury themselves and Europe in the ruins. But even this by itself would not cause the international crisis. What causes it is the fact that in every type of country, the most highly developed and the most backward, have arisen tens of thousands of educated men, organizers, administrators, intellectuals, labor leaders, nationalist leaders, who are ready to do in their own country exactly what the Communists are doing in Russia and look to Russia as their fatherland. This is the problem. The most futile of innumerable futile debates is the quarrel between Democrats and Republicans as to whose policy was responsible for the fact that China has gone Communist. Neither of them could have done one single thing to stop it. The madness spreads irresistibly.

As the theory of the master race and the development of the national economy are merely two inseparable aspects of the national state, so Nazism and Communism are inseparable aspects of the European degeneration. Though they have sprung from such different origins, the Russian Communists are practicing today in the satellite states of Europe the Nazi doctrine of the master race with the thinnest of disguises. If Hitler had been successful and had survived, he would have been driven to adopt some form of the Communist plan. It is now that we can see in his full stature Ahab, embodiment of the totalitarian type. With his purpose clear before him, he is now concerned with two things only: (1) science, the management of things; and (2) politics, the management of men.

In a magnificent chapter entitled, "The Chart," Melville shows us Ahab, the man of purpose, at work. He has at his sole command a whaling-vessel which is one of the most highly developed technological structures of the day. He has catalogued in his brain all the scientific knowledge of navigation accumulated over the centuries. This is one reason why he is so deadly a menace. His purpose may be mad but the weapons that he is using to achieve this purpose are the most advanced achievements of the civilized world, and this purpose gives his already high intelligence a command over them and a power which he never had before. At night he sits alone with his charts. He knows the set of tides and currents, the drift of the sperm whale's food. He has old log books which tell him where Moby Dick has been seen on previous voyages. So he puts marks on his charts with his pencils. And as he marks on the paper, so on his brow appear the lines of care and concentration.

It is too much for any single man or any single body of men. And sometimes late at nights Ahab's madness seemed to overpower him. He would rise and rush out of his cabin. But this is no madness that any doctor can cure. What rushed out, according to Melville, was his common humanity flying from the monster that had overcome it. So that Ahab was then "a vacated thing, a formless somnambulistic being, a ray of living light, to be sure, but without an object to color and therefore a blankness in itself." Humanity would go and there would remain only abstract intellect, abstract science, abstract technology, alive, but blank, serving no human purpose but merely the abstract purpose itself.

Ahab has to manage things, and he has to manage men. "To accomplish his object Ahab must use tools; and of all tools used in the shadow of the moon men are the most apt to get out of order."

Melville pursues the method that he has laid down from the start in his analysis of Ahab. He is by nature a dictatorial personality. But that has not made him a dictator. It is the fact that he has been in command so long, has learned the usages of command at sea which all tend toward creating a dictatorship. Give him now his purpose, and his outstanding ability, and you have the basis of what Melville calls the "tremendous centralization" of power.

The analysis might have been written yesterday. Ahab's problem is contemporary beyond belief. It is stated clearly that the moment Ahab had stated that the purpose of the voyage was different from that for which they had signed, the men were by law entitled to revolt and to take possession of the ship themselves. But what is more important, Ahab has a certain conception of the men, and this, like everything about him, is the result of his years of command. The crew are not human beings but things, as he calls them, "manufactured men." For him their permanent condition is sordidness. For a moment he has lifted them out of themselves by the crusade for achievement of his purpose. And even then he bribed them with a doubloon (for the man who first sighted the White Whale) and grog and ritual. Now he feels that he must for the moment hide the purpose. So he falls back once more on the business of the Pequod as being purely money-making. Later we shall see and recognize the other methods he will use to dominate them. For the time being, however, he concentrates on their sordidness, their incapacity to respond to anything but the meanest motives. The high purpose in reality is for him alone, not for them. So if you read carefully the propaganda of Hitler and Stalin, you will see the purpose tailored to suit the manufactured man. Master race and the planned economy become matters of living space, of defense against enemies who wish to destroy, of the pure blood, of sex, of the living standard in terms of the belly. Here also both have only brought up to the surface what has been the attitude for centuries of educated people to the great masses among whom they live.

That is Ahab—so far. It is certain of course that nobody actually like Ahab ever lived. He is, like Hamlet, Don Quixote, and Satan in Milton's *Paradise Lost*, a creation of the author's mind, based on his observations of life, and history has shown that one such character is more real to us than any single living person whom we know. There is no doubt that people in Europe and in Asia today, once they read *Moby-Dick*, will recognize him and never forget him. We shall show later *how* it was possible for an American writer to portray the totalitarian type as early as 1851.

The question that now immediately presents itself to the reader today is this: if Melville really saw the executives, the managers, the administrators, the popular leaders, and their development into the totalitarian type so clearly, how did he, in 1851, see the ordinary people whom these monsters bind in chains, exploit, corrupt and ultimately ruin? The answer to that is two-fold.

First, Melville is as clear as daylight on this question, far clearer than he is on Ahab.

But, secondly, he felt that here precisely was his problem. He was doubtful if people would understand him. He certainly spared no effort to make himself clear from the very start.

Even before he begins to tell us what Captain Ahab stands for, he describes the officers and the crew of the Pequod in two chapters, both of which have the same name, "Knights and Squires."

The first chapter begins with Starbuck, the first mate. Like Ahab, he is a New Englander. He is a man of principle, high moral qualities, brave and competent. But at the same time, Melville shows how this moral coward is certain to fail before the concentrated purpose and the force of character of Ahab. Melville is sad at the destruction of the dignity of a human being which will be Starbuck's fate. Then, most abruptly, he passes into a totally unexpected panegyric of the working man "that wields a pick or drives a spike." He seems for the moment to have forgotten Starbuck and he rushes on to describe the role the working man, i.e., the crew, will play in his book.

"If, then, to meanest mariners, and renegades and castaways, I shall hereafter ascribe high qualities, though dark; weave round them tragic graces; if even the most mournful, perchance the most abased, among them all, shall at times lift himself to the exalted mounts; if I shall touch that workman's arm with some ethereal light; if I shall spread a rainbow over his disastrous set of sun; then against all mortal critics bear me out in it, thou just Spirit of Equality, which hast spread one royal mantle of humanity over all my kind!"

He refers to John Bunyan, author of the *Pilgrim's Progress* and to Cervantes, the author of *Don Quixote*, as examples of ordinary men who were chosen for greatness by the God of Democracy and Equality. Then on the top of the whole he places Andrew Jackson. "Thou who didst pick up Andrew Jackson from the pebbles; who didst hurl him upon a war-horse; who didst thunder him higher than a throne! Thou who, in all Thy mighty, earthly marchings, ever cullest Thy selectest champions from the kingly commons; bear me out in it, O God!"

The reader can't help feeling that the passage is awkward. It is clear that Melville intends to make the crew the real heroes of his book, but he is afraid of criticism. The next chapter, which, curiously enough, bears the same title as the one we have just examined, will throw more light.

Melville drops the meanest mariners, renegades and castaways, and goes back to the officers. He now describes Stubb, the second mate. He is a man who laughs at everything. And then there is Flask, the third mate, who has no character whatever. But, like Starbuck, they are New Englanders and men of great courage, competence and sobriety.

Next we are introduced (it is all very systematically done) to the three harpooneers. They are first, a South Sea cannibal, Queequeg, by name; the second, Tashtego, a Gay-head Indian from Massachusetts, and the third is Daggoo, a gigantic Negro from the coast of Africa. They are all men of magnificent physique, dazzling skill and striking personality. Now it is true that harpooneers of savage origin were not unknown in the whale fishery at the time, but it is certainly most unusual to find each of the three harpooneers of Ahab's ship a savage, and each a representative of a primitive race.

The crew gives the final proof that Melville is constructing a strictly logical pattern. They are a pack of ragamuffins picked up at random from all parts of the earth. He tells us that in 1851, while white American officers provided the brains, not one in two of the thousands of men in the fishery, in the army, in the navy and the engineering forces employed in the construction of American canals and railroads were Americans. They came from all over the world, were islanders from places like the Azores and the Shetland Islands. Nearly all on Ahab's ship were islanders, and in fact, nearly all the nations of the globe had each its representative. *Isolatoes*, Melville called them, not acknowledging the common continent of men, but each *Isolato* living on a separate continent of his own.

"Yet now, federated along one keel, what a set these Isolatoes were! An Anacharsis Clootz deputation from all the isles of the sea, and all the ends of the earth, accompanying Old Ahab in the Pequod to lay the world's grievances before that bar from which not very many of them ever come back."

Then, astonishing conclusion to an astonishing chapter, Melville tells us what he means by his over-hasty statement in the earlier chapter that the most abased shall lift himself to the most exalted positions. The most abased of the crew on board is Pip, a little Negro from Alabama, the lowest of the low in America of 1851. It is Pip who in the end will be hailed as the greatest hero of all.

To this day people read these chapters and will not understand them. But if these chapters are read and accepted, then right early the book itself can be seen for what it is, the grandest conception that has ever been made to see the modern world, our world, as it was, and the future that lay before it. The voyage of the Pequod is the voyage of modern civilization seeking its destiny.

Ahab, we know, is consumed with anger at that civilization.

The three American officers represent the most competent technological knowledge, brains and leadership. The harpooneers and the crew are the ordinary people of the whole world. The writer of this book confesses frankly that it is only since the end of World War II, that the emergence of the people of the Far East and of Africa into the daily headlines, the spread of Russian totalitarianism, the emergence of America as a power in every quarter of the globe, it is only this that has enabled him to see the range, the power and the boldness of Melville and the certainty with which he wrote down what he intended to do. In this no writer, anywhere, at any time, has ever surpassed him.

His reference to Anacharsis Clootz is decisive.

Anacharsis Clootz was a Prussian nobleman who embraced the French Revolution of 1789. Clootz' ideas went far beyond those of his fellow revolutionaries. He was known as the Orator of the Human Race, he was an ardent advocate of the Universal Republic, and he called on the National Assembly to establish the brotherhood of all men by carrying war to all the tyrants of the world. He gathered together representatives of all the nationalities he could find in Paris, including silent and bewildered Ishmaelites and Chaldeans, and pleaded for the inclusion of all in the brotherhood of nations.

Melville seems to have been fascinated by Clootz, to judge by the references in his works. But whereas Clootz thought of uniting all men in a Universal Republic, based on liberty, equality, fraternity, brother-hood, human rights, etc., Melville, in 1851, had not the faintest trace of these windy abstractions from the beginning of *Moby-Dick* to the end. His candidates for the Universal Republic are bound together by the fact that they work together on a whaling-ship. They are a world-federation of modern industrial workers. They owe allegiance to no nationality. There are Americans among them, but it is the officers who are American. Among the crew nobody is anything. They owe no allegiance to anybody or anything except the work they have to do and the relations with one another on which that work depends. And we may add that they are not to be confused with any labor movement or what is today known as the international solidarity of labor.

If Melville had no use for phrases such as liberty, equality, or frater-nity, he was at the same time, directly or indirectly, the mortal foe of any kind of program which laid down the road by which mankind should act to achieve salvation. If he were alive today, he would turn in horror from Socialists, Communists, Anarchists, Trotskyists and all who set themselves up, not to do this or that particular task, but as the vanguard, the organizers, the educators, the leaders of the workers for the establishment of the Universal Republic. But he was writing in 1851. And what he was concerned with then is what we are increas-ingly concerned with now: what are the conditions of survival of modern civilization? The horrible crises and catastrophes he saw coming, were they rooted in the destructive personality, human na-ture, or did they have other causes? Could mankind overcome them? What were, what would be, or could be the relations between edu-cated people, the technical and executive leaders of an advanced civ-ilization, and the vast millions of ordinary people the world over? Would modern man ever be happy or was he condemned to eternal misery? Would he in the end destroy himself? Melville asked these questions and he answered them as they have never been asked or an-swered within the covers of any single book.

His answers, however, are in terms of human relations. Take the harpooneers. As men of authority, they eat in the captain's cabin. Ahab's meals were a nightmare.

> "In strange contrast to the hardly tolerable constraint and nameless invisible domineerings of the captain's table, was the entire care-free license and ease, the almost frantic democracy

of those inferior fellows the harpooneers. While their masters, the mates, seemed afraid of the sound of the hinges of their own jaws, the harpooneers chewed their food with such relish that there was a report to it. They dined like lords; they filled their bellies like Indian ships all day loading with spices. Such portentous appetites had Queequeg and Tashtego, that to fill out the vacancies made by the previous repast, often the pale Dough-Boy was fain to bring on a great baron of salt-junk, seemingly quarried out of the solid ox. And if he were not lively about it, if he did not go with a nimble hop-skip-and-jump, then Tashtego had an ungentlemanly way of accelerating him by darting a fork at his back, harpoon-wise. And once Daggoo, seized with a sudden humor, assisted Dough-Boy's memory by snatching him up bodily, and thrusting his head into a great empty wooden trencher, while Tashtego, knife in hand, began laying out the circle preliminary to scalping him."

Almost every sentence can be the subject of a comic strip. Melville's language is new and fresh, with an immense vitality. Compare Ahab's Guinea-Coast slavery of solitary command and these three savages.

"It was a sight to see Queequeg seated over against Tashtego, opposing his filed teeth to the Indian's; crosswise to them, Daggoo seated on the floor, for a bench would have brought his hearse-plumed head to the low carlines; at every motion of his colossal limbs, making the low cabin framework to shake, as when an African elephant goes passenger in a ship. But for all this, the great Negro was wonderfully abstemious, not to say dainty. It seemed hardly possible that by such comparatively small mouthfuls he could keep up the vitality diffused through so broad, baronial, and superb a person. But, doubtless, this noble savage fed strong and drank deep of the abounding element of air; and through his dilated nostrils snuffed in the sublime life of the worlds. Not by beef or by the bread, are giants made or nourished. But Queequeg, he had a mortal, barbaric smack of the lip in eating—an ugly sound enough—so much so, that the trembling Dough-Boy almost looked to see whether any marks of teeth lurked in his own lean arms. And when he would hear Tashtego singing out for him to produce himself, that his bones might be picked, the simple-witted Steward all but shattered the crockery hanging round him in the pantry, but his sudden fits of the palsy. Nor did the whetstone which the harpooneers carried in their pockets, for their lances and other weapons; and with which whetstones, at dinner, they would ostentatiously sharpen their knives; that grating sound did not at all tend to tranquillize poor Dough-Boy. How could he forget that in his Island days, Queequeg, for one, must certainly have been guilty of some murderous, convivial indiscretions. . . .

"But, though these barbarians dined in the cabin, and nominally lived there; still, being anything but sedentary in their habits, they were scarcely ever in it except at mealtimes, and just before sleeping-time, when they passed through it to their own peculiar quarters."

In sharp contrast to Ahab's exclusiveness, is the relaxed discipline among the men. As the harpooneers have easy relations with one another, so do they have easy relations with the crew. They hold important positions on the ship. Not only in the boat but, for example, at nights on the whaling-grounds, the command of the deck is theirs. Having such positions, they eat and sleep aft like the other officers. But though their authority is accepted by the men, the men nevertheless always look upon them as their social equal. On board the Pequod as a whole discipline could have been effective and yet not rigorous. On a whale-ship, everyone from captain to pantry-boy was paid in proportion to the profits of the voyage. Thus a voyage in which everyone's wage depended upon the vigilance and intrepidity of each, did not demand the kind of discipline which characterized relations on a merchant-ship. It is after he points out all this that Melville shows Ahab, a grim and gloomy tyrant, his peculiar mentality twisted and hardened by the traditional usages of command at sea.

But the chief thing about Melville's crew is that they work. They are not suffering workers, nor revolutionary workers, nor people who must be organized, nor people who must have more leisure or more education so that they will be able to enjoy their leisure. What matters to them primarily, as it does to all workers, and in fact to all people, is the work they do every day, so many hours a day, nearly every day in the year.

When a whale is sighted, with a dexterity unknown in any other oc-
cupation, the crew leap down like goats into the rolling boats below
from the side of the ship. Flask is a little man and cannot see far
enough. Daggoo offers him his shoulders.

"Whereupon planting his feet firmly against two opposite
planks of the boat, the gigantic Negro, stooping a little, presented his flat palm to Flask's foot, and then putting Flask's
hand on his hearse-plumed head and bidding him spring as he
himself should toss, with one dexterous fling landed the little
man high and dry on his shoulders. And here was Flask now
standing, Daggoo with one lifted arm furnishing him with a
breast-band to lean against and steady himself by.

"At any time it is a strange sight to the tyro to see with what
wondrous habitude of unconscious skill the whaleman will
maintain an erect posture in his boat, even when pitched about
by the most riotously perverse and cross-running seas. Still more
strange to see him giddily perched upon the loggerhead itself,
under such circumstances. But the sight of little Flask mounted
upon gigantic Daggoo was yet more curious; for sustaining himself with a cool, indifferent, easy, unthought of, barbaric majesty,
the noble Negro to every roll of the sea harmoniously rolled his
fine form. On his broad back, flaxen-haired Flask seemed a
snow-flake. The bearer looked nobler than the rider. Though
truly vivacious, tumultous, ostentatious little Flask would now
and then stamp with impatience; but not one added heave did
he thereby give to the Negro's lordly chest. So have I seen Passion and Vanity stamping the living magnanimous earth, but the
earth did not alter her tides and her seasons for that."

The tone is light. But look again at the comparison between New
England Flask and African Daggoo.
There is tension, the tension of strenuous labor, but there is skill
and grace and beauty.

"It was a sight full of quick wonder and awe! The vast swells of
the omnipotent sea; the surging, hollow roar they made, as they
rolled along the eight gunwales, like gigantic bowls in a bound-
less bowling-green; the brief suspended agony of the boat, as it

would tip for an instant on the knife-like edge of the sharper waves, that almost seemed threatening to cut it in two; the sudden profound dip into the water glens and hollows; the keen spurrings and goadings to gain the tip of the opposite hill; the headlong, sled-like slide down its other side;—all these, with the cries of the headsman and harpooneers, and the shuddering gasps of the oarsmen, with the wondrous sight of the ivory Pequod bearing down upon her boats with outstretched sails, like a wild hen after her screaming brood;—all this was thrilling.

"Not the raw recruit, marching from the bosom of his wife into the fever heat of his first battle; not the dead man's ghost encountering the first unknown phantom in the other world;— neither of these can feel stranger and stronger emotions than that man does, who for the first time finds himself pulling into the charmed, churned circle of the hunted sperm whale."

It is all a unity. You cannot distinguish between man and Nature and technology, between sweat and beauty, between an imperative discipline more severe than war, and yet sensations that are as new and powerful as any human experience.

Darkness sets in. Starbuck's boat is swamped. They lose contact with the other boats and with the ship. They have no real hope of being rescued but in the darkness and despair Queequeg holds up a forlorn lantern. Dawn comes, the sea still covered with mist. Suddenly Queequeg starts to his feet, his hand to his ear. It is the ship bearing down on them and they jump for their lives. He boat is smashed, but they are fished from the water.

There is not only physical prowess and tense emotion but spontaneous literary creation of high order. Each mate has his own formula for urging on his crew. Little Flask, mediocrity though he is, uses a fictitious whale which he describes as tantalizing the boat's bow with his tail. So life-like and vivid are his imaginary descriptions that despite the rigid prohibition against looking back, some of his men cannot prevent themselves snatching a fearful look over their shoulders.

Another day Stubb produces a masterpiece of poetic exhortation.

"'Start her, start her, my men! Don't hurry yourselves; take plenty of time—but start her; start her like thunder-claps, that's all,' cried Stubb, spluttering out the smoke as he spoke, 'Start her, now; give 'em the long and strong stroke, Tashtego. Start her, Tash, my boy—start her, all; but keep cool, keep cool—cucumbers is the word—easy, easy—only start her like grim death and grinning devils, and raise the buried dead perpendicular out of their graves, boys—that's all. Start her!'"

The whale-line folds the whole boat in its complicated coils, twisting and writhing around it in almost every direction. When the whale is struck and leaps forward with tremendous speed, the coils must unwind without a kink or else the boat can be jerked over or dragged under. Furthermore, arms, legs and bodies are in imminent peril.

". . . when the line is darting out, to be seated then in the boat, is like being seated in the midst of the manifold whizzings of a steam-engine in full play, when every flying beam, and shaft, and wheel, is grazing you. It is worse; for you cannot sit motionless in the heart of these perils, because the boat is rocking like a cradle, and you are pitched one way and the other, without the slightest warning; and only by a certain self-adjusting buoyancy and simultaneousness of volition and action, can you escape being made a Mazeppa of, and run away with where the all-seeing sun himself could never pierce you out."

"Yet habit—strange thing! what cannot habit accomplish?—Gayer sallies, more merry mirth, better jokes, and brighter repartees, you never heard over your mahogany, than you will hear over the half-inch white cedar of the whale-boat, when thus hung in hangman's nooses; . . ."

Melville is so gay that at a first reading you can easily miss the significance of those last sentences for the world we live in. But re-read them. The humor and the wit of the mariners, renegades and castaways are beyond the cultivated inter-changes of those who sit around mahogany tables. They have to be. Hangman's nooses hang loose around the necks of countless millions today, and for them their unfailing humor is an assertion of life and sanity against the ever-present threat of destruction and a world in chaos. It is about the crew that Melville repeatedly makes such observations. When Ahab for a moment lifts himself out of his tortured soul, it is usually to fall into sentimentality.

When the whale is killed, there begins the complicated laborious task of cutting up and preparing the pieces of blubber for the boiling. Sometimes the work is done by individuals. A harpooner begins the cutting, standing on the back of the half-submerged whale. While Queequeg does this, it is the duty of another mariner to attend to his safety and for this he is attached to Queequeg by a rope. Whenever Queequeg is in danger of being crushed between the rotting carcass and the swinging ship, this other member of the crew must jerk him to safety. Should Queequeg sink to rise no more, usage and honor demand that his protector do not cut the cord, but be dragged down with him.

Queequeg is also in mortal danger from the sharks which attend the carcass in great numbers. To protect Queequeg from these, Tashtego and Daggoo are suspended over the sides with a couple of keen whale spades, with which they strike at the sharks that get too near to Queequeg. But Queequeg and the sharks are hidden at times by the bloody mud of the water, and Queequeg is in as much danger from the whale spades as from the sharks.

At the next stage the work is a combination of mechanism and human labor. Forgotten is the excitement of the chase. But despite the blood and the muck, the sweat and the strain, Melville's clear strong prose without any sentimentality brings out the essential humanity of the process and the absence of any degradation.

"It was a Saturday night, and such a Sabbath as followed! Ex officio professors of Sabbath breaking are all whalemen. The ivory Pequod was turned into what seemed a shamble; every sailor a butcher. You would have thought we were offering up ten thousand red oxen to the sea gods.

"In the first place, the enormous cutting tackles, among other ponderous things comprising a cluster of blocks generally painted green, and which no single man can possibly lift—this vast bunch of grapes was swayed up to the main-top and firmly lashed to the lower mast-head, the strongest point anywhere above a ship's deck. The end of the hawser-like rope winding through these intricacies, was then conducted to the windlass, and the huge lower block of the tackles was swung over the whale; to this block the great blubber hook, weighing some one hundred pounds, was attached.

"And now suspended in stages over the side, Starbuck and Stubb, the mates, armed with their long spades, began cutting a hole in the body for the insertion of the hook just above the nearest of the two side-fins. This done, a broad, semicircular line is cut round the hole, the hook is inserted, and the main body of the crew striking up a wild chorus, now commence heaving in one dense crowd at the windlass. When instantly, the entire ship careens over on her side; every bolt in her starts like the nail-heads of an old house in frosty weather; she trembles, quivers, and nods her frightened mast-heads to the sky.

"More and more she leans over to the whale, while every gasping heave of the windlass is answered by a helping heave from the billows; till at last, a swift, startling snap is heard; with a great swash the ship rolls upwards and backwards from the whale, and the triumphant tackle rises into sight dragging after it the disengaged semicircular end of the first strip of blubber.

"Now as the blubber envelopes the whale precisely as the rind does an orange, so it is stripped off from the body precisely as an orange is sometimes stripped by spiralizing it. For the strain constantly kept up by the windlass continually keeps the whale rolling over and over in the water, and as the blubber in one strip uniformly peels off along the line called the 'scarf,' simultaneously cut by the spades of Starbuck and Stubb, the mates; and just as fast as it is thus peeled off, and indeed by that very act itself, it is all the time being hoisted higher and higher aloft till its upper end grazes the main-top; the men at the windlass then cease heaving, and for a moment or two the prodigious blood-dripping mass sways to and fro as if let down from the sky, and every one present must take good heed to dodge it when it swings, else it may box his ears and pitch him headlong overboard.

"One of the attending harpooneers now advances with a long, keen weapon called a boarding-sword, and watching his chance he dexterously slices out a considerable hole in the lower part of the swaying mass. Into this hole, the end of the second alternating great tackle is then hooked so as to retain a hold upon the blubber, in order to prepare for what follows. Whereupon, this accomplished swordsman, warning all hands to stand off, once more makes a scientific dash at the mass, and with a few sidelong, desperate, lunging slicings, severs it completely in twain; so that while the short lower part is still fast, the long upper strip, called a blanket-piece, swings clear, and is all ready for lowering.

"The heavers forward now resume their song, and while the one tackle is peeling and hoisting a second strip from the whale, the other is slowly slackened away, and down goes the first strip through the main hatch-way right beneath, into an unfurnished parlor called the blubber-room. Into this twilight apartment sundry nimble hands keep coiling away the long blanket-piece as if it were a great live mass of plaited serpents.

"And thus the work proceeds; the two tackles hoisting and lowering simultaneously; both whale and windlass heaving, the heavers singing, the blubber-room gentlemen coiling, the mates scarfing, the ship straining, and all hands swearing occasionally, by way of assuaging the general friction."

It is 1851, but the reference at the start to sacrifices and sea gods, shows how conscious Melville is of the same type of labor being carried out generations ago when the labor was closely associated with religion and sacrifice.

For some two hundred pages this continues. Except when periodically a passing vessel gives Ahab an opportunity to raise again his monomaniac interest in Moby Dick, he and his madness are for the most part excluded.

People write repeatedly that Melville describes the technique of the whaling industry as if he were drawing up some sort of text-book or manual. Melville is doing nothing of the kind. He has painted a body of men at work, the skill and the danger, the laboriousness and the physical and mental mobilization of human resources, the comradeship and the unity, the simplicity and the naturalness.

They are meanest mariners, castaways and renegades. But that is not their fault. They began that way. Their heroism consists in their everyday doing of their work. The only tragic graces with which Melville endows them are the graces of men associated for common labor.

The contrast is between Ahab and the crew, and Melville traces this at every level from the basic human functions to the philosophic conceptions of society. We have seen that they eat differently. They sleep differently. In the forecastle where the off-duty watch is sleeping,

"you would have almost thought you were standing in some illuminated shrine of canonized kings and counsellors. There they lay in
their triangular oaken vaults, each mariner a chiselled muteness; a
score of lamps flashing upon his hooded eyes." Ahab cannot sleep at
all, or when he does, he sleeps standing straight up or in his chair,
shouting about the blood spouting from Moby Dick.

The men pursue whales, responding almost unconsciously to the
rhythm of the sea and Nature, sharing skill, danger, sweat and jokes.
Ahab pursues his whale with foam-glued lips and inflamed distracted
fury. Sometimes the men quarrel and fight, but the essence of their relation with each other at work or at play, is congeniality. Ahab is either
in a state of grim reserve, tragic gloom or hopeless silence, overwhelmed by his isolation and lack of human communication and his
scorn for the great masses of men as manufactured men. The men respond spontaneously to the immediate. Their thoughts are in general
untroubled. Ahab lives perpetually planning and scheming, with his
wrinkled brow and his shoulders humped with the burdens of the centuries since Paradise.

The crew is anonymous, their individual personalities subordinated to the fact that they are all living, working and playing together.
A few of them are mentioned by name a half dozen times, but those
names easily could be left out. Ahab, in defense of his queenly personality, is the most tortured of human beings.

The crew is ignorant and superstitious, but as has been noticed frequently with primitive savages, their ignorance and superstition are
something that they hold quite apart from their immediate responses
to Nature and technology, with both of which they are in perfect harmony. For that harmony is the basis of their efficiency and indeed of
the very preservation of life collectively and individually in the constant perils presented by the fishery. On the other hand, it is Ahab's
education, knowledge and intense consciousness of himself and the
world around him which act directly upon his own life and the safety
of the vessel and the crew which are under his command.

On the night of the great storm, Ahab stands on the deck and
makes his grandiloquent speeches against the fire and the lightning
and the thunder. But immediately after, Melville writes the shortest
chapter in the book, five lines only, in which he makes Tashtego say:
"'What is the use of thunder? Give me some rum instead.'" The contrast is deliberate. And we can be sure that in the same way Tashtego

had the fastest eye on the ship for seeing a whale, so he would be quick in detecting thunder if it affected the ship. Vast philosophical speculations about the meaning of fire and thunder and such like were absolutely foreign to the crew.

It is this weight of consciousness and of knowledge, absence of naturalness, lack of human association, delving into the inner consciousness, seeking to answer problems which cannot be answered, but which the tortured personality in its misery must continue to ask, it is this which Melville condemns. He understands where it comes from and what it is trying to do, but from the beginning is absolutely clear that until modern man, and particularly modern educated man, gets rid of this, the road he travels is the road to disaster.

Melville was not content to rest his point of view upon his description of the crew alone. As against the educated individual in his isolation and inward tortures, he dramatized the basic qualities of the crew in the three harpooneers. What he did was to take the ideal qualities of the crew, and intensify them in these three vivid figures. By making them savages he could emphasize in a manner absolutely unmistakable that break with intellectual and emotional self-torture which he felt was the primary condition for the survival of modern society.

Savages they are but they are not primitive savages. Through them seems to move the very forces of Nature, while at the same time, they are the most skillful seamen and the most generous and magnificent human beings on board.

The first thing about them is that they are the finest workers on the ship. At sea, dignity and danger went hand in hand and the higher you rose, the harder you toiled (until you became a captain). Queequeg faced the rage of the living whale or mounted his dead back in a rolling sea. He descended into the gloom of the hold and, bitterly sweating all day in that subterranean confinement, resolutely manhandled the clumsiest casks and saw to the stowage. Yet, foremost in the routine work, the harpooneers are, as we have already seen, always the ones who respond quickest to any emergency.

The ship is in danger of being pulled over by the weight of a dead whale. Even while a mate calls for a knife, Queequeg has already put his hatchet to the iron chains, they are severed and the perilous moment is passed. Tashtego sees the first whale. If they are being chased by Malay pirates it is Tashtego who sees them first. So it is on every possible occasion. This runs through the whole book. The following episode will give some idea of their personal splendor as men.

Tashtego, perched on the main-yard-arm, is pulling sperm with a bucket out of the great head of a whale when, for some reason, he slips and falls head-foremost into the vast head and begins to sink. "'Man overboard,' cried Daggoo, who, amid the general consternation first comes to his senses." As always. The remaining harpooneers dominate what follows at every turn.

"'Swing the bucket this way!' and putting one foot into it, so as the better to secure his slippery hand-hold on the whip itself, the hoisters ran him high up to the top of the head, almost before Tashtego could have reached its interior bottom. . . .

"At this instant, while Daggoo, on the summit of the head, was clearing the whip . . . to the unspeakable horror of all, one of the two enormous hooks suspending the head tore out, and with a vast vibration the enormous mass sideways swung . . . The one remaining hook, upon which the entire strain now depended, seemed every instant to be on the point of giving way; . . .

"'Come down, come down!' yelled the seamen to Daggoo, but with one hand holding on to the heavy tackles, so that if the head should drop, he would still remain suspended, the Negro having cleared the foul line, rammed down the bucket into the now collapsed well, meaning that the buried harpooner should grasp it, and so be hoisted out.

"'In heaven's name, man,' cried Stubb, 'are you ramming home a cartridge there?—Avast! How will that help him; jamming that iron-bound bucket on top of his head? Avast, will ye!'

"'Stand clear of the tackle!' cried a voice like the bursting of a rocket.

"Almost in the same instant, with a thunder-boom, the enormous mass dropped into the sea, like Niagara's Table-Rock into the whirlpool; the suddenly relieved hull rolled away from it, to far down her glittering copper; and all caught their breath, as half swinging—now over the sailors' heads, and now over the water—Daggoo, through a thick mist of spray, was dimly beheld clinging to the pendulous tackles, while poor, buried-alive Tashtego was sinking utterly down to the bottom of the sea! But hardly had the blinding vapor cleared away, when a naked figure with a boarding-sword in its hand, was for one swift moment seen hovering over the bulwarks. The next, a loud splash announced that my brave Queequeg had dived to the rescue. One packed rush was made to the side, and every eye counted every ripple, as moment followed moment, and no sign of either the sinker or the diver could be seen. Some hands now jumped into a boat alongside, and pushed a little off from the ship.

"'Ha! ha!' cried Daggoo, all at once, from his now quiet, swinging perch overhead; and looking further off from the side, we saw an arm thrust upright from the blue waves; . . .

"'Both! both!—it is both!'—cried Daggoo again with a joyful shout; and soon after, Queequeg was seen boldly striking out with one hand, and with the other clutching the long hair of the Indian. . . .

"Now, how had this noble rescue been accomplished? Why, diving after the slowly descending head, Queequeg with his keen sword had made side lunges near its bottom, so as to scuttle a large hole there; then dropping his sword, had thrust his long arm far inwards and upwards, and so hauled out our poor Tash by the head. He averred, that upon first thrusting in for him, a leg was presented; but well knowing that that was not as it ought to be, and might occasion great troubles;—he had thrust back the leg, and by a dexterous heave and toss, had wrought a somerset upon the Indian; so that with the next trial, he came forth in the good old way—head foremost. . . ."

The spirit of the harpooneers is caught in a single phrase, that, after the rescue "Queequeg did not look very brisk." That is as much as it would have meant to them once the thing had been successfully accomplished.

Once Queequeg was very ill and seemed about to die, but he made a marvellous recovery and declared that it was because he willed it so. A gale or a whale or some violent, ungovernable unintelligent destroyer of that kind could kill him, but otherwise he was master of that situation, by which we presume that the speculation and indecision and moral crisis which weaken civilized men were alien to him. He, through whom pulsed so much life, faced death in his bed with the most methodical preparation. He had a coffin made and placed by his bedside. When he recovered, he spent his spare time copying certain mysterious tattooings from his body on the coffin. Melville is very funny and very subtle about the coffin. He says that the departed prophet who had tattooed Queequeg had written on him a complete theory of the heavens and the earth and a treatise on the art of attaining truth. So that Queequeg in his own person was a wondrous riddle to unfold. The coffin that Queequeg carved will appear again at the end when it will save the life of the solitary person to escape the disaster which overtook the Pequod and everyone on board. In Queequeg therefore was embodied the mystery of the universe and the attainment of truth. But in his nobility of spirit, his relation to Nature, his relation to other beings, and his philosophical attitude to the world, Queequeg was merely a member of the anonymous crew.

But the reader may ask, and even with genuine indignation: Even if all that you say is true, is that all that Melville has to say about America? An American totalitarian and these American officers who cannot stand up against him? What about democracy and the freedom for which this country has been famous for so many years? First, while the captain and the officers are as American as Melville can make them, they are far more than Americans. They represent the science, knowledge, technical skill and ability to lead, of world civilization. That is Melville's vision. That world is heading for a crisis which will be a world crisis, a total crisis in every sense of that word.

But Melville understands what America has given to the world—none better. He has chosen whaling for his unit of demonstration. And in a brilliant page he sums up the grandeur of the American past.

"What wonder, then, that these Nantucketers, born on a beach, should take to the sea for a livelihood! They first caught crabs and quohogs in the sand; grown bolder, they waded out with nets for mackerel; more experienced, they pushed off in boats and captured cod; and at last, launching a navy of great ships on the sea, explored this watery world; put an incessant belt of circumnavigation round it; peeped in at Bhering's Straits; and in all seasons and all oceans declared everlasting war with the mightiest animated mass that has survived the flood; most monstrous and most mountainous; That Himmalehan, salt-sea Mastodon, clothed with such portentousness of unconscious power, that his very panics are more to be dreaded than his most fearless and malicious assaults!

"And thus have these naked Nantucketers, these sea hermits, issuing from their ant-hill in the sea, overrun and conquered the watery world like so many Alexanders; parcelling out among them the Atlantic, Pacific, and Indian oceans, as the three pirate

powers did Poland. Let America add Mexico to Texas, and pile
Cuba upon Canada; let the English overswarm all India, and
hang out their blazing banner from the sun; two-thirds of this
terraqueous globe are the Nantucketer's. For the sea is his; he
owns it, as Emperors own empires; other seamen having but a
right of way through it. Merchant ships are but extension
bridges; armed ones but floating forts; even pirates and priva-
teers, though following the sea as highwaymen the road, they
but plunder other ships, other fragments of the land like themselves, without seeking to draw their living from the bottomless
deep itself. The Nantucketer, he alone resides and riots on the
sea; he alone, in Bible language, goes down to it in ships; to and
fro ploughing it as his own special plantation. *There* is his home;
there lies his business, which a Noah's flood would not interrupt,
though it overwhelmed all the millions in China. He lives on the
sea, as prairie cocks in the prairie; he hides among the waves, he
climbs them as chamois hunters climb the Alps. For years he
knows not the land; so that when he comes to it at last, it smells
like another world, more strangely than the moon would to an
Earthsman. With the landless gull, that at sunset folds her wings
and is rocked to sleep between billows; so at nightfall, the Nantucketer, out of sight of land, furls his sails, and lays him to his
rest, while under his very pillow rush herds of walruses and
whales."

It is his history of America from 1620 to *Moby-Dick*. But note that
Melville, as every truly great writer, sees history in terms of men.
These Nantucketers were heroic men. And they did heroic deeds.
Whalers have explored unknown seas and archipelagoes. People write
of the famous voyages of men like Captain Cook and other heroes of
international exploration. But, says Melville, many an incident to
which these writers devote three chapters in their books, unknown
whaling captains of Nantucket had experienced so often that they
would not have thought them worth putting down in the ship's log-
book. The whaling vessels rounded Cape Horn and established international commerce. They gave impetus to the liberation of Peru,
Chile and Bolivia from the yoke of Spain. They nursed and repeatedly
saved from extinction the infant colonies of Australia. That was America. And because already, in 1851, Melville could see that the social

structure was cramping and thwarting men instead of developing them, he knew that the time had come for the ship of destiny once more to sail and see what the future would be.

He is as systematic as a sociologist, and the first thing he does in *Moby-Dick* is to show the existing world as he saw it.

The story is told by one Ishmael, a young New Yorker who goes to New Bedford and Nantucket, seeking a job on a whaling-ship. He gets one from the owners of the Pequod, Bildad and Peleg, two retired Nantucket sea captains who, like Ahab, had worked their way up from cabin boys. They are Quakers but the moral earnestness of the old Puritans has changed into a piety which but thinly covers their lust for money. Bildad, always reading the Bible, uses Scriptures as an argument to justify the most avaricious deals. From this Quaker whaling-stock with its grand and glorious history, we have as representatives, Bildad and Peleg, and the rebellious Ahab.

Equally unlovely are Nantucket and New Bedford. New Bedford has the finest patrician houses in America and is the place for brilliant weddings. But in its streets are the meanest mariners from all over the world, savages from every part of the South Seas, and green boys from the hills of Vermont and New Hampshire. When Mrs. Hussey, the landlady where Ishmael stays, suspects that someone may have committed suicide in one of her rooms, she prays for his soul, but laments what has happened to her counterpane. She refuses to allow the door to be broken down at once and suggests that a locksmith who lives about a mile away be sent for. She sends a message to the painter asking for a sign, which will say that smoking in the parlor and suicides should not be allowed—might as well kill two birds with one stone, she remarks. In Nantucket, Ishmael is offered the only accommodations available—to share a bed with a savage. When he inquires more as to this man, he receives the laconic reply, "He pays reg'lar." Nothing else matters.

This population, in addition to its lust for money, has a craving for the horrible. A Negro preacher, like a black Angel of Doom, reads a book in his pulpit and his text is the blackness of darkness, and the weeping and wailing and teeth-gnashing there. In one inn a picture shows a vessel half-floundering in the journey round Cape Horn. Only its three dismantled masts are visible, and an exasperated whale, purposing to spring clear over the craft, is in the act of impaling himself upon the three mast-heads. Another piece of furniture consists of a heathenish array of clubs and spears with glittering teeth; others were tufted with knots of human hair. The savage who is to share Ishmael's bed is busy selling dried-up human heads which are in great demand as curios. He carries them knotted on a string, and is very active that afternoon because it is Saturday and it would not look well to be hawking such things in the streets on Sunday when people are going to church.

Whaling, as seen from the shore is the source of death and terror, and the religion of the Nantucketers corresponds. To the mourning widows and the solemn whalemen about to face the perils of the fishery, Father Mapple, himself an old seafaring man, tells the story of Jonah and the whale so that it is more terrifying than it is in the Old Testament. His moral is that the truly and faithfully repentant do not clamor for pardon but are grateful for punishment.

There is wealth of course. In the fine patrician houses there are reservoirs of oil and nightly they recklessly burn the spermacetti candles. But this wealth has been dragged up from the Atlantic and Pacific and the Indian Oceans by whaling men. It is what happens to these men, the men that create the wealth, which will decide the future of society. Melville mentions the owners and the spenders only to brush them aside.

This is life on land.

Like the rest of the story it is all seen through the eyes of Ishmael. Like Ahab, Ishmael lived first in Melville's imagination. Like Ahab, it is the twentieth century, our own, which has its Ishmaels in every city block.

He is a member of a distinguished American family, is well educated and has been a teacher. But he cannot endure the social class in which he was born and reared, so he lives as a worker, digging ditches, or what else comes to hand. He is subject to fits of periodical depression (today we would call him a neurotic) and whenever he feels a fit coming on, he goes to sea. Today they do not go to sea—they join the working class movement or the revolutionary movement instead.

Who does not recognize Ishmael? He wants to be a plain ordinary seaman. He feels himself one of the people. But it isn't that he likes workers. It is that he hates authority and responsibility of any kind. He does not want to be a Commodore but he does not want to be a cook either. Presidential elections, international politics, commerce, all of these he wants no part of. He wants to go to the sea because when life on land is too much for them, men have always gone to sea to find there some explanation of what is baffling them. He wants to go whaling because he wants adventure and peril in far places. And (which sends a shiver down our spines today) he loves the horrible, although he is neither pervert nor degenerate.

Ishmael's description of himself shows that the instinct for violence, the cruelty and the sadism inherent in Western Civilization of the twentieth century are not accidental. They were detected in America over three generations ago.

What is wrong with this young man? He is as isolated and bitter as Ahab and as helpless. He cannot stand the narrow, cramped, limited existence which civilization offers him. He hates the greed, the lies, the hypocrisy. Thus shut out from the world outside, he cannot get out of himself. The only truly civilized person he can find in New Bedford and Nantucket is a cannibal savage, the harpooneer, Queequeg, and the story of their relations is, like all great literature, not only literature but history.

Everyone knows Fenimore Cooper's stories of the white hunter, Deerslayer, and his two Indian comrades, *The Last of the Mohicans.* In these tales Cooper was only following a practice which for centuries had been followed by some of the very great writers of France and Britain. They were using the primitive savage, in his presumed nobility and innocence of vice, as a stick with which to beat the constantly increasing injustices, suffering, deceptions and pretenses which seemed to grow side by side with the growth of civilization. That such a literary device should have been so widespread, so popular and should have lasted so long shows only the terrible need in Western culture for some protest against the burdens which the growth of material wealth was placing on the human personality.

Already a man disillusioned with the world, what he sees in new Bedford and Nantucket so shocks Ishmael that when he goes back to the inn he watches Queequeg, the seller of human heads, with fresh interest. What he sees in him is exactly what he has not been able to find in the world around him.

"Through all his unearthly tattooings, I thought I saw the traces of a simple honest heart; and in his large, deep eyes, fiery black and bold, there seemed tokens of a spirit that would dare a thousand devils. And besides all this, there was a certain lofty bearing about the Pagan, which even his uncouthness could not altogether maim. He looked like a man who had never cringed and never had had a creditor."

Where could one find men like this? The men Ishmael knew were pent up in lath and plaster, tied to counters, nailed to benches, clinched to desks.

Along with Queequeg's untamed and undefeated appearance went an equally distinctive calm and self-reliance.

"He made no advances whatever; appeared to have no desire to enlarge the circle of his acquaintances. All this struck me as mighty singular; yet, upon second thoughts, there was something almost sublime in it. Here was a man some twenty thousand miles from home, by the way of Cape Horn, that is— which was the only way he could get there—thrown among people as strange to him as though he were in the planet Jupiter; and yet he seemed entirely at his ease; preserving the utmost serenity; content with his own companionship; always equal to himself."

Poor lonely Ishmael feels something melting in him. Queequeg is the opposite of everything he has known.

"No more my splintered heart and maddened hand were turned against the wolfish world. This soothing savage had redeemed it. There he sat, his very indifference speaking a nature in which there lurked no civilized hypocrisies and bland deceits. Wild he was; a very sight of sights to see; yet I began to feel myself mysteriously drawn towards him. And those same things that would have repelled most others, they were the very magnets that thus drew me. I'll try a pagan friend, thought I, since Christian kindness has proved but hollow courtesy."

He makes overtures of friendship to Queequeg who returns them with an immediate generosity which knows no bounds.

So far it might seem that Melville is merely repeating the old pattern of noble savage versus corrupt civilization. But he is not doing that. Queequeg is no ideal figure. Queequeg's ignorance often makes his behavior entirely ridiculous. His religious practices, if sincere, are absurd. In his own country he has eaten human flesh. But the thing that matters is that as soon as they get off the land into the boat from New Bedford to Nantucket, Queequeg shows himself what he will later turn out to be, not only brave and ready to risk his life, but a master of his seaman's craft. To his splendid physique, unconquered spirit and spontaneous generosity, this child of Nature has added mastery of one of the most important and authoritative positions in a great modern industry. Thus here with Queequeg, Melville does what he does all through the book, begins with the accepted practices, beliefs and even literary methods of his time, and then consciously and with the utmost sureness leaves them behind or rather takes them over into the world he saw ahead. He saw the future so confidently only because he saw so clearly all that was going on around him.

Ishmaels, we say, live in every city block. And they are dangerous, especially when they actually leave their own environment and work among workers or live among them. For when Ahab, the totalitarian, bribed the men with money and grog and whipped them up to follow him on his monomaniac quest, Ishmael, the man of good family and education, hammered and shouted with the rest. His submission to the totalitarian madness was complete.

Most of the men on the ship at some time or other showed antagonism to Ahab. Ishmael never did—not once. And the analysis of why this type of young man behaves as he does is one of Melville's greatest triumphs.

As usual with Melville's people in *Moby-Dick*, Ishmael at first sight is merely one of those dreamy young men of education and intellect who cannot live in the world. Ishmael's favorite place on board ship is up on the mast-head where he is supposed to be taking his turn at looking for whales. He never sees one, for he is up there dreaming his life away and imagining that his soul is once more at one with the waters that stretch around him to the horizon on every side. But soon it becomes apparent that Ishmael is no mere dreamer. He is a completely modern young intellectual who has broken with society and wavers constantly between totalitarianism and the crew.

First, totalitarianism. Why does Ishmael join Ahab's quest? What overwhelms him in 1851 is what modern psychologists talk about more than anything else, a sense of guilt. But it is not guilt for any sins he has personally committed. He does not feel at home in the world and he is constantly aware of this. Because of this he is dominated by a sense of inadequacy and isolation. In turn, he sees his fellow men as ridden with his own sense of homelessness and despair. As the Pequod sails in far-distant and lonely seas, sea ravens persistently perch on the stays, though repeatedly driven away. For Ishmael these birds see in the ship some drifting uninhabited craft, a thing appointed to desolation and therefore a fit resting-place for their homeless selves. The black sea heaved and heaved as if its vast tides were a conscience and the great soul of the world was in anguish and remorse for the long sin and suffering it had bred. As the Pequod rounded the stormy waters of the Cape of Good Hope these birds and the fish seem to him to be guilty beings condemned to swim on everlastingly without any haven in store or to beat that black air without any horizon. There is no such world, there are no such fish, there are no such birds. Ishmael is an intellectual Ahab. As Ahab is enclosed in the masoned walled-town of the exclusiveness of authority, so Ishmael is enclosed in the solitude of his social and intellectual speculation.

Melville makes a heroic effort to get us to understand this type of mind. Ishmael says that he followed Ahab for a reason peculiar to himself, and he adds, unless he makes us understand this, then the story he is writing will have no meaning. We have to respect what a great writer says about what he is trying to do. Ishmael says that he shouted with the rest because the color of the whale was white.

It is startling but before you have read a page you get an idea of what a great imaginative writer can do, and what philosophers, economists, journalists, historians, however gifted, can never do.

Ishmael begins his explanation with a recognition of the fact that whiteness is the color of religion, of beautiful ceremonials, of weddings, of peace, of things that are beautiful and sincere, and grandly historical and above all, spiritual. After an impressive list acknowledging what the color white has meant, he says that nevertheless it is a color of terror. He reason is clear. For him there is no longer anything beautiful or sincere, or grandly historical, and above all, there is no longer anything of spiritual beauty in the world any more. So that now wherever he sees whiteness, it is a symbol of his spiritual isolation, his loneliness, his revulsion against the world, his deep psychological misery. We understand now why at the very beginning, long before he had seen a whale-ship, far less a whale, he carried already in his mind visions of whales and among them a white hooded monster.

His experience of the world had created in his mind a picture of it which he wanted to pursue and kill because it was torturing him. It was a monster large and powerful. It was hooded, because it saw nothing, paid attention to nothing, merely went its own way. And it was white because white was for him the immediate reminder of a world without any spiritual values, which for him, an intellectual, were the things by which he lived.

In the last paragraph of this famous chapter on the whiteness of the whale, Melville ties together all the social and philosophical themes which he is weaving.

For Ishmael who believes in nothing and therefore constantly analyzes all that he sees to find something, everything in the world is appearance, something superficial, put on. He examines it and below is nothing but bare, dead, white blankness. Whatever is beautiful is only deception, a color added to this dead unending whiteness, as a whore puts paint on her face to cover the rottenness inside. Everyone sees nature in his own way. And this is the Nature that Ishmael sees. And the menace, the deadliness of Ishmael to society can be seen in a few phrases he uses to describe how he sees the natural world: "A dumb blankness, full of meaning, in a wide landscape of snows," and again, "the great principle of light, forever remains white or colorless in itself."

This is his explanation of the universe, seen as he would like us to believe, in the light of science by a thoughtful and sensitive human being. But there is nothing sensitive about it and nothing human. For when, at nights working at his charts, Ahab's humanity was conquered, there remained behind "a ray of living light to be sure, but without an object to color and therefore a blankness in itself." They are the very phrases Ishmael uses to describe his conception of Nature. Thus the totalitarian personality devoid of human feeling and restraint, no longer the master, but the instrument of his purpose, embodies in action the theoretical conclusions of the disoriented intellectual. No wonder that, with terror in his soul, Ishmael follows Ahab, as the guilt-ridden intellectual of today, often with the same terror, finds some refuge in the idea of the one-party totalitarian state.

But if Ishmael, the intellectual, is so strongly attracted to the man of action, equally strong on him is the attraction of the crew. That in fact is what makes him modern. He must decide.

Ishmael begins by clinging to the powerful Queequeg and, in typical modern fashion, his relationship with him on land has all the marks of homosexuality. But as soon as they get on board among the crew, that relationship disappears. Ishmael submits to Ahab's mad purpose. But then over a long period under the influence of daily work with them, he almost becomes one of the anonymous crew. What keeps them apart is his intellectualism, his inability to embrace reality spontaneously, the doubt and fear and guilt and isolation from people, which compel him at all times to seek to find out what is happening to him in relation to the world.

Melville does not let us for one moment escape from this distinction between Ishmael and the crew. Take the first day they see a whale. Ishmael is weaving some cord and Queequeg is helping him by periodically sliding a heavy oaken sword between the threads. As he works, Queequeg, unconsciousness personified, is looking idly at the water but Ishmael is busily constructing some complicated philosophical schema in which the whole operation is the Loom of Time, the cord is necessity and Queequeg's sword represents the free will of men. Suddenly:

"Thus we were weaving and weaving away when I started at a sound so strange, long drawn, and musically wild and unearthly, that the ball of free will dropped from my hand, and I stood gazing up at the clouds whence that voice dropped like a wing. High aloft in the cross-trees was that mad Gay-Header, Tashtego. His body was reaching eagerly forward, his hand stretched out like a wand, and at brief sudden intervals, he continued his cries. To be sure the same sound was that very moment perhaps being heard all over the seas, from hundreds of whalemen's look-outs perched as high in the air; but from few of those lungs could that accustomed old cry have derived such a marvellous cadence as from Tashtego the Indian's."

No wonder the ball of free will drops from Ishmael's hand. The energy, power, and utter concentration of the terrific Tashtego blow Ishmael's philosophical nonsense to the winds. But it does not mean that Tashtego is, philosophically, a barbarian. No. His very lack of self-consciousness in life and work is itself a philosophical attitude to life. Ishmael, looking up at him, is vaguely aware of this.

"As he stood hovering over you half suspended in air, so wildly and eagerly peering towards the horizon, you would have thought him some prophet or seer beholding the shadows of Fate, and by those wild cries announcing their coming."

After his first violent experience of what hunting a whale from an open boat is like, Ishmael almost forgets his preoccupation with himself. He decides that, whatever happens, he will take it in his stride. He goes to his friend Queequeg and makes his will. He is the one who is attached to Queequeg by the rope. He sweats and strains with the rest. One day when they are squeezing spermacetti, all their hands in the soft fluffy mixture together, he experiences a sensation of comradeship and fraternity such as he had never felt before, and he wishes they could all squeeze sperm forever.

But Ishmael can go only so far. There comes a stage in the voyage of the Pequod which breaks him to pieces and leaves him worse than before.

In *Moby-Dick* the process of labor, though very realistically described, is presented as a panorama of labor throughout the ages. The men do not merely collect and prepare the raw material. The whaleship is also a factory. When the blubber is ready, then the try-works, huge cauldrons, are put into place, and the oil is distilled. This is really modern industry. It is the turning point of the book, for everyone is shown for what he is.

That night Ishmael is at the helm and he looks down at the men working below.

"The hatch, removed from the top of the works, now afforded a wide hearth in front of them. Standing on this were the Tartarean shapes of the pagan harpooneers, always the whale-ship's stokers. With huge pronged poles they pitched hissing masses of blubber into the scalding pots, or stirred up the fires beneath, till the snaky flames darted, curling, out of the doors to catch them by the feet. The smoke rolled away in sullen heaps. To every pitch of the ship there was a pitch of the boiling oil, which seemed all eagerness to leap into their faces.

"Opposite the mouth of the works, on the further side of the wide wooden hearth, was the windlass. This served for a sea-sofa. Here lounged the watch, when not otherwise employed, looking into the red heat of the fire, till their eyes felt scorched in their heads. Their tawny features, now all begrimed with smoke and sweat, their matted beards, and the contrasting barbaric brilliancy of their teeth, all these were strangely revealed in the capricious emblazonings of the works.

"As they narrated to each other their unholy adventures, their tales of terror told in words of mirth; as their uncivilized laughter forked upwards out of them, like the flames from the furnace; as to and fro, in their front, the harpooneers wildly gesticulated with their huge pronged forks and dippers; as the wind howled on, and the sea leaped, and the ship groaned and dived, and yet steadfastly shot her red hell further and further into the blackness of the sea and the night, and scornfully champed the white bone in her mouth, and viciously spat round her on all sides; then the rushing Pequod, freighted with savages, and laden with fire, and burning a corpse, and plunging into that blackness of darkness, seemed the material counterpart of her monomaniac commander's soul."

That at first sight is the modern world—the world we live in, the world of the Ruhr, of Pittsburgh, of the Black Country in England. In its symbolism of men turned into devils, of an industrial civilization on fire and plunging blindly into darkness, it is the world of massed bombers, of cities in flames, of Hiroshima and Nagasaki, the world in which we live, the world of Ahab, which he hates and which he will organize or destroy.

But when you look again, you see that the crew is indestructible. There they are, laughing at the terrible things that have happened to them. The three harpooneers are doing their work. True to himself, Ishmael can see the ship only as an expression of Ahab's madness. The men with whom he works, even Queequeg, his splendid friend, all of them are but part of the total madness.

"Wrapped, for that interval, in darkness myself, I but the better saw the redness, the madness, the ghastliness of others. The continual sight of fiend shapes before me, capering half in smoke and half in fire, these at last begat kindred visions in my soul, so soon as I began to yield to that unaccountable drowsiness which ever would come over me at a midnight helm."

Part of his difficulty is that he is guiding the ship; in other words, however temporarily, he is in command of the ship of destiny, and such responsibility always overwhelms this type with terror.

"I thought my eyes were open; I was half conscious of putting my fingers to the lids and mechanically stretching them still further apart. But, spite of all this, I could see no compass before me to steer by; though it seemed but a minute since I had been watching the card, by the steady binnacle lamp illuminating it. Nothing seemed before me but a jet gloom, now and then made ghastly by flashes of redness. Uppermost was the impression, that whatever swift, rushing thing I stood on was not so much bound to any haven ahead as rushing from all havens astern. A stark, bewildered feeling, as of death, came over me . . ."

He caught himself just in time to prevent the ship from perhaps capsizing.

That is the end of Ishmael. Henceforth he will seek refuge from the world in books, particularly in *Ecclesiastes* where it says that "All is vanity. ALL"—in large print. He takes refuge in his philosophical abstractions—he will soar like the eagle in the mountains and even if he has to swoop, his lowest flight will still be higher than that of ordinary men.

How wrong he is is proved but one brief chapter afterwards. The boiling is over and the hatches are replaced and sealed. What follows now is the summation of a whole way of life, the climax of all that Melville has been saying about the meanest mariners, the renegades and the castaways.

"In the sperm fishery, this is perhaps one of the most remarkable incidents in all the business of whaling. One day the planks stream with freshets of blood and oil; on the sacred quarterdeck enormous masses of the whale's head are profanely piled; great rusty casks lie about, as in a brewery yard; the smoke from the try-works has besooted all the bulwarks; the mariners go about suffused with unctiousness; the entire ship seems great leviathan himself; while on all hands the din is deafening.

"But a day or two after, you look about you, and prick your ears in this self-same ship; and were it not for the tell-tale boats and try-works, you would all but swear you trod some silent merchant vessel, with a most scrupulously neat commander. The unmanufactured sperm oil possesses a singularly cleansing virtue. This is the reason why the decks never look so white as just after what they call an affair of oil. Besides, from the ashes of the burned scrapes of the whale, a potent ley is readily made; and whenever any adhesiveness from the back of the whale remains clinging to the side, that ley quickly exterminates it. Hands go diligently along the bulwarks, and with buckets of water and rags restore them to their full tidiness. The soot is brushed from the lower rigging. All the numerous implements which have been in use are likewise faithfully cleansed and put away. The great hatch is scrubbed and placed upon the try-works, completely hiding the pots; every cask is out of sight; all tackles are coiled in unseen nooks; and when by the combined and simultaneous industry of almost the entire ship's company, the whole of this conscientious duty is at last concluded, then the crew themselves proceed to their own ablutions; shift themselves from top to toe; and finally issue to the immaculate deck, fresh and all aglow, as bridegrooms new-leaped from out the daintiest Holland.

"Now, with elated step, they pace the planks in twos and threes, and humorously discourse of parlors, sofas, carpets, and fine cambrics; propose to mat the deck; think of having hangings to the top; object not to taking tea by moonlight on the piazza of the forecastle. To hint to such musked mariners of oil, and bone, and blubber, were little short of audacity. They know not the thing you distantly allude to. Away and bring us napkins!

"But mark: aloft there, at the three mast heads, stand three men intent on spying out more whales, which, if caught infallibly will again soil the old oaken furniture, and drop at least one small grease-spot somewhere. Yes; and many is the time, when, after the severest uninterrupted labors, which know no night; continuing straight through for ninety-six hours; when from the boat, where they have swelled their wrists with all day rowing on the Line,—they only step to the deck to carry vast chains, and heave the heavy windlass, and cut and slash, yea, and in their very sweatings to be smoked and burned anew by the combined fires of the equatorial sun and the equatorial try-works; when, on the heel of all this, they have finally bestirred themselves to cleanse the ship, and make a spotless dairy room of it; many is the time the poor fellows, just buttoning the necks of their clean frocks, are startled by the cry of 'There she blows!' and away they fly to fight another whale, and go through the whole weary thing again."

Thus, around the try-works, there comes to a head the hopelesss madness, the rush to destruction of Ahab, and the revulsion from the world of Ishmael. Ahab sat in his cabin marking his charts; Ishmael, thinking of books and dreaming of how he would soar above it all like an eagle, will become in his imagination as destructive as his mono-maniac leader. But the Anacharsis Clootz deputation, the meanest mariners, renegades and castaways, remain sane and human, in their ever-present sense of community, their scrupulous cleanliness, their grace and wit and humor, and their good-humored contempt of those for whom life consists of nothing else but fine cambrics and tea on the piazza.

Chapter III

THE CATASTROPHE

The try-works is the turning point. Immediately after this comes the stowing-down and cleaning-up, and from there begins the rapid decline to the final catastrophe. What we shall see from now on is the rapid unfolding, layer by layer, of the innermost depths of the individuals and groups with whom we are now acquainted.

First, Ahab.

He spends all his time now preparing. But if the rise of totalitarianism follows a logic of its own, equally relentless is the logic of its collapse.

From the beginning Ahab was, and to the end remained, a master of his science of whaling. But rapidly he narrows the very concept of science down to what serves his purpose simply and directly. Any other kind of science he will destroy.

One day he has just taken the daily reckoning from the sun with the quadrant when in a sudden rage he dashes it to the deck. " 'Science! I curse thee, thou vain toy,' " he yells and stamps upon the instrument.

His reason is one of Melville's profoundest penetrations into the nature of totalitarianism. The quadrant, Ahab says, can tell where the sun is. But it cannot tell man what he wants to know, and that is where he will be tomorrow. It lifts man's eyes up to the great and glorious sun. But man by doing so only ruins himself. Man was made to live with his eyes limited to the earth's horizons.

" 'Aye, thus I trample on thee, thou paltry thing that feebly pointest on high; thus I split and destroy thee!' " Here is the ruthless limitation of social aspirations which totalitarianism imposes on the masses of its followers. Their eyes must be kept level with the horizon until after the purpose is achieved. It is on the same evening that the storm breaks, the fires burn on the masts, and Ahab defies the fires of industry. Thus, within one day, Industry and Science, the twin gods of the nineteenth century, have been deposed.

What Ahab really wants in order to advance his purpose is to finish away altogether with men who think. This is what he tells the carpenter: "'I'll order a complete man after a desirable pattern. Imprimis, fifty feet high in his socks; then, chest modelled after the Thames Tunnel; then, legs with roots to 'em, to stay in one place; then, arms three feet through the wrist; no heart at all, brass forehead, and about a quarter of an acre of fine brains; and let me see—shall I order eyes to see outwards? No, but put a sky-light on top of his head to illuminate inwards.'"

It is a joke. Or it was a joke in 1851. But it is precisely this that is the aim of every totalitarian dictator—hundreds of millions of inhumanly strong, capable, technically efficient men with no heart to feel, without aspirations, except what their masters tell them.

And with this hatred of anything which will elevate men, and this need for men who will do nothing but respond automatically to his will, there goes of necessity an extreme subjectivism. Ahab goes to the carpenter to get a new leg and curses the interdebtedness between mortals that makes him, proud as a Greek god, indebted to the blockhead of a carpenter for a leg to stand on.

In its great days, individualism prided itself on the fact that the more individualistic it was, the more civilization progressed and the more men developed as a community. Now this monomaniac shows in an elementary thing like a new leg that he is losing all sense of reality. Henceforward we shall watch his degeneration to the point where he so identifies himself with the purpose that his own ideas, his own feelings, his own needs become the standard by which reality is tested and whatever does not fit into that must be excluded. So, early in World War II, Hitler took over the direction of the war for Germany, and repeatedly over-rode the opinions of trained diplomats and the German General Staff, committing blunder after blunder. This intense subjectivism he called his "intuition."

The question now arises, if it has not already arisen in the mind of the reader: Why didn't the men revolt? It is a question of which Melville is aware from the very beginning and he gives it his habitual systematic treatment. Ahab, we remember, knew that by law the men were entitled to revolt. Melville places the first responsibility upon the three officers and, above all, on Starbuck. The crew was "morally enfeebled" by "the incompetence of mere unaided virtue or rightmindedness in Starbuck." And so yet again Melville has anatomized for us a contemporary type.

Why is Starbuck's virtue and rightmindedness called "unaided"? Because although Starbuck talked always the traditional words about business and the rights of ownership, he did not believe in them as Ahab believes in his purpose. He knew that Ahab was mad and he protested continuously. But every protest was followed by a capitulation. That Ahab was so passionately devoted to something (no matter what it was) this was what overwhelmed Starbuck.

His story is the story of the liberals and democrats who during the last quarter of a century have led the capitulation to the totalitarians in country after country. On the night of the great storm, Starbuck, forgetting himself, shouts to Ahab before all the men, to turn back. He points to Ahab's harpoon which has caught fire from the magnetic flame on the mast. The voyage, he says, is doomed to disaster. For a moment, it seemed that Starbuck was saying what the men were thinking. They raise a half-mutinous cry and rush to the sails. One word from Starbuck and Ahab would be over the side. But Ahab seizes his harpoon and swearing to transfix with it any man who moves, tells them that he will blow out the flame and blows it out with one breath. His fearlessness, his skillful pretense of being able to command the mysterious, magnetic flame, terrify the men. It is characteristic of Starbuck that, having missed his chance when he has the men behind him, he seeks out Ahab that night, alone, to plead with him. Ahab dismisses him contemptuously. No need to emphasize that in reality, Starbuck hates the men and looks upon them as uncouth, barbarous sub-human beings.

But Ahab is running a course whose end Starbuck cannot but foresee. One night he stands in front of Ahab's cabin, and sees on the wall a musket which Ahab had threatened him with one day when he was protesting about the rights of owners. He takes the musket in his hands and reviews the situation. Ahab, he says, if not stopped, will infallibly cause the loss of the ship and all on board. One shot, and the vessel and everybody is saved. But, reasons Starbuck, there is "no lawful way" in which to stop him. That is it. There is no legal force by which to stop Ahab. So? Let him sink the ship with all on board. Why not take him prisoner? It is quite clear that Starbuck knows the men are with him. But Ahab dominates him in his innermost soul. For he admits that even if Ahab were imprisoned and fastened tight in the hold, his howls of anger and rage would be such that Starbuck would never be able to stand it. He puts the musket back on the rack and returns to the deck.

Ahab, like all totalitarians, understands a man like Starbuck to the last inch. Late in the voyage Ahab can trust no one. He has himself hoisted up to the mast-head for he does not believe that the sailors now will shout if Moby Dick appears. The line which attaches him to his high perch must obviously be entrusted to someone he can depend on. A sailor only has to let it slip, down will come Ahab crashing to the deck, and the crazy voyage, which all now dread so much, will be over. It is to the protesting Starbuck that Ahab entrusts the line and his life.

The second officer is Stubb. Observers of Communist totalitarianism in particular will have noted that most of its followers have an extraordinary capacity for accepting and accepting with apparent joy and enthusiasm policies which they execrated up to the very day they were announced. Stubb is their prototype.

He goes up to Ahab one day and makes a perfectly reasonable and civil request. Ahab threatens to kick him if he does not go away. Stubb, personally a very brave man, says that he is not accustomed to being spoken to in that way. Ahab does not budge and Stubb goes away. Next day Stubb tells Flask a dream he has had. He dreamed that Ahab had kicked him after all. But, he reasons in his dream, he was kicked only by the ivory leg. A really insulting kick could come only from a living leg. So that kick was only playful. And later in the dream someone else tells him not only that a kick with an ivory leg was a playful kick, but it was an honor to be kicked by so great a man. Stubb should consider Ahab's kicks honors. That dream, continues Stubb, made a wise man of me. And he advises Flask that in future whatever Ahab says, they should do, and never question it.

The night after the scene on the deck with the magnetic flames, it is clear that disaster is not far off. Flask pleads with Stubb.

"'Didn't you once say that whatever ship Ahab sails in, that ship should pay something extra on its insurance policy, just as though it were loaded with powder barrels aft and boxes of lucifers forward? Stop, now; didn't you say so?'"

Stubb's reply shows how deeply Melville saw into the type.

"'Well, suppose I did? What then? I've part changed my flesh since that time, why not my mind? Besides, supposing we *are* loaded with powder barrels aft and lucifers forward; how the devil could the lucifers get afire in this drenching spray here?'"

It is most likely that Melville, working on board ship, had observed closely how men rationalized their subservience to tyranny, and from there plunged into an imaginative projection of the process carried to its logical conclusion. But whatever the process of creation, nowhere does there exist a more penetrating description of how the Communist makes a virtue and a pleasure of accepting what to the ordinary human being would be degradation and self-destruction, and at the same time ties any doubters into knots of confusion and sophistry. Needless to say, the mediocre Flask goes along with Stubb. These are the three men who represent competence, sanity, tradition, against monomaniac Ahab. Melville claims that they did not help the men, they demoralized them. And we of this day and generation have seen it happen often enough.

The reader of today, however, may still ask: But if Starbuck, Stubb and Flask were incapable of resisting Ahab, why didn't the men revolt? But to ask this question is not merely to see the book of 1851 with the eyes of 1952 which, however we try, we cannot avoid doing. It is to do much worse, it is to inject the social problems of 1952 into the social problems of 1851. Whereby it becomes impossible to understand either literature or society.

Let us remind ourselves of Melville's view of his problem in 1851. The Pequod is taking a voyage that humanity has periodically to take into the open sea, into the unknown, because of the problems posed to it by life on the safe sheltered land. The Pequod set out on that voyage. But, as always on these journeys, mankind finds reflected in the water only the image of what it has brought with it. When the Pequod set out so bravely and boldly, it carried in its very heart, in the captain's cabin, the monomaniac Ahab, as genuine a part of that society as is Starbuck. Ahab will lead the vessel to inevitable destruction and those whose responsibility it is to defend the society will be completely incapable of doing so.

Melville took great pains to show that revolt was no answer to the question he asked. As soon as his narrative gave him the opportunity, he introduces a story of a revolt on another vessel. The great length of the story and the power Melville put into it showed how important it was for him. Steelkilt, a magnificent specimen of manhood and a sailor of heroic mould, leads a revolt against a tyrannical mate and a weak captain. The revolt is in the end successful. But what happens? Steelkilt and some of his fellow-mutineers escape and get back home again. That's all. Everything goes back to just where it was before. That is exactly what would have happened in 1851 if there had been a revolt on the Pequod. We would have been left in the end exactly where we had been at the beginning.

As a creative artist, Melville went further to indicate what humanity would inevitably produce. With profound philosophical insight, he indicated what were the elements of a new reorganization of society and where they were to be found. To accomplish this he achieved a miracle of artistic subtlety in the treatment of the crew and artistic audacity in his creation of the harpooneers. But he left all this subordinate to his main theme, how the society of free individualism would give birth to totalitarianism and be unable to defend itself against it.

Melville's theme is totalitarianism, its rise and fall, its power and its weakness. For long before Moby Dick actually destroys him, Ahab begins to show the fatal weaknesses of the course he has embarked upon. He begins to weaken on the side of Fedallah and he begins to weaken on the side of Pip.

Few dictators, however well-established, depend entirely on a regular army, a regular police, and the normal protection of power. They usually create a special force, loyal to themselves alone, men totally alien from the population, who are dependent entirely upon the dictator for life, for livelihood, and for ideas to live by. Ahab has such a force. He has hidden on board a boat's crew of savages from the Manillas, a tribe notorious for evil, and at their head is Fedallah, a Parsee fire-worshipper. Fedallah is a horrible creature, with a single tooth in his mouth, and a white turban, consisting of his own hair, wrapped around his head. He is one of those persons you still meet in the Far East who seem to have survived from the days when men still asked why the sun and moon were created.

This evil monster, Fedallah, poses in a very sharp way the relation between a writer's creation and a reader. No one can say what *exactly* Fedallah is. And if Melville himself had tried to analyze and explain Fedallah, he would in all probability have made a mess of it and given up the attempt. His strength is not analysis but creation. Yet Fedallah is an extraordinarily vivid, perfectly logical, perfectly consistent character. He lives. And as such we shall say what he means to us.

Totalitarianism is utterly alien to the vast majority of modern men, alien to the way they work, alien to the social environment in which they live, alien to their sense of individual personality, alien to their need for free expression. Thus the totalitarian power must find, create, educate a special staff of men who are psychologically primitive, aborigines, with the added horror that they use modern weapons and modern science. It is impossible to account otherwise for the desperate inhuman cruelties which systematically are carried out day after day in, for example, totalitarian concentration camps. This is the literal reversion to barbarism. Unless one understands that men are such highly social creatures, so highly civilized, even when individually they are only meanest mariners, renegades and castaways, that only the most monstrous barbarism can hold them down, then one has to fall back into the theory of the inherent evil in human nature as such, and the hopelessness and despair which are so rampant today. Totalitarianism and barbarism are inseparable, twin sides of the same coin, and Melville makes Ahab and Fedallah inseparable.

One midnight when all the crew is asleep, Ahab starts from his slumbers to face the Parsee. "Hooped round by the gloom of the night they seemed the last men in a flooded world." The superb phrase is, as it is always, not something to admire, but a beacon-light in the illumination of Fedallah. Together he and Ahab are leading society to its destruction.

Henceforth at every new appearance, Fedallah's relation to Ahab becomes clearer. When Ahab smashed the quadrant, Fedallah exhibits a sense of triumph for Ahab and despair for himself. In his own twisted way, Ahab is elevating men above things. That day Ahab speaks to the fires burning on the masts. It is his greatest moment, he is defying fire in the name of humanity, limited though his conception of humanity is. During that scene Fedallah is crouched on the deck, and Ahab's foot is on him. Fedallah, who as a primitive aboriginal worships fire for fire's sake, is completely defeated.

But as they learn from passing ships that Moby Dick is near, and Ahab begins to be dragged down by the weight of his purpose, Fedallah establishes his now permanent relation with Ahab. Though they do not speak, at night in particular, they stand for hours looking at each other. In Fedallah Ahab sees his forethrown shadow; in Ahab Fedallah sees his abandoned substance. Sometimes Ahab seems independent of him, sometimes they seem joined together. Ahab is power, Fedallah only a shade, but the shadow is always before him. Fedallah is certain that Ahab is doomed, that Ahab's attempt to humanize industry and science is doomed to failure. Fedallah waits the moment when once more man will bow down to fire, completely and abjectly. That is the way aboriginal man worshipped it. That is the substance which Ahab has abandoned. Fedallah waits. Ahab, he is sure, will come back to him. Hemp, he prophesies, will kill Ahab. But by this time Ahab is incapable of any reasoning which runs counter to his purpose. Hemp is most obviously the whale-line. But Ahab, thinking he means the gallows, laughs at the prophecy.

Fedallah prophesies also that the wood of Ahab's hearse can only be American. He means the ship. Ahab will bury himself in the wreck of American industrial civilization, symbolized by the line and the whaling-vessel. At this also Ahab jeers. But he falls silent and he and Fedallah continue to watch one another in silence day after day.

Your whole interpretation of Fedallah depends upon recognizing Ahab for what he is. You can call him the spirit of evil, the diabolical in Ahab's character, etc., only if you see Ahab as some private individual suffering from megalomania, sexual crisis, or some such personalized difficulty, symbolical, but symbolical of human nature in general. But once he is seen as a specific type of person, at a specific point of historical time, produced by specific historical circumstances, then Fedallah becomes the spectre of barbarism, of modern man on his knees before economic plans, charts of production and numbers of planes, of productivity quotas, and all the multifarious paraphernalia of modern civilization, with man at the center, bowing down before it, as blind, as hopeless, as self-destructive, as the savage who bowed down before five thousand years ago.

If in Fedallah, Melville has dramatized the extreme form of the return to barbarism that is dragging Ahab down on the one side, he has on the other side created an equally daring dramatization of the unattainable vision that floats in Ahab's disordered mind. Pip, the little Negro boy, is its exponent. Pip has gone mad. Frightened by the line, he jumped out of the whale-boat once and was warned. He jumped a second time, and this time the boat went on after the whale and left him behind. He was fished up by another boat but by that time he had lost his reason. With the loss of his reason he attains the ultimate wisdom. He looks down into the bottom of the sea and sees the origin of the universe. He does not disturb himself any more about the search for ultimate truths which permeate the human consciousness. Pip becomes as indifferent and as uncompromised as God. This is madness so-called. It is in reality the wisdom of heaven. It is Melville's way of saying that the perpetual preoccupation with human destiny, the thing that was eating the heart out of Ahab, Ishmael and Starbuck, the profundities of philosophy and religion, *this* was madness. And madness it is, for men torment themselves about these abstractions only when they cannot make satisfactory contact with the reality around them.

But Pip learned even greater wisdom. He lost fear. Alone of all the crew he now spoke to the terrible Ahab as one human being to another. The effect is startling. Profoundly moved by this direct assault upon the traditional usages that had shaped his whole character, Ahab befriended Pip and took him into his cabin. There was some sociability in that cabin at last. Yet Ahab remains Ahab. When Pip weeps at Ahab's leaving him to go on deck, Ahab threatens to crush him, for he feels that if Pip continues in that way, his purpose will be weakened. Pip subsides and Ahab puts him to sit in Ahab's own chair. Then occurs one of the most strangely moving passages in the whole book. Crazy little Pip imagines that he, the little Alabama Negro, is entertaining great Admirals with high hats and gold-braid and lace. A black boy, he says, is host to white men with gold lace upon their coat. He invites them to fill up and drink and put their feet on the table. In his mad world, even Pip, the little Negro and the little coward, can meet great Admirals on terms of equality and good fellowship.

Pip is modelled on a famous Shakespearean character, the Fool in Shakespeare's *King Lear*. Lear is also an old man who has gone mad and the Fool is Lear's jester, himself a half-wit. Both Shakespeare and Melville knew that at all times and in all places there are certain simple people who are outside the normal categories of society and think and act with a simple directness that takes no interest in the great problems for which the majority of intelligent men destroy themselves and lay the world in ruins. These usually half-witted folk think simply and directly of what is humanly right or wrong. No one who is active in practical affairs can follow the advice they give because it is not realistic, their simplicity often being the result of mental weakness. But somehow what they say haunts the mind as it contemplates the pain and woe and catastrophes which able and powerful and realistic men, following worldly wisdom, bring upon themselves and the world. And this advice very often turns out to be not only humane but wise. The only thing wrong with it is that men cannot follow it. So the crazy Cassandra in the *Oresteia*, the greatest play of ancient times, prophesies, but no one will listen to her. The fool plays the same role in *King Lear*, and Pip in *Moby-Dick*. So the Biblical author of Revelations prophesied a time when the lion and the lamb will lie down in peace. At the back of the minds of the very greatest writers is always this vision. It would not be difficult to prove that without it they would not be the men they are.

Pip did not think in terms of the nationalization of production or of the political reorganization of society. In his ignorance he thought that it would be a wonderful world if a little American Negro boy who was a proven coward could entertain great Admirals in gold-braid and ask them to pass the bottle and put their feet on the table. And his simple faith and good-fellowship nearly broke Ahab's unbreakable will. Pip plays no great part in the book, as the Pips play no great part in the world. But his importance is in the mind of his creator. When Melville, who understood the complicated modern world as few men have ever done, nevertheless introduced Pip at the very beginning of his book, he uncompromisingly stated that when Pip went crazy, the highest place would be his. It is enough that Melville, writing his great book a hundred years ago, found a place in it for Pip. We today can judge better than he whether he was justified or not.

Even in such a mind as Ahab's Pip can find a response. But Pips never turn Ahabs aside from their purpose. The captain of the *Rachel*, one of the many symbolical ships that meet the Pequod on its long journey, now informs Ahab that he saw Moby Dick the day before, and at the same time begs him to stay and cruise with them in search of a boat's crew that is lost. On it is the captain's son, a boy of twelve. Ahab refuses. He has cut himself off from all humanity.

He is now regularly up in the mast-head himself scanning the sea for his enemy. One day a sea-hawk, a type of bird which often troubles men in this high spot, makes off with his hat and soars into the skies. Somehow this episode reminds us of Ishmael, that intellectual running away from the try-works by promising himself that he will soar like an eagle. But at last the sea-hawk drops the hat and every one can see the small black object falling from that great height into the sea. All these marvelous ideas of these mind-ridden individualists are going to find their proper place before long.

. . .

So the Pequod meets Moby Dick at last. Moby Dick is what he has always been—an exceptional but by no means solitary example of a whale who attacks his pursuers with cunning and ferocity. But grand fighter though he is, in the great battle with the Pequod, whenever Moby Dick sees a chance, he tries to run away. Destiny is on the Pequod, not in the whale who glides in the sunshine.

"As they neared him, the ocean grew still more smooth; seemed drawing a carpet over its waves; seemed a noon-meadow, so serenely it spread. At length the breathless hunter came so nigh his seemingly unsuspecting prey, that his entire dazzling hump was distinctly visible, sliding along the sea as if an isolated thing, and continually set in a revolving ring of finest, fleecy, greenish foam. He saw the vast, involved wrinkles of the slightly projecting head beyond.

"Before it, far out on the soft Turkish-rugged waters, went the glistening white shadow from his broad, milky forehead, a musical rippling playfully accompanying the shade; and behind, the blue waters interchangeably flowed over into the moving valley of his steady wake; and on either hand bright bubbles arose and danced at his side. But these were broken again by the light toes of hundreds of gay fowls softly feathering the sea, alternate with their fitful flight; and like to some flag-staff rising from the painted hull of an argosy, the tall but shattered pole of a recent lance projected from the white whale's back; and at intervals one of the cloud of soft-toed fowls hovering, and to and fro skimming like a canopy over the fish, silently perched and rocked on this pole, the long tail feathers streaming like pennons.

"A gentle joyousness—a mighty mildness of repose in swiftness, invested the gliding whale. Not the white bull Jupiter swimming away with ravished Europa clinging to his graceful horns; his lovely, leering eyes sideways intent upon the maid; with smooth bewitching fleetness, rippling straight for the nuptial bower in Crete; not Jove, not that great majesty Supreme! did surpass the glorified White Whale as he so divinely swam."

This is the way a Greek in his happy sunny civilization would have seen Moby Dick. But to the Pequod the sight of him means Armageddon—the war of wars. The struggle rages for three days. It extends from the far reaches of the sky to the depths of the ocean, the boats, the deck, the ship, within the horizon to windward and to leeward, the bottom of the ocean. Never before and never since have been reproduced in literature such energy, such violence, such rage and hate. But equally powerful, if less spectacularly presented, is the power of human association for a common purpose, the unconquerable spirit of man, the answer that the Pequod set out to seek.

Moby Dick is a power. On that first day he holds Ahab's boat in his mouth and bites it in two. Ahab is spilled into the sea and floats helplessly in the foam of the whale's tail. The Pequod itself has to sail on Moby Dick to part him from his victim.

That night Moby Dick tries to put as much distance as possible between him and his pursuers. But such is the scientific knowledge of whaling geniuses like Ahab, that he can foretell where Moby will be at dawn the next day.

That day, as if to strike quick terror into pursuers who will not leave him alone, Moby Dick attacks all the boats simultaneously, rushing among them with open jaws and lashing tail. Three lines are fastened into him. But the White Whale crossed and recrossed and in a thousand ways entangled the slack of the lines, then in a mass of discarded harpoons and lances dashed together two of the boats like rolling husks on a surf-beaten beach. Moby Dick then dives down and shooting up perpendicularly from the depths sends Ahab's boat tossing round and round in the air. Trailing the irons in him and the lines still attached to them, he once more sets out upon his own way at a traveller's methodic pace.

That night they discover that Fedallah is gone and the next day, when Moby Dick appears, they see the body of the Parsee lashed to the body of the whale by the convolutions of the line. A man must be chosen to replace Fedallah in Ahab's diabolical crew and the man chosen is Ishmael. Blown by the beneficient Trade Winds, the Pequod again pursues the whale during the night. On the third day the boats dash to the attack and, maddened perhaps by the irons that now corrode in him, Moby Dick seems combinedly possessed by all the angels that fell from heaven. He disables the boats and once more starts to swim away, though not as fast as before. This time perhaps it is a maneuver, or he may be tired after nearly three days of being pursued. Ahab's boat is still unharmed. It has been overturned, and three men have been thrown out, but two have scrambled back. The third man, left swimming, is Ishmael.

The actual positions of everyone must now be well understood. Despite the terrible battles of the three days, not one man, except Fedallah, has been lost and all are safely aboard the ship. Ahab is alone with his crew of devils on the water. Ishmael is, as usual, neither with the crew nor with Ahab—he is still swimming in the water. Moby Dick is swimming away.

Starbuck is in charge of the ship. He calls agonizingly to Ahab to desist, shows him that Moby Dick is not chasing him, that it is he, Ahab, who is chasing Moby Dick. Ahab dashes a harpoon into Moby Dick, but the line breaks. Once more Ahab urges his oarsmen up to the whale. It is then that Moby Dick wheels round and charges the ship itself. As a really gigantic sperm whale is able to do, the White Whale rams the vessel with its head, and then charges it again, so that the ship is soon sinking. But Ahab hurls still one more harpoon into Moby Dick. The harpoon goes home, but the line runs foul. He stoops to clear it, he does clear it, but it catches him around the neck, and without a word he is shot out of the boat and is gone before even his boat's crew realizes it. The ship goes down and drags the boat and all the crew with it, except Ishmael, who is rescued, and lives to tell the story.

It is to this crisis that they have been heading ever since they started on the quest. The final answer lies in how each meets it.

First, Ahab.

Tragedy shows the will of man at its most indomitable scope, and Ahab's spirit is unconquerable. His skill, his energy, his leadership are at their highest. But Ahab is a doomed man and he goes into battle knowing this. Having the highest technical and social achievements of his age under his command, he is completely isolated from them except as they serve his purpose.

In this final crisis his isolation becomes so complete that he no longer has any sense of relation with other human beings at all. Ahab is the first to see Moby Dick, though he defeats Tashtego only by a fraction of a second. "'Fate reserved the doubloon for me,'" says Ahab. "'*I* only . . .'" He only, that is his theme.

He makes his most devastating criticism of Starbuck and Stubb—Stubb is Starbuck and Starbuck is Stubb, reversed. This is perhaps as profound a thing as Ahab has said in all that journey, that Stubb's indifference and perpetual good humor and Starbuck's life of unremitting moral crisis are merely different responses to the same weakness—the inability to make of life a creative adventure. But Ahab thinks that all men are like Stubb and Starbuck, and he, Ahab, stands alone among all the millions of the earth, neither of God (because gods have not these troubles) but more than a man.

He loses all sense of objectivity and sees himself in such subjective terms that he is now a mortal danger to all around him in the very thing in which he is so skilled, whaling. By the second day he is saying, "'Nor white whale, nor man, nor fiend, can so much as graze old Ahab in his own proper and inaccessible being.'"

He lives entirely in abstractions. He is the "unconquerable captain" of his soul. His "soul is a centipede that moves on a hundred legs." Before he breaks, they will hear him crack and until they hear that, let them know that "Ahab's hawser tows his purpose yet." Fedallah's death is a riddle that may baffle all the lawyers backed by the ghosts of the whole line of judges. But: "*I'll, I'll* solve it though!" He will solve everything. It is the biography of the last days of Adolf Hitler.

This is the end reached by the mechanization through science and industry which he so hates but which he, and no other, has carried to its logical extremity. His world is divided into the men of education, thought, feeling, soul and spirit, and the mass who must obey. Ahab sees himself entirely in terms of spirit and intelligence. In this matter of the whale, he tells Starbuck that Starbuck's face should be as the palm of his hand, a blank without lips or features. The climax is reached on the third day when he tells the crew of his boat that they are not other men but his arms and legs. This is not Ahab's personal character. It is the final end of his attack, in the name of individual personality, upon the society which to the end he denounces as mechanical. *He* will be soul and brains and spirit, and the rest of mankind will be arms and legs. It is the elite theory of totalitarianism, whatever its origins, shapes or forms.

But, as always, counter to this ultimate climax of individualism, this frenzy of subjectivity, megalomania and fatalistic despair, stands the crew.

When Melville first introduces them at the very beginning of the voyage, he said that they followed Ahab because to some degree they saw in the White Whale the great gliding demon of the sea of life. A hasty reader might easily have fallen into the belief that they too suffered from the social system which so tortured Ahab, and therefore saw the White Whale as crazy Ahab saw it. But first Ahab was mad. They were sane. And in any case Melville stops this line of thought at once by going on to say that why exactly they follow Ahab, he does not really know. As the Pequod approached Moby Dick, the crew becomes gloomy and terror-stricken. But now suddenly on the second day a transformation takes place that leaves them indeed still under Ahab's command but at one stroke makes the separation between him and them total and complete.

"The ship tore on; leaving such a furrow in the sea as when a cannonball, missent, becomes a plough-share and turns up the level field.

" 'By salt and hemp!' cried Stubb, 'but this swift motion of the deck creeps upon one's legs and tingles at the heart. This ship and I are two brave fellows!—Ha! ha! Some one take me up, and launch me, spine-wise, on the sea,—for by live-oaks! my spine's a keel. Ha, ha! we go the gait that leaves no dust behind!'

" 'There she blows—she blows!—she blows!—right ahead!' was now the mast-head cry.

" 'Aye, aye!' cried Stubb, 'I knew it—ye can't escape—blow on and split your spout, O whale! the mad fiend himself is after ye! blow your trumpet, blister your lungs!—Ahab will dam off your blood, as a miller shuts his water-gate upon the stream!'

"And Stubb did but speak out for well nigh all that crew. The frenzies of the chase had by this time worked them bubblingly up, like old wine worked anew. Whatever pale fears and forebodings some of them might have felt before; these were not only now kept out of sight through the growing awe of Ahab, but they were broken up, and on all sides routed, as timid prairie hares that scatter before the bounding bison. The hand of Fate had snatched all their souls; and by the stirring perils of the previous day; the rack of the past night's suspense; the fixed, unfearing, blind, reckless way in which their wild craft went plunging towards its flying mark; by all these things, their hearts were bowled along. The wind that made great bellies of their sails, and rushed the vessel on by arms invisible as irresistible; this seemed the symbol of that unseen agency which so enslaved them to the race.

"They were one man, not thirty. For as the one ship that held them all; though it was put together of all contrasting things— oak, and maple, and pine wood; iron, and pitch, and hemp— yet all these ran into each other in the one concrete hull, which shot on its way, both balanced and directed by the long central keel; even so, all the individualities of the crew, this man's valor, that man's fear; guilt and guiltiness, all varieties were welded into oneness, and were all directed to that fatal goal which Ahab their one lord and keel did point to.

"The rigging lived. The mast-heads, like the tops of tall palms, were outspreadingly tufted with arms and legs. Clinging to a spar with one hand, some reached forth the other with impatient wavings; others, shading their eyes from the vivid sunlight, sat far out on the rocking yards; all the spars in full bearing of mortals, ready and ripe for their fate. Ah! how they still strove through that infinite blueness to seek out the thing that might destroy them!

"'Why sing ye not out for him, if ye see him?' cried Ahab, when, after the lapse of some minutes since the first cry, no more had been heard. 'Sway me up, men; ye have been deceived; not Moby Dick casts one odd jet that way, and then disappears.'

"It was even so; in their headlong eagerness, the men had mistaken some other thing for the whale-spout, as the event itself soon proved; for hardly had Ahab reached his perch; hardly was the rope belayed to its pin on deck, when he struck the keynote to an orchestra that made the air vibrate as with the combined discharges of rifles.

"The triumphant halloo of thirty buckskin lungs was heard, as—much nearer to the ship than the place of the imaginary jet, less than a mile ahead—Moby Dick bodily burst into view! For not by any calm and indolent spoutings; not by the peaceable gush of that mystic fountain in his head, did the White Whale now reveal his vicinity; but by the far more wondrous phenomenon of breaching. Rising with his utmost velocity from the furthest depths, the Sperm Whale thus booms his entire bulk into the pure element of air, and piling up a mountain of dazzling foam, shows his place to the distance of seven miles and more. In those moments, the torn, enraged waves he shakes

off, seem his mane; in some cases, this breaching is his act of defiance.
"'There she breaches! there she breaches!' was the cry, as in his immeasurable bravadoes the White Whale tossed himself salmon-like to Heaven."

It is the noblest piece of writing in the book and fittingly so. This is modern man, one with Nature, master of technology, all personal individuality freely subordinated to the excitement of achieving a common goal. They have reached it at last by the complete integration of the ship and the wind and the sea and their own activity. True, it has been achieved under the whip of Ahab. But whereas Ahab is all isolation, all loneliness, all megalomania and irresponsible madness, the men, in no way inferior to him in technical skill, endurance and determination, are moved by feelings common to all humanity in its greatest moments. This is the reason why they followed Ahab, though at the beginning Melville says he does not know. Once before we have been given a hint of it, that is when Melville says that the thing that appealed to Queequeg, Tashtego and Daggoo in Ahab was his inflexible determination to conquer the whale.

This separation of the men from Ahab is objectively placed before us. Towards the end of the third day, Ahab's boat is the only one in the sea. Starbuck, we remember, in charge of the ship, tells Ahab that the whale is swimming away—to let him go. Ahab as usual ignores Starbuck. But in the pursuit of Moby Dick, he has to pass by the ship.

"Glancing upwards, he saw Tashtego, Queequeg, and Daggoo, eagerly mounting to the three mast-heads; while the oarsmen were rocking in the two staved boats which had but just been hoisted to the side, and were busily at work in repairing them. One after the other, through the portholes, as he sped, he also caught flying glimpses of Stubb and Flask, busying themselves on deck among bundles of new irons and lances. As he saw all this; as he heard the hammers in the broken boats; far other hammers seemed driving a nail into his heart. But he rallied. And now marking that the vane or flag was gone from the main-mast-head, he shouted to Tashtego, who had just gained that perch, to descend again for another flag, and a hammer and nails, and so nail it to the mast."

That is really the end. Stubb and Flask have joined the crew and are all excitement and activity. Ahab, already a broken man, and Ishmael, his intellectual counterpart, are in the boat with Ahab's diabolical crew. Starbuck, as usual, is in between, pleading with Ahab.

That the ship actually goes down, therefore, is because Starbuck in charge of it, would not, could not, recognize that Ahab and his diabolical crew no longer had any place in it, and that if he continued to follow Ahab, then complete catastrophe would be the result. He did not even have to capture or to bind Ahab now. But by this time the miserable Starbuck, chief representative and defender in words of Nantucket civilization, had become Ahab's slave. He has called him, "my captain, my captain!—noble heart," and "heart of wrought steel." He has begged Ahab to note how Starbuck, a brave man, weeps. Ahab has brushed him aside.

Starbuck can be in no doubt of the end. Ahab, sinking inside, tells him how some men die at ebb tide, others at low tide, some at the full of the flood, and he, Ahab, feels like a billow that is all one crested comb. He is old, he says, and asks Starbuck to shake hands with him. Starbuck himself feels the dampness of the ocean which will entomb him. But he remains enslaved and does his duty, carries out Ahab's orders.

One swift episode shows Melville's understanding of men like Starbuck. Starbuck will betray a whole way of life and the lives of a ship's crew. But he flares up once only, when he believes, mistakenly, that Ahab has called him a coward. As death approaches, he pulls himself together to die bravely and not like a fainting woman. He has no social sense whatever and all that he is really interested in is his own sense of personal righteousness. Stubb says that his approaching death will be somewhat salty and wishes he had some red cherries to eat. Flask, mediocre to the last, says he is not interested in cherries. He hopes his mother has drawn some of his pay in advance. So die three men, representatives, and very capable representatives, of what the old Nantucketers had built up and left behind in his hands of Bildad and Peleg.

The issue rests between Ahab and the crew, and in the last two pages, Melville draws to a conclusion and makes external the deep innermost structure of his gigantic creation. For a moment it looks as if the final word will be Ahab's, as if Ahab will dominate to the end. As the whale rams the ship, the men stand watching it in a peculiar silence and inaction, most of them in the bows, and the three harpooneers in the three mast-heads. Thus they take the shock.

Ahab hurls his last harpoon in bitterness and a conviction of defeat and despair.

"'Towards thee I roll, thou all-destroying but unconquering whale; to the last I grapple with thee; from hell's heart I stab at thee; for hate's sake I spit my last breath at thee. Sink all coffins and all hearses to one common pool! and since neither can be mine, let me then tow to pieces, while still chasing thee, though tied to thee, thou damned whale! *Thus,* I give up the spear!'"

His last words are in the same rhythm he uses when he stamps upon the quadrant, the rhythm of frustration and defeat. He has seen his ship smashed. His last hope is that he will be attached to his enemy and tow forever behind him. But even that he is denied. It is the line which takes him around the neck and kills him, throwing him out of the boat.

But the last word is not with Ahab. All through that afternoon we have been kept aware that Ahab's ship is in danger of losing its commander's flag. Starbuck notices it first. A sea hawk, a bird of the same kind which had symbolically soared into the highest heavens with Ahab's hat, kept pecking at the flag, and Starbuck saw it soar away with the cloth. For him it was an omen to make Ahab "shudder, shudder." Ahab did not shudder. He shouted to Tashtego who had climbed up to the main-mast-head to come down again for another flag and hammer and nails and so nail the flag up again to the mast. Tashtego did so and was up there nailing when Moby Dick turned to charge the ship.

"Meantime, for that one beholding instant, Tashtego's mast-head hammer remained suspended in his hand; and the red flag, half-wrapping him as with a plaid, then streamed itself straight out from him, as his own forward-flowing heart; while Starbuck and Stubb, standing upon the bow-spirit beneath, caught sight of the down-coming monster just as soon as he."

The last five words are crucial for it is at the sight of Moby Dick bearing down upon them that Starbuck pulls himself together not to die like a fainting woman and Stubb feels his need for cherries. They are crumpling, Ahab's heart is cracking, but while the flag streams forward from Tashtego's still forward-flowing heart, the Indian had stopped hammering for that one moment only. His spirit was undaunted. After his one glance, he continued to hammer. With the shock of the whale's attack he seems to have stopped, for Ahab calls to him that he wants to hear his hammer.

The ship sinks until only the uppermost masts are out of the water, where, "fixed by infatuation, or fidelity, or fate," the pagan harpooneers still maintain their look-outs upon the sea. The water finally covers the masts and carries everything out of sight, every floating oar, every lance-pole, and human being. All seems over.

"But as the last whelmings intermixingly poured themselves over the sunken head of the Indian at the mainmast, leaving a few inches of the erect spar yet visible, together with long streaming yards of the flag, which calmly undulated, with ironical coincidings, over the destroying billows they almost touched;—at that instant, a red arm and a hammer hovered backwardly uplifted in the open air, in the act of nailing the flag faster and yet faster to the subsiding spar. A sky-hawk that tauntingly had followed the main-truck downwards from its natural home among the stars, pecking at the flag, and incommoding Tashtego there; this bird now chanced to intercept its broad fluttering wing between the hammer and the wood; and simultaneously feeling that etherial thrill, the submerged savage beneath, in his death-grasp, kept his hammer frozen there; and so the bird of heaven, with archangelic shrieks, and his imperial beak thrust upwards, and his whole captive form folded in the flag of Ahab, went down with his ship, which, like Satan, would not sink to hell till she had dragged a living part of heaven along with her, and helmeted herself with it."

That world, the world of Bildad, Peleg and Starbuck, had gone down forever. Ahab's attempt to make it tolerable for himself had ruined both himself and them. It had gone to its own concept of hell. And Tashtego, that splendid savage, had seen to it that its banner, and its archangelic bird, with its vain soarings into the heavens, should go down too, so that every vestige of that world, its heaven or its hell, should be destroyed.

"Now small fowls flew screaming over the yet yawning gulf; a sullen white surf beat against its steep sides; then all collapsed, and the great shroud of the sea rolled on as it rolled five thousand years ago."

Chapter IV

FICTION AND REALITY

The question of questions is: how could a book from the world of 1850 contain so much of the world of the 1950s? The best answer is given by Melville himself. He once explained how great writers wrote great books. A character like Ahab is an original character. And by original character Melville meant a type of human being that had never existed before in the world. Such characters come once in many centuries and are as rare as men who found new religions, philosophers who revolutionize human thinking, and statesmen who create new political forms. Melville mentions three: Satan from Milton's *Paradise Lost,* Hamlet from Shakespeare's play and the Don Quixote of Cervantes. That is how rare they are. According to Melville, many a gifted writer can create dozens of interesting, sprightly, clever, intriguing characters. But original characters? No. A writer is very lucky if in his lifetime he creates one.

Where does a writer find such characters? And here Melville is categorical. He finds them in the world around him, in the world *outside.* They do not originate in his head.

The process seems to be as follows. The originality, the newness, in the actual human beings a great writer sees, are half-formed, partial, incomplete. Starting from these hints, the great writer creates the type as it would be if its originality were perfected. As a fully developed human personality, a character like Hamlet, Don Quixote, Ahab never existed, and in fact could not exist. He is a composite of a realistic base from which imagination and logic build a complete whole. But if something new in personality has really come into the world, if the writer observes closely enough, and his creative power is great enough, then future generations will be able actually to see and recognize the type in a manner the author himself was not able to do.

But almost as important is the second aspect of the process. As the artist clarifies the newness, the originality of the character, the character itself becomes a kind of revolving light illuminating what is around it. Everything else grows and develops to correspond to this central figure so that the original character, so to speak, helps the artist to create a portrait not only of a new type of human being but also of the society and the people who correspond to him.

Melville does not say this about Ahab and *Moby-Dick* in so many words. But the evidence is overwhelming that when writing about characters like Hamlet and Don Quixote, and how they were created, he was drawing on his own experience in creating Ahab. Except for Aristotle, nearly 2500 years ago, and Hegel who wrote a generation before Melville, no critic of literature has written so profoundly of the art of great writing.

What is most important in this theory is the idea that the great tragic writer has to work out an adequate conception of the character, to create the character in its perfection. It is a process that lasts for years until finally a great masterpiece is written. To follow this in the case of Melville, we need only the bare elementary facts of his life before *Moby-Dick* and these can be told in less than a hundred words.

Melville was born in New York in 1819, of a good family. But his people lost their money and after doing various odd jobs, he went to sea as a common sailor, first to England and then to the Pacific on a whaling-vessel. He deserted, lived among the natives, and finally, after four years came home as a seaman on board a ship of the United States navy. He was twenty-five years old. He began to write, his first book was a success, and between 1845 and 1850 he published five books. In 1851 he wrote *Moby-Dick*.

No one except scholars and people specially interested in literature need read any of these books. They are not worth it. But it is in them that lies the answer as to how Melville came to write *Moby-Dick*. It is no miracle. You can trace the same process in the writings of Shakespeare.

The first book, *Typee,* is an account of Melville's life among that cannibal people. But quite early in the book we who are familiar with *Moby-Dick* come across the following episode.

The hero is plotting to escape from the ship, and he decides to ask another man to accompany him, one Toby. Toby "was one of that class of rovers you sometimes meet at sea, who never reveal their origin, never allude to home, and go rambling over the world as if pursued by some mysterious fate they cannot possibly elude. . . . He was a strange wayward being, moody, fitful, and melancholy—at times almost morose. He had a quick and fiery temper too, which, when thoroughly roused, transported him into a state bordering on delirium. It is strange the power that a mind of deep passion has over feebler natures. I have seen a brawny fellow, with no lack of ordinary courage, fairly quail before this slender stripling, when in one of his furious fits. . . .

"No one ever saw Toby laugh. . . ."

Now there was a real person, Toby, who shared Melville's adventure. He settled down on land. He lost no leg, captained no ship and pursued no whales. But here, already, Melville's mind is struck by the type of person who will eventually become Ahab. Deep resentment against the world, solitude, gloom, power over men.

At the same time his mind thus early is open. In *Typee* he holds up to admiration the civilization of the Typees and makes the most damaging comparisons with Western civilization. Melville says that during the weeks he lived among the Typees, no one was ever put on trial for any public offense. As far as he could see there were no courts of law or equity. No police. Yet everything went on in the valley with a perfect harmony and smoothness. He denounces missionaries, white traders and government officials for degrading and corrupting this ideal civilization, cannibalistic as it was.

"I will frankly declare," he writes, "that after passing a few weeks in this valley of the Marquesas, I formed a higher estimate of human nature than I had ever before entertained. But alas! since then I have become one of a crew of a man-of-war and the pent-up wickedness of five hundred men has nearly overturned all my previous theories."

The book was a success both in England and the United States and Melville immediately began a continuation, *Omoo*. This one, as he says in the introduction, is to describe the whale-fishery and the sailors who work at it.

The attack upon the crew is even more savage than in *Typee*. "The crew manning vessels like these are for the most part villains of all nations and dyes; picked up in the lawless ports of the Spanish Main, and among the savages of the islands. Like galley-slaves, they are only to be governed by scourges and chains. Their officers go among them with dirk and pistol—concealed, but ready at a grasp."

Among the sailors there is one memorable figure—a native harpooneer, powerful, fearless and ferocious. Being insulted by a seaman, he does his best to wreck the ship with all on board, including himself. Here is another of these Ahab-like types.

Then Melville drops the real business of an artist, the study of human personality and human relations, and writes a book whose special value is that it shows how very close his mind was to ours.

Mardi is an ill-constructed, ill-written book, and on the whole, for the average reader, is today, even more than when it was published, almost unreadable. Its importance is that in the course of writing this book Melville became convinced that the world as he knew it was headed for disaster.

This is the story. An intellectual who is at the same time a common sailor deserts from a ship. This time his companion is an old Scandinavian sailor, Jarl, ignorant and superstitious, but a man of skill, bravery, loyalty and sterling character. In Jarl are the first signs of the crew of *Moby-Dick*, except for the fact that he is an individual. Their voyage is also a quest. Here for the first time appears the idea of a ship setting out to search for an answer to the problems of human destiny. After some realistic adventures, they are joined by a native savage, Samoa, a man of great bravery who has lost his arm. Very, very faintly the outline of *Moby-Dick* is beginning to appear.

In a fight with natives they gain possession of a beautiful white girl, Yillah. The young man falls in love with her and woos her successfully.

They land on territory inhabited by natives. The young sailor poses as a god, Taji, they are all welcomed by the native ruler, King Media, and entertained in his palace.

While they are there, a body of natives comes to petition King Media, demanding that thereafter all differences between man and man, together with all alleged offenses against the state, be tried by twelve good men and true. They are demanding what is in effect trial by jury. King Media laughs long, loudly and scornfully: "I am King, ye are slaves. Mine to command, yours to obey."

Thus we are plunged violently and without warning into a satirical novel whose subject matter is the fundamentals of political democracy.

Yillah is abducted from media's kingdom by enemies and it is soon clear that Yillah is a symbolical figure, signifying peace, happiness, beauty and whatnot.

To help find her King Media himself sets out with Taji to visit the neighboring countries. Taji is determined to find his Yillah who for a moment seems to be the answer to his quest. This time he is assisted by philosophy, history, poetry, and experience, in the persons of Mohi, the historian, Babbalanja, the philosopher, Yoomy, the poet, and King Media himself. Together they visit country after country in Poorpheero, which turns out to be Europe, and then they visit Vivenza, which turns out to be America. It is a foretaste of things to come that Jarl, the sailor and Samoa, the native, have no interest in this search for individual happiness. They stay behind and are soon murdered. In the intervals of their examination of these countries and their interview with their rulers, the travelers talk incessantly about religion, philosophy, poetry, history and politics.

Melville's correspondence shows us that when he started *Mardi*, he had seriously intended to write some sort of continuation of *Typee* and *Omoo*. It is obvious therefore that he had yielded to what was an irresistible impulse to write down his views on the philosophy, literature and politics of Europe and America. Melville had been reading hard, ancient and modern history, classical literature, modern literature, philosophy and religion, the arguments for and against Christianity. Since his success as an author he corresponded and talked regularly with educated and informed people. *Mardi* shows the results.

Country after country in Europe is rapidly visited. The poverty of the majority; the tyranny of the rich; aristocracy, organized religion, the Papacy, law, medicine, war, the immoral rivalries of national states, the deception of the people by their rulers, the emptiness of philosophy, the uselessness of poetry, all these are mercilessly castigated by Melville. A great deal of it had been said before. Melville's writing is not very brilliant. At times he is quite superficial. But his rejection of what the people of his time were doing and thinking is as complete as he can make it.

How close his experience was to ours is proved by the fact that the two things that interested him most were (a) the world revolution and (b) the future of American democracy.

The travellers visit Vivenza, the United States. No Republican in the campaign of 1952 has said anything so savage against graft, greed and corruption in Washington politics as Melville did. Melville does not denounce one party. He denounces the whole Congress and his attitude is that it is and always will be the same. Downstairs where great affairs of state are being carried out, the party leaders sit around a huge bowl. "They were all chiefs of immense capacity—how many gallons there was no finding out."

Next day they visit that section of Vivenza again. News had just come of the 1848 revolutions in Europe. Here we must remember that when the news of the French revolution of 1848 came to Washington, not only did the populace rejoice, but the White House itself was illuminated. This is the scene to which Melville is referring. People are delirious, awaiting and greeting with wild cheers and wild excitement the successive news of the fate of monarchical governments. "Who may withstand the people? The times tell terrible tales to tyrants! Ere we die, freemen, all Mardi will be free."

Amidst the tumult the excited people discover a scroll written by an anonymous person, and after much discussion, it is decided to read it aloud. Melville leaves the question of who wrote the scroll a mystery, but there is no doubt that it contains his essential views.

According to the scroll, the great error of the people of the United States is to believe that Europe is now in the last scene of her drama and that all preceding historical events were ordained to bring "a universal and permanent Republic." People who think that way are fools. History teaches that everything collapses in the end. It was so with the Republic of Rome. It was so with the Republic of the French Revolution. If America is different, it is only because it has a vast western territory. When that is over-run, the crisis must come. If its population had been packed tight as that of Britain, then the great experiment might have resulted in explosion. The people are free because they are young, but age overtakes all things. Do not think that America will "forever remain as liberal as now."

Equality is an illusion. No equality of knowledge can get rid of the inbred servility of mortal to mortal. Men inevitably are divided into brigades and battalions, with captains at their head.

It is not the primary aim and chief blessing to be politically free. Freedom is only good as a means. It is not an end in itself. If men fought it out against tyrants until the knife was plunged in to the handle, they would not thereby free themselves from the yoke of slavery. In no stable democracy do all men govern themselves. Though an army be all volunteers, it must be ruled by martial law. People who live in association with each other must delegate power.

"Freedom is the name for a thing that is *not* freedom."

All over Europe "poverty is abased before riches . . . everywhere, suffering is found."

"Thus, freedom is more social than political. And its real felicity is not to be shared. *That* is of a man's own individual getting and holding. It is not, who rules the state, but who rules me. Better be secure under one king, than exposed to violence from twenty millions of monarchs, though oneself be of the number."

Though great reforms are needed, nowhere are bloody revolutions required. People believed that the old ages of blood and sword were over and the world was settling down. That is an illusion. The world is on fire once more. America should cut herself away from Europe in deed and word.

When the travellers leave Washington they go to the South where they see slavery. They all burn with anger but they cannot agree on whether revolution by the slaves is justified. And yet, if they do not think it is, they are, they admit, no better than Calhoun, the apologist for slavery. Their anger fizzles out in frustration. It was not the first time that the travellers had been baffled by this question of revolution. When the French Revolution of 1848 broke out, they had been torn between fears of the violence and destruction and hope that something valuable for mankind might come of it.

It is obvious that the Universal Republic of 1848 was a far cry from the World Revolution as we have known it since 1917. It is also extremely dangerous to take these ideas as specific political policies of Melville. He was an artist, and had made no consistent studies of economics and politics. He was for example an extreme, in fact a fanatical democrat. Some of the views he expressed he would change in his next book. But *Mardi* shows that already he believed that a future of continually expanding democracy was an illusion, for America as for the rest of the world, that he considered politics a game played by politicians, and that he was grappling seriously with the question of what exactly did men mean by freedom. It is not too much to say that he was thinking about the very things that the vast majority of men are thinking about today.

Yillah is never found. Instead Taji is tempted by the dark-haired Hautia who is a very crude symbol for wealth, sensuality, luxury and power. He nearly succumbs, but in the end he flies from her, alone in an open boat, pursued by three of Hautia's soldiers. "And thus, pursuers and pursued, fled on, over an endless sea." That is the last sentence of the novel. What the sailor-intellectual was looking for he has not found.

Mardi was a failure. Melville was now very broke. He had to write for money and write fast. But it is precisely this sitting down and scribbling exactly what is in his mind that allows us to see how he is developing. In his next two books before *Moby-Dick* we see him strengthening his rejection of the world as he knows it, and working out what will take its place. And it is here that he begins to work again on the type which will become Ahab.

Redburn is an account of his first voyage to England. Like his first two books it is fiction on a solid ground-work of fact. He is once more living through his early experiences. Dominating *Redburn* is the character of Jackson. Jackson is a man of passion, of spiritual force, and a man in revolt against the whole world for what it has done to him. He is the best seaman on board. Despite physical weakness he is so overpowering a personality that all the men on board are afraid of him. Without education, he is marvellously quick and cunning, and understands human nature and those he had to deal with. And finally there was his eye, "the most deep, subtle, infernal looking eye, that I ever saw lodged in a human head."

He might have been thirty or fifty. He had travelled all over the world as a sailor and had horrible experiences to tell, full of piracies, plagues and poisonings. Broken in health from the consequences of the evil life he had lived, he hated the young and healthy. He seemed determined to die with a curse on his lips. The world seemed to him to be one person, which had done him some dreadful harm and his hatred was rankling and festering in his heart. And Melville gives the reason. One day a sailor, in Jackson's hearing, talks about the heaven which is awaiting all men, including sailors, who will then be repaid for their sufferings on earth. All Jackson's hatred seems to fly out of him at one breath. The sailor is a fool to talk like that. All talk of heaven is lies. "I know it!" And all who believe in it are fools. Heaven for sailors? Will they let a sailor in, with tar on his hands and oil in his hair? Death swallows a sailor as a sailor swallows a pill and he wishes that some tempest would swallow down the whole ship.

Here at first sight is the genuine totalitarian consciousness of injustice, the totalitarian hatred and totalitarian readiness to destroy the whole world in revenge, which will be the basis of Ahab's character. But Jackson is no Ahab. Jackson is a worker whose evil character

Melville attributes to the suffering and misery which society imposed upon the class to which he belonged. Just here some of the greatest writers of the nineteenth century stopped and never went a step further. It is precisely here, however, that Melville's originality begins. Melville knew workers and workers are not people who in revenge wish to destroy the world.

In his account of how a great writer finally arrives at portraying a great character, he had written that, beginning with the character, everything around seems to start up to meet it, to correspond to it. It seems, as far as one can work out such things, that this was the way Melville got to the crew of *Moby-Dick*. This much is certain. When the future creator of the crew of *Moby-Dick* sat down to write his first book, *Typee*, all he had to say about the sailors was their coarseness of mind and body, their debauchery, their unholy passions, their gross licentiousness, their shameful drunkenness. When he wrote about the whale-fishery and whaling-vessels in *Omoo*, it was worse. In *Mardi*, there is a change. But now in *Redburn* he begins seriously to examine the crew. He still portrays them as ignorant and cruel men, but he begins to talk about their skill. More important, he launches into a long defense of sailors as a class of workers. They carry around the globe missionaries, ambassadors, opera-singers, armies, merchants. The business of the world depends upon them; if they were suddenly to emigrate to the navies of the moon everything on earth would stop except its revolution on its axis and the orators in the American Congress. Respectable people and pious hypocrites give a little charity to sailors and speak of the improvement in their condition. There is no real improvement and there can never be. The world is constituted in such a way that the working poor have to bear the burdens, and the sailors are among those who have to bear them.

In *Redburn* also three new things appear. He paints a horrible picture of the misery of the population of Liverpool and the general cruelty. We shall see this again in the opening chapters of *Moby-Dick*. The account of the voyage home describes at length the sufferings of a body of Irish immigrants, and the cruelty and selfishness of the captain and the cabin passengers.

Also he changes his mind about America cutting itself away from Europe. Now he looks forward to America being in future years a society of liberty and freedom, composed of all the races of the earth.

"There is something in the contemplation of the mode in which America has been settled that, in a noble breast, should forever extinguish the prejudices of national dislikes. Settled by the people of all nations, all nations may claim her for their own. You cannot spill a drop of American blood without spilling the blood of the whole world. . . . Our blood is as the flood of the Amazon, made up of a thousand noble currents all pouring into one. We are not a nation, so much as a world. . . . Our ancestry is lost in the universal pageantry; and Caesar and Alfred, St. Paul and Luther, and Homer and Shakespeare are as much ours as Washington, who is as much the world's as our own. We are the heirs of all time, and with all nations we divide our inheritance. On this Western Hemisphere all tribes and peoples are forming into one federated whole; and there is a future which shall see the estranged children of Adam restored as to the old hearthstone in Eden."

All this we shall meet again in the conception of the crew of the Pequod as an Anacharsis Clootz deputation, seeking the universal republic of liberty and fraternity under the leadership of American officers.

But his main preoccupation is still the individual character of passionate revolt, who for the time being is Jackson.

He compares Jackson to the Emperor Tiberius, an embodiment of evil in ancient times, and to Satan of Milton's *Paradise Lost.* This Yankee sailor, Jackson, he says, is worthy to rank with these historic figures. But Melville is as yet still somewhat confused. He has not seen the character in its perfection. There is, he says, no dignity in evil. Yet it is a credit to Milton's genius that out of such a monster as Satan, he could create so magnificent a poem. Melville has not solved his problem but he is already conscious of what it is. He has to show how genuine and deeply-rooted is this fearful desire for revenge upon the world by embittered men, the men of his century— the Yankees he knows. He feels that this is a mighty force in the world around him, and that the world will have to reckon with it sooner or later. He is already certain that this destructive passion is not characteristic of aristocrats, financiers and property-owners. For them he has a general contempt. It is to be found among men concerned with work.

If you have read *Moby-Dick* you can feel the uncertainty in *Redburn.*

But the man of passionate revolt who will reorganize or destroy, and the crew, if only in Melville's new attitude to it, are there.

In his next book, *White-Jacket*, he crosses the bridge from his own time into ours. His greatest discovery is to push individual characteristics aside and see men in terms of the work that they do. A warship is an organization where men perform special functions. This man may be a drunkard, that one a thief, the other one writes poetry, another is a splendid, fine sailor, a born leader of men and charming. But a ship is in reality nothing more than various groups of men who do certain types of work, without which there would be complete chaos. It is this specific type of work which determines their social characteristics. And the ship is only a miniature of the world in which we live.

It is this discovery which leads him to perhaps his greatest single step, taking the character of Jackson from out of the crew and placing him among the officers, where we will see him as Ahab.

What is the bitterest personal cry of Ahab? It is his isolation, the isolation inseparable from the function of authority in the modern world. Melville found it in writing about the officers on the warship. Take the Commodore. He was perhaps dumb, for the author of the book never heard him utter a word. But not only was he dumb himself but his mere appearance on the deck seemed to give everyone the lock-jaw. The real reason was perhaps that like all high functionaries he had to preserve his dignity, and inasmuch as apart from the common dignity of manhood, Commodores have no real dignity at all, Commodores, like crowned heads, generalissimos, lord-high admirals, have to carry themselves straight, which is uncomfortable to themselves and ridiculous to an enlightened generation. Melville is very light-hearted about it but before two years Ahab will speak from the depths of his heart about the Guinea-Coast slavery of solitary command.

On the Pequod, Ahab's word is law and it is this which paralyzes resistance. Next to the Commodore on the man-of-war is the captain. His word is law. He never speaks but in the imperative mood. He commands even the sun. For when the noon observation is taken, it is officially twelve o'clock only when the captain says "*Make* it so." Ahab will smash the quadrant and denounce the whole procedure and all science included.

Ahab's dinner-table is the symbol of his social isolation. The dinner-table of a man-of-war is the criterion of rank. The Commodore dines alone at four or five o'clock; the captain at three; the younger men at two. A captain once dined at five when the Commodore dined at four. A note from the Commodore made him change to half-past three.

It is the relations between men at work that shape human character. And the most decisive relation on board ship is the relation between officers and men.

There are marines on board. Why? Because the officers want to use the marines against the sailors and the sailors against the marines. And Melville condemns the whole system not only as evil but as incurable.

"The immutable ceremonies and iron etiquette of a man-of-war; the spiked barriers separating the various grades of rank; the delegated absolutism of authority on all hands; the impossibility, on the part of the common seaman, of appeal from incidental abuses, and many more things that might be enumerated, all tend to beget in most armed ships a general social condition which is the precise reverse of what any Christian could desire. And though there are vessels that in some measure furnish exceptions to this; and though, in other ships, the thing may be glazed over by a guarded, punctilious exterior, almost completely hiding the truth from casual visitors, while the worst facts touching the common sailor are systematically kept in the background, yet it is certain that what has here been said of the domestic interior of a man-of-war will, in a greater or less degree, apply to most vessels in the navy. It is not that the officers are so malevolent, nor, altogether, that the man-of-war's-man is so vicious. Some of these evils are unavoidably generated through the operation of the naval code; others are absolutely organic to a navy establishment, and, like other organic evils, are incurable, except when they dissolve with the body they live in."

War? "The whole matter of war is a thing that smites common sense and Christianity in the face; so every thing connected with it is utterly foolish, unchristian, barbarous, brutal and savoring of the Feejee Islands, cannibalism, saltpetre and the devil." But what if your country is attacked? That has nothing to do with it. If you profess Christianity, be then Christians.

The chaplain is a hypocrite; the surgeon a bloodthirsty maniac and his subordinates cowards and self-seekers; the master-at-arms (the civilian responsible for discipline) is a crook, a smuggler and an unmitigated scoundrel; the purser is a thief.

But Melville's most intriguing step forward is the manner in which he now treats the crew. *White-Jacket* is full of their shortcomings and their crimes. But he now gives a detailed description of the various types of work that they do and the kind of men who do it. To give two examples:

The sheet-anchor men are veterans all, fine sailors, feared by the officers and all fanatical worshippers of Andrew Jackson. Three decks down are the troglodytes, people who live below the surface among the water-tanks, casks and cables. You never get to know their names. But: "In times of tempests, when all hands are called to save ship, they issue forth into the gale, like the mysterious men of Paris, during the massacre of the Three Days of September; every one marvels who they are, and whence they come; they disappear as mysteriously; and are seen no more, until another general commotion."

The reference is of course to the September massacres, one of the best-known events in the French Revolution and it is impossible to believe that Melville is not aware of the overtones of what he is writing.

For him now the crew embodies some type of social order. Their association at work gives them interests, ideas and attitudes that separate them entirely from the rest of society.

He has not got the differences between the crew and officers nearly so clear as he will in *Moby-Dick*, where Ahab, Starbuck and Ishmael, on the one hand, and the anonymous crew on the other react to things, large and small, in such consistent opposition. But once you have read *Moby-Dick*, then the line of division in *White-Jacket* is already clear.

The whole of the last chapter sums up the ship as symbolical of the real world. "Outwardly regarded, our craft is a lie; for all that is outwardly seen of it is the clean-swept deck, and oft-painted planks comprised above the water-line; whereas, the vast mass of our fabric, with all its store-rooms of secrets, forever slides along far under the surface." The great majority are far below deck and no one knows what is happening to them. Commodores and Captains and Lord High Admirals parade as leaders, but neither they nor anybody else knows where the vessel is going. Characteristic of Melville's attitude is the fact that he praises the Commodore as a brave old man who had fought gallantly for his country. The captain, as captains go, was not a

bad or vindictive man. They lived in a world in which they had to behave as they did. Very striking is his good humor and high spirits
which he rarely loses, except on the question of flogging. He does not
urge action. As in *Mardi* he is clearing his mind. There is very little of
this type of rebelliousness in *Moby-Dick*.

Melville is not an agitator. He is a creative artist who is moving
steadily towards that rarest of achievements—the creation of a character which will sum up a whole epoch of human history. And twice in
White-Jacket he once more tackles the type.

The first is old Ushant, captain of the forecastle. He is a man in
his sixties, always alert to his duty and boldly mounting the fore-yard
in a gale. But when not required by duty he was staid, reserved and
a majestic old man, who frequently talked philosophy to the men
around him.

> "Nor was his philosophy to be despised; it abounded in wisdom.
> For this Ushant was an old man, of strong natural sense, who
> had seen nearly the whole terraqueous globe, and could reason
> of civilized and savage, of gentile and Jew, of Christian and
> Moslem. The long night-watches of the sailor are eminently
> adapted to draw out the reflective faculties of any serious-
> minded man, however humble or uneducated. Judge, then,
> what half a century of battling out watches on the ocean must
> have done for this fine old tar. He was a sort of sea Socrates, in
> his old age 'pouring out his last philosophy and life,' as sweet
> Spencer has it; and I never could look at him and survey his
> right reverend beard, without bestowing upon him that title
> which, in one of his satires, Persius gives to the immortal quaffer
> of the hemlock."

Strange and contradictory (but profoundly logical) are the ways by
which writers arrive at their masterpieces. The very first reference to
Ahab in *Moby-Dick* is as follows:

> ". . . a man of greatly superior force, with a globular brain and
> a ponderous heart; who has also by the stillness and seclusion of
> many long night-watches in the remotest waters, and beneath
> constellations never seen here at the north, been led to think un-
> traditionally and independently; receiving all nature's sweet or

savage impressions fresh from her own virgin voluntary and confiding breast, and thereby chiefly, but with some help from accidental advantages to learn a bold and nervous lofty language—that man makes one in a whole nation's census—a mighty pageant creature, formed for noble tragedies."

One model for Ahab is clearly this delightful old man. But this old man too has much of the defiance of Ahab in him. As the ship nears home an order comes down that all beards are to be shaved. The men have been preparing magnificent beards for their homecoming and are furious. An insurrection almost breaks out and is averted in fact only by the experience and popularity of Jack Chase, a sailor beloved by all on board. Finally, however, the men give in, all except Old Ushant. He is threatened with flogging. He replies that his beard is his own. The old man is flogged and placed in irons, and though these are removed after a few days he remains confined for the rest of the voyage. His time of service was up, and when the ship reached port Ushant took a boat and went ashore, amid the unsuppressible cheers of all hands. The episode of the beards and Ushant fills four chapters and is the emotional climax of the book. Somehow that old man's beard had become the test of his manhood. They could have killed him but he would have died with his face unshaven.

The second example is none other than the hero of the book, young White Jacket himself. The young fellow is called up one day to be flogged, as usual before the crew. He is innocent but he explains in vain. The sentence will be carried out. White Jacket, however, is determined not to be flogged. Behind the spot where the captain is standing, there is no rail. He plans to rush at him and sweep him overboard. He himself will go overboard too. But that price he is prepared to pay. However, just as he is preparing to carry out this desperate measure, one of the leading marines does an unheard-of thing. He steps out of the assembled crew and tells the captain that he does not think White Jacket is guilty. The leader of the seamen, encouraged by this, does the same. Taken aback, the captain hesitates for a moment and then dismisses White Jacket and saunters off "while I who in the desperation of my soul had but just escaped being a murderer and a suicide almost burst into tears of thanksgiving where I stood."

Suicide and murder. Destroy yourself and everything you can take with you rather than submit. Even after he had written *Moby-Dick*,

Melville for years pondered on this peculiar type of character which seemed to him new in the world, and which he thought, and so rightly, would increasingly dominate human society. But *White-Jacket* was the end of his apprenticeship.

Is it possible now to have any doubt as to what Melville had in mind when he wrote *Moby-Dick*? These early books of his are not an account of his life from 1839, when he first shipped, to 1844 when he returned home. They are an account of the development of a mind from 1844 to 1850, the finest mind that has ever functioned in the New World and the greatest since Shakespeare's that has ever concerned itself with literature. It must not be thought that he consciously plotted his course from book to book as it has been described here. But the books show how logically the process developed, and if not at the time, then years after *Moby-Dick*, Melville recognized how it had happened and sketched it out in his book, *The Confidence Man*.

Yet the ultimate question is not how Melville did it, but what he did. And the proof of that is in the world around us. It is not what he had in mind when he wrote that is important. If he were to return today, how would the author of *Moby-Dick* see the world in which we live and which he divined in relation to the world he actually knew? The answer to that question lies in his books and in the world around us.

As Melville gets rid of traditional conceptions, he begins to recapture his own individual experiences. He begins to realize that his contact with Nature is made through his work on the ship. And something new is born in literature, as new as Ahab is among men. Redburn climbs the mast in a storm. There is a wild delirium about it, a rushing of the blood, a thrilling and throbbing of the whole system, to find yourself tossed up at every pitch into the clouds of a stormy sky and hovering like a judgment angel between heaven and earth, both hands free, with one foot in the rigging and one somewhat behind you in the air.

The attitude is still romantic. Melville is still describing Redburn's feelings as a literary intellectual would. But this is not Rousseau flying to Nature from the evils of society or Wordsworth meditating over a yellow primrose, or Shelley pouring out verses about liberty to the West Wind, or Keats following a nightingale over Hampstead Heath and drowning himself in thoughts of death and countless generations of dead men, or Whitman, shocked at the death of Lincoln, going off by himself to look at the water and dream of death. This is not personal emotion or reflection or play. Redburn has to get up there as a matter of business whenever it is needed, calm or storm, and, as Melville warned Ishmael dreaming on the mast-head, if he misses, he will fall and lose his life.

By *White-Jacket* Melville has moments in which he gets rid of all literary self-consciousness. They are rounding Cape Horn, and on that journey no one ever knows when a destructive squall may leap out of the calm and sink the ship with every soul on board. A storm bursts. The men who are holding the double-wheel are jumping up and down with their hands on the spokes "for the whole helm and galvanized keel were fiercely feverish, with the life imparted to them by the tempest." Fifty men are ordered aloft to furl the main-sail. The rigging is coated with ice. For three-quarters of an hour they remain in the darkness clinging for dear life and finally have to abandon the task. But they cannot get back so easily. Some have to throw themselves prostrate along the yard, and embrace it with arms and legs and just hold on. Yet no one was afraid.

"The truth is, that, in circumstances like these, the sense of fear is annihilated in the unutterable sights that fill all the eye, and the sounds that fill all the ear. You become identified with the tempest; your insignificance is lost in the riot of the stormy universe around."

You cannot find anything like this in all the Romantic writers, from Rousseau to Whitman.

And, very significantly, the next paragraph is:

"Below us, our noble frigate seemed thrice its real length—a vast black wedge, opposing its widest end to the combined fury of the sea and wind."

No wonder in *Moby-Dick* and elsewhere Melville makes jokes at Byron with his rhapsodic:

"Roll on, thou dark and deep blue ocean, roll,
Ten thousand fleets roll over thee in vain."

But as with so many of Melville's jokes, new conceptions of the world lay behind them. In the world which Melville saw, and more particularly saw was coming, there was no place any more for these outpourings of the individual soul. The dissatisfied intellectual would either join the crew with its social and practically scientific attitude to

Nature or guilt would drive him to where it drove Ishmael. Hence Melville's totally new sense of Nature, as incessantly influencing men and shaping every aspect of their lives and characters. Nature is not a background to men's activity or something to be conquered and used. It is a part of man, at every turn physically, intellectually and emotionally, and man is a part of it. And if man does not integrate his daily life with his natural surroundings and his technical achievements, they will turn on him and destroy him. It was Ishmael who was tortured by the immensity of the universe and Ahab by the magnetic lights and the thunder. Not Tashtego.

Ishmael is a character in *Moby-Dick* and sometimes it is impossible to tell whether Ishmael is writing or Melville himself is speaking in his own name. But by *Moby-Dick* Melville has created for himself a total philosophy of life to replace the one he has rejected. It is not organized, but it is not in the slightest degree unconscious. This, one of the best-read of all Americans, says that if he should ever leave any literary work of importance behind him, the honor should go to whaling for "a whale-ship was my Yale college and my Harvard." These are not passing words. His qualification for attempting the enormous but neglected task of classifying the whales of the ocean is that he had read enormously and: "I have had to do with whales with these visible hands." He will try to portray the whale as he appears to the eye of the whaleman when the whale is moored alongside the whale-ship. Most drawings and paintings of the whale he denounces as inaccurate and fanciful—the living whale in his full majesty and significance is to be seen at sea only in unfathomable waters. So with scientific writers. They have seldom had the benefit of a whaling voyage. Pictures of whales and whaling he judges as an expert whaleman would; his standard is the fidelity with which they represent the facts and the spirit of whaling. It is common sailors, he finds, who with their simple jack-knife will carve and engrave sketches of whaling-scenes, not quite up to the mark technically but close-packed in design and full of barbaric spirit and suggestiveness.

It might be thought that this undeviating reference back of everything to a body of men working would result in narrowness and limitation. The exact opposite is the case. It is he who attempts the first classification of the sperm whale because as he says the sperm whale lives not complete in any literature neither as science nor as poetry. He begins his book with some seventy quotations about whales, from the literature of the world. His analysis of the anatomy and physiology of every separate part of the whale is as complete as he can make it. But always from the point of view of men working with whales every day. He is inexhaustible at the business of using his practical experiences and knowledge of whaling to make sometimes serious, at other times deliberately fanciful interpretations of ancient mythology and history. In the end the whale and whaling turn out to be a thread on which is hung a succession of pictures portraying the history of the world: before time; the mating and birth and domesticity of whales as they must have been before man; the social habits of whales and cannibal savagery of sharks, in all of which sailors can see daily the primary instincts and the drives of what has become civilized man; the primitive aboriginalness of early civilizations; phallic-worship; the civilizations and writers of Greece and Rome; the succession of modern European nations who as whalemen ruled the seas. He wishes to include in his book everything.

"Friends, hold my arms! For in the mere act of penning my thoughts of this Leviathan, they weary me, and make me faint with their outreaching comprehensiveness of sweep, as if to include the whole circle of the sciences, and all the generations of whales, and men, and mastodons, past, present, and to come, with all the revolving panoramas of empire on earth, and throughout the whole universe, not excluding its suburbs."

But it is all as a whale-man, a common sailor, one who writes and reads and studies but always on the basis of "the living experiences of living men," and by this he means people who work with their hands. Man has to become a total, complete being, participating in all aspects and phases of a modern existence or the modern world would crush his divided personality.

He ranges the universe, groping down into the bottom of the sea where he has his hands "among the unspeakable foundations, ribs and very pelvis of the world." And from there he soars into the lyric outbursts which none of the Romantics can exceed.

"At some old gable-roofed country houses you will see brass whales hung by the tail for knockers to the road-side door.... On the spires of some old-fashioned churches you will see sheet-iron whales placed there for weather-cocks; ...

"In bony, ribby regions of the earth, where at the base of high broken cliffs masses of rock lie strewn in fantastic groupings upon the plain, you will often discover images as of the petrified forms of the Leviathan partly merged in grass, which of a windy day breaks against them in a surf of green surges.

"Then, again, in mountainous countries where the traveller is continually girdled by amphitheatrical heights; here and there from some lucky point of view you will catch passing glimpses of the profiles of whales defined along the undulating ridges. But you must be a thorough whaleman, to see these sights. . . .

"Nor when expandingly lifted by your subject, can you fail to trace out great whales in the starry heavens, and boats in pursuit of them; as when long filled with thoughts of war the Eastern nations saw armies locked in battle among the clouds. Thus at the North have I chased Leviathan round and round the Pole with the revolutions of the bright points that first defined him to me. And beneath the effulgent Antarctic skies I have boarded the Argo-Navis, and joined the chase against the starry Cetus far beyond the utmost stretch of Hydrus and the Flying Fish."

And here the poet of an industrial civilization speaks.

"With a frigate's anchors for my bridle-bitts and fasces of harpoons for spurs, would I could mount that whale and leap the topmost skies, to see whether the fabled heavens with all their countless tents really lie encamped beyond my mortal sight!"

Only a man who has thoroughly integrated his conception of life into modern industry could create so simple and yet so daring an image. Beginning with a certain type of mind, i.e., the mind of a man of genius, and fortunate enough to live at a time when some new type of personality has come into the world, Melville worked out an entirely new conception of society, not dealing with profits and the rights of private property (Ahab was utterly contemptuous of both), but with new conceptions of the relations between man and man, between man and his technology and between man and Nature. We can see Melville, in book after book, working them out until he arrives at the ultimate profundities of *Moby-Dick*.

Melville is not only the representative writer of industrial civilization. He is the only one that there is. In his great book the division and antagonisms and madnesses of an outworn civilization are mercilessly dissected and cast aside. Nature, technology, the community of men, science and knowledge, literature and ideas are fused into a new humanism, opening a vast expansion of human capacity and human achievement. *Moby-Dick* will either be universally burnt or be universally known in every language as the first comprehensive statement in literature of the conditions and perspectives for the survival of Western Civilization.

Chapter V

NEUROSIS AND THE INTELLECTUALS

Melville had now completed his vision of the world to come—our world. He did not see it in 1851 exactly as we see it today. There is always, when reading great masterpieces of the past, a difference in the emphasis of the author and the reader. Many places when Melville was of necessity feeling his way and going by creative instinct, we, after the last twenty years, can be absolutely sure—we have seen it written across continents in letters of blood and iron. He saw the elements of the heroic in Ahab in a way that we cannot see it. He was diffident and discreet about the crew in a manner that no one of our age can be. It does not mean that he was wrong in his judgments. In a hundred years people may agree with him instead of with us.

But there was one specialized feature of the age to come which Melville knew but could find no place for in his conception of *Moby-Dick*. It is what we know today as psychoanalysis. And as soon as *Moby-Dick* was finished, Melville in a few months wrote another novel, *Pierre*, which to this day is the finest and most profound study in existence of what the Freudians call the neurosis. It is the most profound because Melville not only knew the thing itself. He knew what the psychoanalysts do not know. He knew where it came from.

Psychoanalytic theories are as numerous as berries on a tree. We can deal with only a few aspects. First, Freud himself, the originator, who is in our opinion still the master. His view is quite categorical: Neurosis is the prevailing condition of mankind. The foundation of the neurosis is the incestuous sexual desire of the child for the parent of the opposite sex. It is in this desire and its history that must be sought the roots of individual personality. This, Freud claims, has always been so in civilized society, but it was first scientifically discovered and expounded by him and his assistants at the turn of the century.

That is where the thing began fifty years ago. By today, however much his disciples and successors may have differed with him and with one another, the total result is undeniable. The idea of the unconscious, and particularly the sexual unconscious, the struggle between the unconscious and the need for disciplined behavior, the influence upon adult personality of the relations between parents and children, the pervading consciousness of sickness, of guilt, of crisis, in the individual personality, these psychological preoccupations dominate the thinking of educated people in the twentieth century. History has never seen anything like it.

This is what Melville deals with in *Pierre*. But, although he had anticipated Freud by fifty years, Melville is no Freudian. In fact, he is today, more than ever, the deadliest enemy the Freudians have ever had, because for Melville this preoccupation with personality, this tendency to incest and homosexuality was not human nature but a disease, a horrible sickness, rooted, as was the sickness of Ahab and Ishmael, in an unbearable sense of social crisis.

Secondly, the disease is confined to a special class of people, chiefly intellectuals and the idle rich who cannot decide what attitude they should take to a changing society.

Thirdly, this disease is no mere personal sickness. Its tortured victims explode in the tendency to destruction, suicide, murder and violence of all kinds which distinguish our age.

Finally, Melville though very much aware of the unconscious, was very cautious about it. And he certainly did not believe that it represented the animal, the primitive, the lustful drives in man which had to be constantly fought and kept in check. It would seem that he thought exactly the opposite; that in civilized man, the unconscious was the source of immense creative energy and power, which was repressed by the discipline of society as he knew it.

Thus, while he saw very clearly the facts which the psychoanalysts discovered fifty years after, his interpretation of them clashes with theirs at every point.

Pierre, where his main ideas are dramatized, is a very different type of book from *Moby-Dick*. For one thing scholars have been able to discover clear and apparently striking resemblances and parallels between the characters and members of Melville's family. Furthermore it is possible to make connections between important episodes in the book and events in the life of Melville, his parents and his wife. All this is not very important. The astonishing similarity between the plot of Shakespeare's *Hamlet* and the plot of *Pierre* is of infinitely greater significance than any resemblances between Pierre and Melville's own life. The greater the writer, the less important is his personal biography. Yet the biography of Melville is important for *Pierre* and we give a brief sketch of it. Both his grandfathers were heroes of the Revolutionary War. His father was a merchant, an importer of foreign merchandise. Melville was thus by birth a member of that landed and commercial aristocracy which, even after 1776, held the first place in American society until Andrew Jackson gave it a mortal wound in 1828. The Melville family felt this personally. Herman's grandfather, Major Thomas Melville, was removed as Naval officer for the Port of Boston by the new Jackson administration. Other calamities were in store. In 1832 a depression ruined his father and the blow caused his death. The Melvilles were ruined. Herman was then thirteen years old. Around him, henceforward, the old America was passing, and a new America was taking its place in a turmoil that grew increasingly.

Machine production was breaking up the old artisan industry. Between 1840 and 1850, far from the frontier offering an outlet for the bold and energetic in the East, there was a movement back from the farms to the cities. The old sense that men had of being members of an integrated community, which the winning of Independence had not destroyed, was now in process of dissolution. This is the society in which young Melville grew up. Unchecked individualism was coming to maturity and Emerson, a favorite author of Henry Ford, understood the change and celebrated it.

Herman touched this crisis at all points. He had taken a commercial course and got a job in a bank. In 1833 and 1834 he worked on the farm of his uncle Thomas, who was filled with reminiscences of the life in Paris in the old days. A year later he was a clerk at his uncle's store. In 1837 another depression ruined the business his brother was trying to build up. Herman taught in a village school. Next year he took a course in surveying and engineering and tried and failed to get a job in the Engineering Department of the Erie Canal. In June 1839 he took a job as a common sailor on a boat that went to Liverpool. In the fall he was teaching again. The school did not pay him his salary and in December 1840 he signed on the crew of the whaling-vessel, the *Acushnet*. There are millions of young intellectuals in the world today, who, born in 1919 instead of 1819, went through experiences similar to Melville's, beginning with the Depression of 1929. We can presume that this young man, gifted with a unique genius, was at least as acutely conscious of social instability as they were.

Herman worked on the whaling-vessel until on July 9, he and a companion deserted the ship and escaped to the interior of Nukhawa, one of the Marquesas Islands. He lived with the Typee natives for some weeks and in August signed on an Australian whaler. The men on board mutinied and were imprisoned, Melville with them. Melville escaped and signed on a Nantucket whaler. In May 1843 he was discharged and went to Honolulu where he found various jobs. If we can trust his account in *Omoo*, he, in the company of a disreputable but charming doctor, spent a great deal of his time chasing women, both white and native.

In August he shipped on the American frigate, the *United States*, as an ordinary seaman. In October 1844, his ship reached Boston. He was discharged, and, rejoining his family, he began to write *Typee*.

In 1847 he married, his wife being a member of the same social class from which he had sprung. She was the daughter of the Chief Justice of Massachusetts. Children began to come. But *Mardi* was a failure, *Redburn* and *White-Jacket* did just well enough, and *Moby-Dick* was a terrible failure.

Melville now lived on a farm at Pittsfield, New York. He did the work on his farm himself and wrote at the same time. He was not only in constant financial difficulties, but *Moby-Dick* tells us the eyes with which he looked on the world. He was neither an Ahab nor an Ishmael nor a Starbuck but neither was he a member of any crew. He was outside of everything. His literary friends tried to make him one of their social groups of writing, criticizing, discussing intellectuals, but he kept them at a distance. Meanwhile America heaved around him in the throes of the crisis which finally exploded in the Civil War.

Redburn shows his sympathy for immigrants and his hope that America might become a banner and a refuge for all the world. He was in his personal attitude to people a fanatical democrat. He wrote once that for him "a thief in jail is as honorable a person as Gen. George Washington." The total picture is unmistakable. Here was a man who had seen much of a world in crisis, had reflected deeply on it, foresaw catastrophe, and believed in nothing. Were he able to sit by listening to the intimate conversations of the many puzzled, bewildered

Americans who grew up in the Depression, he would have no difficulty whatever in understanding them. Whether he looked deep into his own heart, or whether, as he always insisted, he saw the outline of Pierre's character in people around him, we do not know. But the mood of personal frustration in which he wrote is obvious. What should be even more obvious today is that the book he wrote has no significance whatever as personal revelation but faithfully portrays a section of the society in which we live.

The story of *Pierre* takes place in America a few years before 1850. Pierre is a young man of eighteen who lives in the Hudson Valley with his widowed mother. Handsome, intelligent, with a high spirit, he is heir to the estate which is one of the few where the tenants still pay feudal dues as in many parts of Europe.

His grandfather was a famous hero in the revolutionary wars. His dead father was a rich, respected and solid citizen. His mother is a woman of fifty but still strikingly handsome. She maintains the aristocratic traditions of the family.

The relation between mother and son is an extraordinary one. They treat each other like brother and sister. Mrs. Glendinning has refused many offers to marry. Pierre is engaged to Lucy Tartan, beautiful, blonde, and also belonging to a rich family. Mrs. Glendinning approves of the match, for Lucy is a quiet, submissive girl, and through her, Mrs. Glendinning wishes to continue her domination of her son even after his marriage. Pierre, she says to herself a dozen times in as many minutes, is a docile boy. May he ever remain so. She does not want her beautiful life to be disturbed.

Pierre seems very much in love with Lucy. Melville indulges in a number of rhapsodies about love being the redeemer of the world, which are so patently ridiculous that it is obvious that he is playing a game of which he was very fond—writing down with a straight face things which he cannot possibly believe.

Into this idyll, there is suddenly injected a ghost from the past. At a village sewing party, a girl had screamed and fainted when Pierre and his mother entered the room. The mysterious incident loses all its mystery, when the girl writes to him that she is the illegitimate daughter of his revered father. Pierre feels in his bones that it is true and that he faces a crisis which will alter his whole life. A Black Knight with the visor of its helmet down seems to confront him and mock at him. But he will strike through the helmet and see the face even if it is the face of the evil spirit. The reader is at once reminded of Ahab for whom the whale was a mask through which he would strike to the hidden truth about the universe. Pierre now must seek truth. From the time Pierre sees "the face," Melville stops his gibing and his rather careless writing, and is once more a master of his business of writing.

Pierre is suddenly possessed of a piercing and ruthless vision into his past life. He knows at once that he dare not appeal to his mother. She loves him, but he knows it is her own proud and pampered self that she loves in her love for her son. She will never acknowledge the girl.

His father was a seducer who deserted mother and child. His mother is a proud, unfeeling selfish woman. From this corruption covered over by wealth and gracious living, Pierre turns in horror. He will break with all that life his mother represents. Henceforth will be welcome to him Ugliness, Poverty, Infamy. He now knows why of old the men of Truth went barefoot and why Christ said, "Blessed are the poor in spirit, and blessed they that mourn." He will follow henceforth the dictates of his heart.

So Melville, having glamorized to the extreme the old aristocratic society to which he belonged by birth, has made youth and strength and intelligence and vitality and moral earnestness reject it utterly. What now will take its place? The answer is obviously with his half-sister and Pierre goes with burning eagerness to see Isabel.

She is a woman of strange and compelling beauty. She tells Pierre her story in two successive evenings. She never knew a mother. Her first memory is of an old half-ruined house which in after life she guessed was a French chateau. Its only occupants are an old man and an old woman who treated her brutally. Then, she vaguely remembers, she found herself in another house. In both houses she spoke childishly in two different languages. Still vaguer is a memory as of crossing the sea. Then, there was a third house with cultivated fields and farmhouses around, which she felt sure was in the United States. There were people in it, young men and young women and children. It seemed a happy place for some, but it was not for her. She stayed there six or seven years and gradually during that time things changed. Some of the occupants departed, some changed from smiles to tears, some grew savage and outrageous, some were dragged away by dumb men into deep places below—the child is living in a lunatic asylum. She drifts on to another house, a cottage this time. She became beautiful. A strange gentleman visited her at times and whispered into her ear the word, father. But after a while she learns that he is dead. The farmer and his wife who lived in the house grew impatient with her and she got permission to work. She bought herself a guitar which she taught herself to play. She interrupts her story to play for him. With her beauty and her raven-black hair and the strange music that she plays, she is for Pierre a being of wonder and mystery and enchantment. It is late and he leaves for the night.

Modern psychologists have accurately divined what Isabel signifies in psychological terms. She is the inward dream of Pierre come to life. He has revolted against all that way of life that his mother represents. Lucy is fair. Isabel is dark. His mother and Lucy are women who have all the advantages that wealth and culture can give. Isabel has grown up a homeless waif drifting from place to place. His mother and Lucy have lived and live entirely by the work of others. Isabel has earned her own living and lives in the humblest of circumstances. His mother's life and the life she has mapped for him with Lucy is a life that moves according to set rules and patterns. Isabel is a mystery.

A human spirit which finds itself cramped in a situation where it can find no outlet for its energies and yet is unable to find any objective reason for a dissatisfaction of which it is often not conscious, builds up in itself an image which is the direct opposite of what it hates. Often at the first sign of someone who corresponds to that internal image, the internal needs, hitherto cramped, explode, and the individual undergoes a change that is totally inexplicable to observers of the merely external facts of his life. A very capable professional psychologist and a man versed in literature as well has written that this phenomenon, a comparatively recent discovery in psychology, has never been so well and so fully and accurately described as by Melville in *Pierre*.

So far so good. That tells us much. But it does not help us to understand Melville's story. What is decisive is the dramatic representation of the same world crisis Melville has just treated in *Moby-Dick*.

Melville has carefully and explicitly made Pierre a proud representative of the combined cultures of Europe and America. And equally carefully and explicitly he has made Isabel an immigrant from the continent of Europe—one of the largest and most despised social groups in the United States of that time. The magnificent young Pierre must find truth from Isabel who comes penniless and destitute from the decay and dissolution of Europe. Once again a young American, rejecting the official world he has known, goes towards the meanest and lowest in the land. But Isabel has American blood in her veins too. Limited in scope as is his plot, Melville, as in *Moby-Dick*, is writing of America, but he is thinking of the world. Did Melville have this in mind? There can be much useless talk on this. But for the time being we shall say what has been said before: it is not important whether it was in his mind or not. What matters is that this, on the page, is what has come out of his mind. He could have made Isabel a prostitute from the streets of New York—Dostoevsky would have done that. Or he could have made her a girl from a ranch in the Far West or a dozen other things. He made her what we have seen and that is what we have to deal with.

What is Isabel like? On this first night she has expressed her hopes. She wants to feel herself an integral part of life. Individualism she does not want. "I feel there can be no perfect peace in individualness." Work has civilized her. It was when she first worked that she knew she was human. But human beings she sees as harmless people in a world of snakes and lightnings, of horrible and inscrutable inhumanities. She is ignorant and what she wants from Pierre is help and guidance. Whatever he says she will do. She is not a developed character, but undeveloped as she is, she has in her all the elements of a personality such as the world has never seen before. This is quite apparent to Pierre on the following night. She awakens in him the elemental awe that sometimes overwhelms man at the inscrutable mystery of human existence—that feeling which is the foundation of all religions.

"To Pierre, the deep oaken recess of the double casement, before which Isabel was kneeling seemed now the immediate vestibule of some awful shrine, mystically revealed through the obscurely open window, which ever and anon was still softly illumined by the mild heat-lightnings and ground-lightnings, that wove their wonderfulness without, in the unsearchable air of that ebony warm and most noiseless summer night."

What is a human being? Already in 1852 Melville was saying that a human being, the most advanced of Nature's creation, was in reality a distilled concentration of all of the elemental forces of Nature, earth, air, fire, lightning, physical magnetism, sexual energy.

"To Pierre's dilated senses Isabel seemed to swim in an electric fluid; the vivid buckler of her brow seemed as a magnetic plate. Now first this night was Pierre made aware of what, in the superstitiousness of his rapt enthusiasm, he could not help believing was an extraordinary physical magnetism in Isabel. And—as it were derived from this marvelous quality thus imputed to her—he now first became vaguely sensible of a certain still more marvelous power in the girl over himself and his most interior thoughts and motions;—a power so hovering upon the confines of the invisible world, that it seemed more inclined that way than this;—a power which not only seemed irresistibly to draw him toward Isabel, but to draw him away from another quarter—wantonly as it were, and yet quite ignorantly and unintendingly; and, besides, without respect apparently to anything ulterior, and yet again, only under cover of drawing him to her. For over all these things, and interfusing itself with the sparkling electricity in which she seemed to swim, was an ever-creeping and condensing haze of ambiguities.

"Often, in after-times with her, did he recall this first magnetic night, and would seem to see that she then had bound him to her by an extraordinary atmospheric spell—both physical and spiritual—which henceforth it had become impossible for him to break, but whose full potency he never recognized till long after he had become habituated to its sway. This spell seemed one with that Pantheistic master-spell, which eternally looks in mystery and in muteness the universal subject world, and the physical electricalness of Isabel seemed reciprocal with the heat-lightnings and the ground-lightnings nigh to which it had first become revealed to Pierre. She seemed moulded from fire and air, and vivified at some Voltaic pile of August thunder-clouds heaped against the sunset."

In her own way, Isabel reminds us of Tashtego, that child of Nature who seems also a spirit of the air. But she is a very human woman. First, in her simplicity.

"The occasional sweet simplicity, and innocence, and humbleness of her story; her often serene and open aspect; her deep-

seated, but mostly quiet, unobtrusive sadness, and that touch-
ingness of her less unwonted tone and air;—these only the
more signalized and contrastingly emphasized the profounder,
subtler, and more mystic part of her. Especially did Pierre feel
this, when after another silent interval, she now proceeded with
her story in a manner so gently confiding, so entirely artless, so
almost peasant-like in its simplicity, and dealing in some details
so little sublimated in themselves, that it seemed well-nigh impossible that this unassuming maid should be the same dark,
regal being who had but just now bade Pierre be silent in so im-
perious a tone, and around whose wondrous temples the strange
electric glory had been playing. Yet not very long did she now
thus innocently proceed, ere, at times, some fainter flashes of
her electricalness came from her, but only to be followed by such
melting, human, and most feminine traits as brought all his soft,
enthusiast tears into the sympathetic but still unshedding eyes of
Pierre."

But here is no nature of docile domesticity. She is a gallant fight-
ing spirit. When Pierre tells her that he will crush the disdainful
down on their knees if they do not acknowledge her, she rises to the
challenge and promises to fight it out with him, "Her changed attitude of beautiful audacity; her long scornful hair, that trailed out a
disheveled banner; her wonderful transfigured eyes, in which some
meteors seemed playing up; all this now seemed to Pierre the work of
an invisible enchanter. Transformed she stood before him; and
Pierre, bowing low over to her, owned that irrespective, darting majesty of humanity, which can be majestical and menacing in woman
as in man.

"But her gentler sex returned to Isabel at last; and she sat silent in
the casement's niche, looking out upon the soft ground-lightnings of
the electric summer night."

She will fight, but she is not interested in wealth and position. If
Pierre will do what he thinks is right, she will agree, whatever it may
be. Thus her submission is the submission of poverty, ignorance and
inexperience to intellect, education and social knowledge.

Here is a magnificent woman, ready to help Pierre find the truth he
is now looking for. All he has to do is to acknowledge her before the
world as his sister.

Pierre is an intellectual pure and simple, a man of ideas and feelings. After the first part of Isabel's story, he cannot stay in the house with his thoughts. He must walk outside. But outside he cannot stand even the sight of anything connected with civilization.

"He could not bring himself to confront any face or house; a plowed field, any sign of tillage, the rotted stump of a long-felled pine, the slightest passing trace of man was uncongenial and repelling to him. Likewise in his own mind all remembrances and imaginings that had to do with the common and general humanity had become, for the time, in the most singular manner distasteful to him."

His life now consisted entirely in the thoughts and emotions waked in him by the appearance and personality of Isabel. Immemorial Nature and Time and the eternal freshness and mysteriousness of uncorrupted life weave through him.

"Still wandering through the forest, his eye pursuing its ever shifting shadowy vistas; remote from all visible haunts and traces of that strangely willful race, who, in the sordid traffickings of clay and mud, are ever seeking to denationalize the natural heavenliness of their souls; there came into the mind of Pierre, thoughts and fancies never imbibed within the gates of towns; but only given forth by the atmosphere of primeval forests, which, with the eternal ocean, are the only unchanged general objects remaining to this day, from those that originally met the gaze of Adam. For so it is, that the apparently most inflammable or evaporable of all earthly things, wood and water, are, in this view, immensely the most endurable."

He thought of Space and he thought of Time, but all in connection with Isabel. She was older than he, but she seemed to be everlastingly young, even child-like, but with the child-like innocence of those who have experienced the world and passed safely through it.
But above all, she was mysterious—the mystery of the unknown.

"Now, unending as the wonderful rivers, which once bathed the feet of primeval generations, and still remain to flow fast by the graves of all succeeding men, and by the beds of all now living; unending, everflowing, ran through the soul of Pierre, fresh and fresher, further and still further, thoughts of Isabel. But the more his thoughtful river ran, the more mysteriousness it floated to him; and yet the more certainty that the mysteriousness was unchangeable. In her life there was an unraveled plot; and he felt that unraveled it would eternally remain to him. No slightest hope or dream had he, that what was dark and mournful in her would ever be cleared up into some coming atmosphere of light and mirth."

He can feel no passionate love such as he feels for Lucy, because she is his sister. Yet she is the subject of the most ardent and deepest emotions of his soul. She therefore soars out of the realms of mortality and for Pierre becomes transfigured into the highest heaven of Uncorrupted Love.

The old life is behind and this is the vision of the new: Nature, physical magnetism, the sense of history, of space and time, of rejecting social corruption and searching for truth, ethics, i.e., what is the correct thing to do. For a few hours Pierre's soul, cramped by his docile life with his wealthy mother, expands boundlessly. Nor is Pierre just any young man. All his sensations become part of one great central experience, his meeting with Isabel. The personality divided into separate parts, of which the early nineteenth century already was so acutely conscious, is now a totality.

It is splendid, but it is dangerous. For Pierre is a literary intellectual. His one chance is to commit himself completely to this immigrant girl. He needs her as much as she needs him. What is he going to do? When Pierre goes home that first night he finds his copy of *Hamlet* open on the table at Hamlet's famous lines:

> "The time is out of joint: O cursed spite,
> That ever I was born to set it right!"

That is his situation exactly. The world he has known is out of joint, rotten as the state of Denmark. He must build a new one. But to do so requires that he break up the old one, ruin his mother and discredit his father forever. That is what the acknowledgment of Isabel will mean. And Pierre cannot do it. He can give up his fine home and his wealth and his easy life and his beautiful prospects. For an idealistic young man, that kind of personal sacrifice is easy enough to make. But for him to take the step which will break that world to pieces, that step is beyond his powers.

This is his plan. He will announce to his mother and to Lucy that he is already married. Then he will take Isabel away with him to New York. There she will live with him under pretense of being his wife, and thus he will be able to take care of her. He will save the old from ruin and at the same time help the new.

The plan is fantastic and brings immediate disaster. His mother drives him out of the house; Lucy collapses. This he expects. When he tells Isabel his plan she agrees. But at that moment, a terrible self-revelation comes to him. He becomes aware that he has an incestuous passion for her and she responds willingly to a long and passionate embrace. At that moment in the story Western Civilization took a long stride in the consciousness of its own degeneration.

This is the crisis of the nineteenth century intellectual and his descendants of the twentieth century. Melville does not have to be interpreted. He says that for the growing child, its mother is the world and its father is god. But when it finds itself alone in the world, it "still clamors for the support of its mother the world, and its father the Deity." If its isolation and its crisis become too much for it, it becomes overwhelmed with the need to return back to the mother-protection of childhood, back, say the psychoanalysts, to the safety of the womb. Maybe. But for a grown man this rush back to childhood is the road of incest. That is what happened to Hamlet. And that is what happens to Pierre.

He cannot ruin the memory of his dead father. But he must help Isabel. So, in a situation which allows of no compromise, the only way out he can find is compromise.

That is the sickness of this generation of intellectuals; not so much that they commit incest but that they preoccupy themselves unceasingly with incestuous desires, father-complex, mother-fixation as the foundation of human personality and human behaviour. As is usual with them (for they do most of the literary work of the world) they transform their preoccupation into a characteristic of the whole world and seek to account through this for the inability of modern man, i.e., themselves, to solve his problems. What Freud discovered at the turn of the century and thought was eternal human nature, was in reality the reaction of the crisis which now has mankind by the throat upon the middle classes and the intellectuals.

That the elements of incestuous desires exist in children from their early associations with their parents seems to be true. But whether these are shed as easily as other childhood diseases or remain to become the refuge of guilt and indecision and fear and shame, that is a social question. What Melville saw was the way in which the traditional, the accepted, the established, however admittedly corrupt, retains its grip on those who want to break with it, or seem to have broken with it,—and the consequences to personality.

As you follow the story of Pierre, you see that whenever Pierre makes a cowardly or dishonest decision, he is almost immediately overwhelmed by the perverse passion he is striving to conquer. Melville does not claim to understand the internal processes whereby Pierre fell into this pit of degradation, but he says if he may venture one superficial reason, it is because Pierre was prepared for it by playing brother and sister with his mother. And that we know was Mrs. Glendinning's method of keeping a grip on her son, i.e., ensuring the continuation of her way of life. There is a passing but suggestive remark on homosexuality: young boys, wealthy and full of spirit, often show the external signs of being in love with one another. But, says Melville, that soon passes off, if everything else goes well with them. It should be noted that in *White-Jacket* Melville mentions homosexuality among the sailors, but it is clear that there it is simple vice, brought on by the fact that they have been away from women for long periods of time. The incestuous desires of Pierre are strictly an intellectual disease.

Pierre goes to New York with Isabel. There he decides to write a novel and teach the world the great truths he has learned. The proposal is preposterous and Melville himself does not take the novel-writing business seriously. Isabel remains ready to do whatever Pierre asks. Lucy, a brave girl, leaves behind family, money and reputation and comes to live with Pierre and Isabel who she thinks, of course, are married. She is also ready to do whatever Pierre wants. But Pierre cannot take the simple step which is needed to clear up the situation. He shrinks rapidly into a monster of selfishness, self-pity and hate. His unconscious is not lust and animal drives for primitive self-satisfaction. It is nothing; there is nothing there. It is his frustration, his social dilemma and not primitive lust inherent in human nature, which drives him to crime and ruin.

His mother dies from grief and leaves the estate and the money to a nephew. Pierre's publishers reject his novel. He gets into a quarrel with his rich cousin and Lucy's brother. He kills them both, is arrested and commits suicide in prison. Isabel, who takes poison, and Lucy, from shock and sorrow, die with him in his cell. Pierre therefore causes the destruction of every member of that very family which in the first place he had sought to preserve. But what is worse, he has ruined Isabel and Lucy, the two girls, the one immigrant and the other a member of a rich and ruling family, who were ready to leave the old behind and go wherever Pierre led.

In that part of the book where he states the case, Melville writes magnificently but once Pierre sets out for New York, Melville's creative power rapidly declines. All that Melville knows is that Pierre is headed for disaster. And he does not care very much how he gets him there.

Such is this remarkable novel, with all its faults, unique, unapproached for a hundred years. As with *Moby-Dick*, the world of 1850–1914 had to be shattered before what Melville was driving at could be seen. Intellectuals like Ishmael would go directly to the working class. Pierre was a different type, the man of ideas and sensitivity. Violently alienated from the old world by its corruption and its selfishness, he would turn to the poor and the humble, seeking to regenerate the world by new discoveries in Truth, and Wisdom and ethical principles. There are none such to be found anywhere. Hence Pierre clung to the old conceptions, could not break once and for all with his father's world. His incestuous desires for Isabel were the only means by which the tempestuous social passions and visions aroused in him would find an outlet. She was half-Glendinning and half-immigrant. It was his only means of reconciling irreconcilable worlds.

As Melville was careful to say, he did not really know the interior processes by which this would take place. All he was sure of was that people in Pierre's situation would behave that way. It is possible that Melville may have dived into his own personality to find the basic material for that novel. But even if he did, it is clear that he did not capitulate to the ingrown incest-sickness and he wrote of it as a social phenomenon. The psychoanalyst's couch is the favorite resting-place of many Pierres as the mast-head was for Ishmael. The Pierres are of both sexes. Anyone familiar with that section of society where meet together the left-wing of the liberal movement, the radical intellectuals,

the rising labor leaders and a small section of workers who aim at rais-
ing themselves above the workers' status can see the Pierres and the Is-
abels by the hundreds. One fastens on to the other and all the burdens
of social decision, or half-decision, of the personality disintegrating
under the pressures, these are piled by Pierre, male or female, upon Isabel. They need not end in suicide. By the time they reach the divorce
court, the ruin of each personality is sealed. There is always Ahab
waiting to give them that protection from having to make choices and
from the constant struggles of a world that is too much for them.

Those who read Pierre in 1852, needless to say, were scandalized.
Many years were to pass before men were educated to believe that incestuous desires were a permanent part of their personalities.

What now happened to Melville is a story very strange, very sad,
and yet, as everything about this extraordinary man, very significant
for the history of our times.

Melville has nothing more to say that is new. Hard up for money he
begins to write stories for magazines. But whenever he finds his favorite theme, the revulsion of modern man from an intolerable world, all
his old mastery seems to return. Three of these stories are among the
finest short stories that have ever been written; and so much is his literary genius by now a part of the world he has created, that these stories seem to belong to the world of 1914 to 1952. The first deals with
the revolt of the white-collar workers, another, with the revolt of
backward races, and a third with the revolt of man against civilization
itself, the fear that the long climb out of the primeval slime has been in
vain, and man is headed back for the swamps and the jungle.

The first story is entitled *Bartleby*. Bartleby is a scrivener, and the
millions of girls who spend their lives typing and retyping documents
every day will understand Bartleby well. In the days before typewriters
these documents were written by hand, and that is the type of work
done by Bartleby in a Wall Street lawyer's office. He is a young man,
ill-dressed, thin, pale and silent. However, he copies documents well.

But one day his employer asks him to check some papers. Bartleby
replies: "I would prefer not to." Had he been rude, angry or rebellious
he would have been sacked on the spot. But he is extremely, in fact,
inhumanly calm. His employer is struck with astonishment. But he decides that maybe Bartleby is not well or something. Bartleby is a good
worker. So the lawyer lets the incident pass.

Bartleby continues to do his work, but his employer, who tells the story, now observes Bartleby a little more closely than before. He notices that Bartleby never leaves the office. He sends the office-boy out for a handful of ginger-nuts on which to lunch. The employer, a successful, robust aggressive type, feels sympathy for him. But very soon, on another day, when called upon to do some work, Bartleby again replies: "I would prefer not to," and will not do what he is asked to do.

Bartleby's employer has never in his life experienced anything like this. Now, only now, he sees for the first time the shabbiness, the friendlessness, the loneliness of Bartleby. He seems removed from the life of ordinary men. But Bartleby continues to disrupt the office periodically with his adamant: "I would prefer not to."

This cannot go on. Soon Bartleby refuses to write any more. His employer attempts to dismiss him. But Bartleby will not leave. He prefers not to. His employer discovers by accident that Bartleby actually lives on the premises. By this time the pale, mild-mannered clerk is haunting the lawyer. He offers to take Bartleby into his house for a time where he can live decently. Bartleby prefers not to. The lawyer at another time fears that he will lose his temper and by an unpremeditated blow, murder Bartleby.

Finally in despair he abandons the office and moves to another one. Bartleby is arrested as a vagrant and sent to the Tombs among the murderers and thieves. His employer, in deep distress, rushes there to see him and to arrange that he should have decent meals. But Bartleby rejects his help with some strange words: "I know you, and I want nothing to say to you." He will not eat, and they find him lying on the grass one day. He is asleep? asks the grub-man. He sleeps "with kings and counsellors," says the lawyer. Bartleby is dead.

Kings and counsellors. It is the same phrase used of the crew of the Pequod as they slept in the forecastle. Somewhere this active go-getting Wall Street lawyer has recognized that in Bartleby's life and death are some heroism and grandeur far above the actual miserable existence of the clerk and his own worldly success. Melville concludes his story with a little epilogue. No one knows anything about Bartleby except that he once worked in the Dead Letter Office at Washington. His work was to sort and burn letters addressed to people who were dead by the time they were located. "Dead letters! Does it not sound like dead men?" This dismal work it was which

had demoralized Bartleby and, perhaps, explained his strange behavior. The story ends: "Ah, Bartleby! Ah, humanity!"
What are we to make of this story? First of all this is still the old Melville of *Moby-Dick*. Melville's story is realistic to the last comma. You live in a Wall Street office. Bartleby is presented with a touch of fantasy but he is as real as an ink-pot. But though he is writing in 1853 and short as the story is, Melville has in his remorselessly scientific manner isolated a section of society in his own time which has grown to immense importance in our own day—those millions of human beings who spend their strength, vitality and capacity for living, day after day, taking down, typing, checking, filing and then looking for documents which are to them as dead as the dead letters Bartleby handled. This today has reached a stage which Melville could hardly have envisaged. But he saw the tendency of things, and over and over again the words he uses bring to mind the contemporary millions who constitute the hewers of wood and drawers of water for the vast administrative machines that now dominate modern life.

But, perhaps because of the very coldness of his scientific dissection, within this drab commonplace realism Melville is heroic in the grandest of heroic traditions. Long, long ago he had decided that an ordinary Yankee sailor was worthy to rank with the Emperor Tiberius and Milton's Satan as the embodiment of audacious and heroic evil. So, Bartleby, at first, is a half-comic, half-pathetic figure. He has been turned into a clerical machine, a human typewriter who gave so much of his life to copying documents that he might as well eat and sleep in the office. But by degrees, Bartleby becomes the embodiment of a gigantic protest against this waste, this degradation of human life. At the end he looms up as a man of epic stature. With all the strength of his ill-fed, ill-clad, ill-housed body, he protested. His protest was absolute. He wanted no charity from his employer, no help because that would not alter his basic condition. And in the only way open to him, though at the cost of life itself, he asserted that he was a human being and not a thing. Even the origin of Bartleby's character comes from the method used in regard to Ahab in *Moby-Dick*. Bartleby, by nature and unfortunate upbringing, was inclined to a pallid hopelessness. Then the type of work he did intensified these characteristics and made him what he was.

Bartleby is an apparently simple story. But even when you have grasped the inhumanity of the type of existence lived by Bartleby, and the humanity of his protest, though you have grasped much, you are still far away from Melville's total conception. As presented at first, the Wall Street lawyer and his clerks are normal, Bartleby is crazy. In time it will be seen that it is Bartleby who is a normal human being—they are the crazy ones. Some glimmer of this bothers the lawyer from the very beginning and in the end conquers him although he never understands it. That is why he puts up with Bartleby's insubordination.

Melville is as confident as any man can be that the life of Bartleby and people like Bartleby is a monstrous denial of what is human in human beings. But Melville does not believe that anything can be done to alter such fundamental relations of a modern society. So that the only way it can be made bearable is by humor. To the reader who has thoroughly entered into *Moby-Dick,* the comedy of *Bartleby* is Melville's own brand of humor in the hangman's noose. There is no bitterness. The story must be told with humor or it cannot be told at all.

The story also explains Melville's life-long distrust and skepticism of liberals, radicals and revolutionaries, and his permanent disrespect for the Congress of the United States. What did all these people have to say, what could they do about a life such as Bartleby's? His answer was: nothing. And lives like Bartleby's were for the mature Melville one of the pillars on which modern civilization rested. This he had known at least since *Redburn.*

In 1854, Melville wrote *Las Encantadas,* and today, looking back, it seems that in it he said farewell. He has come finally to the conclusion that modern civilization is doomed. But his method of saying it is his own.

He does not play with the question, but is as uncompromising and absolute as ever. He does not go digging into his own feelings and weeping and wailing about them in the modern manner. He retains his habit of seeing the world objectively.

The Encantadas are a group of islands or rather, extinct volcanoes, which lie off the beaten track of vessels in the Pacific Ocean. Cut by the Equator, they know not autumn and they know not spring. In those islands rain never falls. Off and on through the centuries pirates have used them as hiding-places and a few individual attempts have been made to settle in them.

It is of these islands that Melville writes a series of sketches, an account of a visit he is supposed to have paid to them. He describes their appearance, the birds, animals, and reptiles who make these islands their home, the few people who for one reason or another have tried to live there. In reality, the sketches are one long poetic meditation on the theme that man's effort has been in vain and he is destined to begin again where once he did before.

One form of life prevalent on the islands is the tortoise. Melville is fascinated by it. Of the tortoises he writes haunting sentences. "they seemed newly crawled forth from beneath the foundation of the world." It is as if everything was beginning all over again.

He describes tortoises on the deck.

"As I lay in my hammock that night, overhead I heard the slow weary draggings of the three ponderous strangers along the encumbered deck. Their stupidity or their resolution was so great, that they never went aside for any impediment. One ceased his movements altogether just before the mid-watch. At sunrise I found him butted like a battering-ram against the immovable foot of the fore-mast, and still striving, tooth and nail, to force the impossible passage. That these tortoises are the victims of a penal, or malignant, or perhaps a downright diabolical enchanter, seems in nothing more likely than in that strange infatuation of hopeless toil which so often possesses them. I have known them in their journeyings ram themselves heroically against rocks, and long abide there, nudging, wriggling, wedging, in order to displace them, and so hold on their inflexible path. Their crowning curse is their drudging impulse to straightforwardness in a belittered world."

We do not need the last sentence to see that it is man, man struggling through the ages, struggling hopelessly, blindly, that Melville has in mind when writing about tortoises. He sees signs and has visions of them when he has run away from New York and sits among the trees in the Adirondacks. And in the midst of the most elegant and graceful culture that American civilization can show, they reappear to haunt him.

"For, often in scenes of social merriment, and especially at revels held by candle-light in old-fashioned mansions, so that shadows are thrown into the further recesses of an angular and spacious room, making them put on a look of haunted undergrowth of lonely woods, I have drawn the attention of my comrades by my fixed gaze and sudden change of air, as I have seemed to see, slowly emerging from these imagined solitudes, and heavily crawling along the floor, the ghost of a gigantic tortoise, with 'Memento Mori' [memory of death] burning in live letters upon his back."

He takes politics and religion, love, friendship and faith; one by one he places them in *Las Encantadas* and shows how they are destroyed. He does not complain. He is even good-tempered, but the destruction is not the less thorough.

There was still one more masterpiece to come from him. He was reading a book of travels and a story that not one writer in a hundred would have noticed caught his eye. But it set his mind to work, the same mind that wrote *Moby-Dick, Pierre,* and *Bartleby.* It has the peculiarity characteristic of all his finest work. It seems as if it was written not even after World War I but after Word War II.

A Yankee captain, competent, jolly and good-humored, is at anchor one morning in a harbor off the coast of Chile. He sees a strange vessel come into port and he goes off to pay it a visit. The vessel is a Spanish slaver, with slaves on board and the captain, Benito Cereno, whose name gives the title to the story, tells a sad tale of unfavorable weather, sickness and a hard voyage. The Yankee captain is full of sympathy.

Benito Cereno is followed everywhere by a Negro, Babo, who is unfailingly solicitous in his attentions to his master. The Yankee captain, reminding himself how well suited by nature Negroes are to be domestic servants, is very pleased by this.

Benito Cereno is a sick man and at times his behavior is strange. Captain Delono is mystified at many unusual incidents on the ship. But he makes allowances. The Negroes on board and the characteristics of Negroes occupy much of his attention. The slaves are in tumult but some are working. Six blacks in particular, elevated above the general throng, are busy cleaning rusty hatchets. Periodically they clash the hatchets together and the captain recognizes how fond Negroes are of uniting industry with pastime. He sees a mulatto steward on board. Is it true, he asks, that mulattoes are hostile to being placed in a subordinate position to blacks? He sees a Negro slave woman sleeping on deck while her baby sucks at the nipple, and he is pleased at this glimpse of the natural relation between a primitive mother and child. He is so impressed with Babo's unceasing attentions to his master that he offers to buy Babo as his personal servant, a proposal which, as could have been expected, the faithful Babo indignantly opposes. Captain Delano is one of those white men who not only understands but who loves Negroes.

Finally Captain Delano leaves the ship and goes back into his own boat. Suddenly, as the climax of his somewhat strange behavior all day, Benito Cereno leaps into the boat and Babo leaps after him with a knife. Captain Delano fears that his own life is in danger from the ever-faithful Babo, who perhaps believes that his beloved master is being kidnapped. But he soon learns the truth. Babo's knife is intended for Benito Cereno, and after the black is overpowered, the whole story comes out.

The slaves had revolted and seized the ship. They had tried to escape to freedom, but had not succeeded. When they came into the harbor, Babo, the leader, organized a new plot. They would pretend that Benito Cereno was still captain. But he, Babo, would be in attendance on him all day, and if he so much as tried to say a word, he would be immediately killed. All on board, slaves and white sailors, had been instructed by Babo what to do. The slaves kept watch on the sailors. The hatchet-polishers were not Negroes uniting industry with pastime as is the habit of Negroes. They were on guard, ready to intervene in any disturbance. The mulatto steward did not object to Negroes being over him—he was Babo's faithful lieutenant. The Negro women were not kindly primitives—they had taken a leading part in the revolt.

Delano's men finally recaptured the ship and Babo was beheaded. But here, as early as 1855, Melville had, in the opinions of the capable, well-meaning, Negro-loving Captain Delano, itemized every single belief cherished by an advanced civilization (we have selected only a few) about a backward people and then one by one showed that they were not merely false but were the direct cause of his own blindness and stupidity. Under his very nose, Babo had been forcing Benito Cereno to participate in a new plot, aimed at capturing Delano's own ship.

Melville, with his usual scientific precision, does not write of Negro slaves. He writes of the Negro race, civilized and uncivilized alike.

Harriet Beecher Stowe, who wrote a few years before, wrote about Negroes, about Uncle Tom and Eva, who mean nothing today. Melville's interest is in a vast section of the modern world, the backward peoples, and today from the continents of Asia and Africa, their doings fill the front pages of our newspapers. As is usual with him, his protest is uncompromising, absolute. The Negroes fight to a finish, Babo is the most heroic character in Melville's fiction. He is a man of unbending will, a natural leader, an organizer of large schemes but a master of detail, ruthless against his enemies but without personal weakness, as was proved by his behavior after he was captured. Melville purposely makes him physically small, a man of internal power with a brain that is a "hive of subtlety."

Masterpiece though *Benito Cereno* is, yet the story is a stage on the road of Melville's decline into the shallowness of modern literature. It is a propaganda story, a mystery, written to prove a particular social or political point. It is true that idea and story are perfectly fused. It is true also that Melville is master of his plan, he plays cat and mouse with the reader until he is ready to tell the secret; no one could guess it, and it would be interesting to know the opinions of modern masters like Dashiell Hammett or Raymond Chandler, if this is not really the first and best mystery of its kind in modern literature. But propaganda stories are of necessity limited. Ahab, for example, is a new type of human being. Bartleby is not. Still less is Babo. The Negro slaves and their leaders are shown to be human. But from Spartacus to Zapata, history tells us ten thousand such stories. Melville had ceased to be creative, and he had lost his vision of the future. Without such vision no writer can describe existing reality, for without it he does not know what is important or what is not, what will endure and what will pass.

Melville was finished and he knew it. But his future history continues to be symbolical. He wrote two more novels, but one of them he did not finish and one was very carelessly written. He got himself a job as an inspector of customs, and for twenty years he wrote not a line of fiction. He wrote poetry, but it is not very good poetry. After his death, among his papers was found a novel, *Billy Budd*, written during the brief period of life which remained to him after he retired from his job. It is a book which, the more it is studied, the more mysterious it becomes. Yet it gains most of its importance, not from its own intrinsic value, but because its author is the author of *Moby-Dick*.

Yet so much was he a man of our age that he could not write a line, good or bad, without showing it. Among the writings of his last twenty years is a poem called *Clarel*, very long and very tiresome. It is mentioned here because the spirit of it is modern to the last degree. A group of educated people are seeking salvation and some answer to the riddle of modern society. All are intellectuals or middle-class. They observe and analyze one another and their ideas for endless verses, and in the end, find no satisfactory answer. The talkers discuss Science and Religion, War and Politics, Revolution and Democracy. In the poem Melville, who had created the crew of the Pequod and the harpooneers, refers to workers as "the masses." He had completely lost what distinguished him in the great years—the sense of society as a whole. Yet the book is important for what it teaches about Melville in reverse. *Carel* deals with what was always on the outer surface of Melville's mind, the things you will find in his correspondence and the reports of his conversations with people. But ten thousand intellectuals of his day thought and spoke and wrote about just such things. The unique genius was the man who created out of his own experience and reflection characters and conceptions of which you will find little or no trace in his conversations or in his letters.

Nevertheless, in his decline as in his greatness, Melville remains a man of our time. *Clarel* is the work of a contemporary intellectual. Much of our contemporary literature is the work of intellectuals without vision. They do not know what inhumanity is, they do not know what humanity is. Although a hundred years have passed, few of them understand *Moby-Dick*, few of them understand a simple, straightforward elementary character like Babo.

Just look at the names of the famous books which will be handed to future generations as a picture of our times: *The Waste Land*, *Journey to the End of the Night*, *Darkness at Noon*, *Farewell to Arms*, *The Counterfeiters*, *In Remembrance of Things Past*—a catalogue of misery or self-centered hopelessness. These are the books Ishmael and Pierre would write if they wrote novels. One thing unites these authors. They know nothing about work and workers, the living experience of the vast majority of living men. Only when war compels them to associate with the great mass of their fellows and sweat and die with them in common association do we get isolated books like *The Naked and the Dead* and *From Here to Eternity*. Since World War II the catalogue continues, more dreary than ever. We have had *Nausea*, *The Flies*, *Reprieve*, *The Plague*,

The Stranger. In the two or three words which is all the narrow back of a book will take, the intellectuals of our time have placed their diseased stamp upon the literature of our age, as they have placed their diseased stamp upon its psychology. Some of them are men of very great gifts, but for all of them, human beings are the naked and the dead, for whom there is nothing between here and eternity, life is a journey to the end of the night, where in the darkness of midday, the neurotic personality of our time escapes from freedom into a wasteland of guilt and hopelessness. Melville describes the same world in which they live, and Ishmael and Pierre are sick to the heart with the modern sickness. Yet how light in the scales is the contemporary mountain of self-examination and self-pity against the warmth, the humor, the sanity, the anonymous but unfailing humanity of the renegades and castaways and savages of the Pequod, rooted in the whole historical past of man, doing what they have to do, facing what they have to face.

Chapter VI

THE WORK, THE AUTHOR AND THE TIMES

We have now analyzed the most important of Melville's writings. But in all such analysis, and particularly when it is related, as it must be related, to the social movement, there is one great danger. This is that the book, as a work of art, fades into the background, and it becomes a mere expression of social and political ideas. This is fatal because the social and political ideas in a great work of imagination are embodied in human personalities, in the way they are presented, in the clash of passions, the struggle for happiness, the avoidance of misery.

With the disappearance of the work as an imaginative creation of human relations, the author also tends to disappear, the supreme author, a unique individual, the type of human being who appears but rarely in the history of civilization. Yet he and his life are rooted in the life of their time. No book on Melville would be complete which did not attempt to place in their proper relation the work, the author, and the period.

The ancient Greeks in the great days of Greek civilization looked upon their great writers as second to none in the state. Here also, as in so many other judgments, they were wiser than we. For consider. What Melville did was to place within the covers of one book a presentation of a whole civilization so that any ordinary human being today can read it in a few days and grasp the essentials of the world he lived in. To do this a man must contain within his single self, at one and the same time, the whole history of the past, the most significant experiences of the world around him, and a clear vision of the future. Of all this he creates an ordered whole. No philosopher, statesman, scientist or soldier exceeds him in creative effort.

Melville knew how rarely such writers appear, and as usual, he has given the best description of these gigantic efforts of individual human beings.

The great author begins, as we have seen, by seeing the elements of his characters in the world around him. Melville tolerates no nonsense on that question. But after that an entirely individual personal process begins. The great author has read the great creative works of the past, and it is in this way that he absorbs the great characters and experiences of previous civilizations. He is mature, according to Melville, only when these writings are a part of him, and his own mind, so nourished, functions with complete independence.

Then follows his own original creation. It seems that really new characters with original instincts cannot be developed adequately within the framework of the consciousness of the age. The great author must find in his mind new depths of consciousness, hitherto unprobed, to fill out these original characters. Melville actually uses the term, "strange stuff" which upheaves and upgushes in the writer's soul. This strange stuff the author has to resolve into its primitive elements. Thus these rare original characters seem to demand for their creation an extension of the range of consciousness of their creators, and through him this extended consciousness is transferred to the rest of mankind, when they are ready to listen.

It is impossible to test whether all this is true or not. All we can do is to examine some other great creative works of the past and great authors of the past and see if any light is thereby thrown upon Melville in this combination of observing actual human character, reading the great works of the past and then digging down into the consciousness.

Two writers immediately come to mind—the great Greek tragedian, Aeschylus, and his *Prometheus Bound,* and the still more famous Shakespeare and his play *King Lear.*

Ahab is a rebel, i.e., a man who is dissatisfied with the old and must have something new. So is Prometheus. So is Lear. Ahab defies science and industrial power, the gods of the nineteenth century. Prometheus was nailed to a rock because he had stolen fire from heaven and given it to primitive, backward, suffering mankind to start them on the road to civilization by means of the arts and sciences. For this, Zeus, King of Gods and men, chained him to a rock for 30,000 years. But still Prometheus defied him. Lear believed that Nature was a beneficent goddess in whose name he ruled, and by whom all his actions were blessed. When he discovered that it was not so, he defied Nature.

Then going mad, he denounced the whole society of which he had been ruler and gave a vision of the future.

When Ahab defies the spirit of fire, he is way out in distant seas, thousands of miles away from civilization, standing on the deck of the Pequod, with the meanest mariners, renegades and castaways around him. When Prometheus defies Zeus, he is chained to a rock, on a wild expanse of land at the very ends of the earth. Around him are some young women from all parts of the world who are determined to share his fate. When Lear defies the thunder and the lightning, the most powerful manifestations of the forces of Nature, he is also on an open heath, and with him are a retainer whom he himself had banished; a crazy fool; and another fugitive from justice, disguised as an agricultural vagrant. Zeus hurls Prometheus and his followers into the lower regions with the thunderbolts and lightning of a great storm. Lear is driven mad by the thunder and lightning. These breaking upon him after his grievous experiences seem to be the final culmination of his sufferings. Ahab escapes the lightning and the thunder and the corpusants only to fall victim to his own madness. At times the three characters use almost the same words. These similarities cannot possibly be accidental.

It seems that at very great crises in human history, and they must be very great, an author appears who becomes aware that one great age is passing and another beginning. But he becomes aware of this primarily in terms of new types of human character, with new desires, new needs, new passions. The great writer, at least each of the three greatest writers the author of this book knows, conceives a situation in which this character is brought right up against things that symbolize the old and oppose the new. The scene is set outside the confines of civilization. What is old is established, it has existed for centuries, it is accepted. But the new will not be denied. It is not fully conscious of itself, but it is certain that it is right. A gigantic conflict is inevitable.

It is here that Melville's description of the creative process may help us.

Prometheus, though in the play he is one of the Gods, is an Athenian of the fifth century before Christ. Amidst the surrounding primitiveness and savagery, a wonderful civilization had flowered with almost marvellous suddenness, a civilization based on the development of industry and commerce, practicing democracy, gifted in architecture, sculpture, philosophy and the drama. We have not got the complete drama on Prometheus written by Aeschylus. We have only what amounts to Act II of a play of three acts. But it seems fairly clear that Prometheus stood for the new, the splendid civilization, against the apathy, the ignorance, and perhaps the brutal tyranny of the old regime, or more probably the readiness of the first founders of the new regime to compromise with the old and leave things much as they were before. The history of Athens shows us figures who could have served as a model for him. How far he, from this model, was the creation of his author, we cannot at this distance tell. But this much we know. While the ancient Greeks understood the character, to this very day Prometheus is still the prototype of the revolutionary leader, benefactor of humanity, bold, defiant, confident. It would seem that Aeschylus went far beyond his actual model or models, and created the type in such perfection that it lives to this day.

With Lear we can get closer to Melville's theories. Lear was created at the beginning of the seventeenth century about a dozen years before the founding of New England. A new world was on its way, the world of free individualism, of the conquest of Nature, of social revolution against tyrannical monarchy, of open conflicts over the distribution of the national income, when new concepts of justice would be battled over, and scientific explanations would be sought for human crime and error. Now this is what Lear spoke about when, driven mad by the wrongs inflicted upon him, he defied the storm on the heath.

Where did Shakespeare get all this from? How did he conceive of it all in the person of one single character? All we can say is that Melville's explanation is as good as any, and we should not forget that it is a great writer himself speaking. It took literally centuries before the modern world began to understand Lear. Shakespeare, having been given the initial impetus from outside, had to dig down into his own consciousness for the new feelings and the new ideas needed to complete his portrayal.

Melville says more than once and with great emphasis that what a great author like Shakespeare writes down is only a partial, inadequate, poor representation of what is in his mind. He says that there are two books, the one the author sees in his mind and the one he writes. And the one in the mind is as sluggish as an elephant, it will not move when called upon, and it sucks away the life-blood of the writer. It is too big and in places too obscure for accurate reproduction. It would seem then that the author does create within himself the character and its world and gives the best account of it he can.

The achievement of a great writer who writes an immortal book now stands before us in all its magnitude. He creates a world of human beings and an environment to correspond. He has read and absorbed how great characters in previous critical situations acted. He recognizes the similarity of emotions. He can use them to help his own structure. But what matters in his work is what is new, and that he must dig out for himself. What matters to us in Ahab is not his heroic determination. It is the sense of purpose, the attitude to science and industry, the defense of individual personality, the attitude to the men around him. There is not, and could not be anything like this in Aeschylus or in Shakespeare.

It is the completeness of the creation in the mind that seems to be the most astonishing thing. Just as from the real world of human beings, one can abstract philosophy, political economy, scientific theory, so from the partial account that is written down of this inherent world, one can deduce scientific theories of which the author was not at all directly conscious. Melville wrote *Moby-Dick* in 1851. Yet in it today can be seen the anticipations of Darwin's theory of man's relation to the natural world, of Marx's theory of the relation of the individual to the economic and social structure, of Freud's theory of the irrational and primitive forces which lie just below the surface of human behavior.

He does not only anticipate the work of scientists. He is himself a scientist in human relations. Ahab is of the race of Prometheus. But it seems as if, for Melville, that type was now doomed. Great men, leading their fellows from one stage of civilization to another, there have always been and will always be, but the Promethean individual, containing in himself, his ideas, his plans, the chart of the future, he seems finished. In the world of affairs he leads only to disaster, which is why perhaps in literature he no longer appears at all.

The world of the author's creation is his own world in a very precise sense. Though rooted in reality, it is not a real world. No man ever chased or would chase a White Whale as Ahab did. No intellectual ever followed a totalitarian because of the whiteness of anything. The great writer is dealing in human emotions. The world he creates is designed to portray emotions. Those are real enough. And he will use anything that will bring those emotions vividly before his reader. The

White Whale seems infinitely remote from the idea of the master race or the master plan. But within Melville's world the reasoning and feelings and actions and effects of the men who follow this fantasy are as real as those in the actual world of men.

The greatest scene in *King Lear* is that scene in which the old man defies the storm and then begins to speak like a prophet inspired with a vision of three centuries to come. Very fortunately we are fairly certain where Shakespeare got the idea. A few months before he wrote this play, a tremendous storm swept over Western Europe by sea and land and dealt such damage as had never been experienced within the memory of living man. For the men of Shakespeare's day, a Nature giving its blessings to men was an integral part of their philosophy of life, their concept of the world. Already in *Hamlet* Shakespeare had drawn a picture of a man whose personality was in insoluble conflict with the world in which he lived. In *Lear* Shakespeare was to carry this to its logical conclusion. Here in the storm was a symbol of a Nature that, far from being beneficent, had turned on man and wrecked his civilization. Shakespeare seized upon this and found in it the perfect foil which would dramatize the sufferings and the defiance and the vision of Lear. So impressed was Shakespeare's imagination by the storm that he used it in another play, *Macbeth*, written about the same time. The references to the great storm are unmistakable.

This was the procedure that Melville seems to have followed in *Moby-Dick*. As a young man he had been enormously impressed by the story of a whale which had turned on its pursuers and smashed their ship to pieces. Years passed and he began the writing of *Moby-Dick*. The central character is Ahab with his purpose. But Melville had to find an opposition. He found it in an actual whale, Moocha Dick, a gigantic monster which sought its pursuers on sight to given them deadly battle. Thus whales, the traditional source of wealth and power of men of that age, in the shape of the malignant Moocha Dick, became the symbol of a civilization which was no longer beneficent, but had turned against man.

Once the writer has got hold of his characters and their environment, then that world dominates everything, including himself. Structure, style, ideas, phrases fit into or spring from this distinct creation. For convenience we have spoken of characters, then of environment, here of reality, there of logical imagination. But in these great creative works these things are no more separate than, in the real world, a man's political activity can be separated from his personality. The artist's world is a total whole and its effect on the reader is designed to be total. Ahab for example is eaten up inside by his speculations on the nature of the universe and his scientific plans to capture Moby Dick. This is shown on his physical person by the great lines of thought on his forehead which are constantly brought to the notice of the reader. Again, on two dramatic occasions, first Melville and then Ahab himself refer to the weight upon Ahab's back of the countless miseries men have endured since the days of Adam. Ahab's words are worth repeating, "I feel deadly faint, bowed, and humped, as though I were Adam, staggering beneath the piled centuries since Paradise."

But on at least twenty-five occasions in the book, from the chapter in which we first see him to the last pages in which he destroys the Pequod, Moby Dick is persistently described for us as a whale with a wrinkled forehead and a hump on his back. Those and his whiteness are his distinguishing features. Thus by degrees it dawns upon us that Moby Dick is the physical embodiment of Ahab's inward crisis. His determination to slay Moby Dick is his determination to slay the demons which are torturing him. But Melville at the same time makes it consistently clear that Moby Dick is actually just a big fish in the sea. It is crazy Ahab who makes of him this fantastic symbol. Similarly the evil effect of the whiteness of the whale is felt by Ishmael who had brought with him from his life on land the vision of a white monster.

If within this world the writer feels that characters or events are needed to make his conception logical, he creates them, often in direct contradiction with ordinary experience and ordinary sense. He is guided by one fact—his world needs them. The writer of this book feels that it is out of some such need that there came figures like Queequeg, Daggoo and Tashtego.

This is the type of world created by the great writer. These are the effects he seeks and these are the means he uses to achieve them. This is his book, his own individual creation, and it is by means of the wrinkled brow and the whiteness of the whale, and the flag streaming forward from Tashtego's own forward-flowing heart that Melville says what he has to say.

And yet at the same time, this most intense individuality of creation is moulded not only out of the general social environment but of the very nationality of the author. Melville establishes in the most unequivocal form that his theme is world civilization. But Aeschylus was in every line of his work an Athenian of the fifth century B.C. Similarly Shakespeare was an Elizabethan Englishman, and Melville is the most American of all writers. It is not only his original character that is rooted in the external world. He himself is rooted in that world. We have tried to show this in the slight biographical sketches, and the attempt to outline the growth of his mind. But the roots are deeper.

We have given examples of Melville's strictly scientific method of selecting and defining his theme. All of *Moby-Dick* is built on this principle. From Chapter I to the last chapter he has his plan plotted and worked out in order, item after item stated, almost like a bill of lading. When he finished with one topic he takes up another. He constantly classifies. From Chapter I to Chapter XXII he describes the land. Chapter XXIII describes the purpose of the voyage and describes mankind in general. Chapters XXV to L describe all on board and Moby Dick. Chapters LI–XCV are almost entirely devoted to the crew. Chapter XCVI describes the Try-Works and the collapse of Ishmael. Two chapters later we have the stowing-down and the clearing-up and then the next chapter, XCIX, the Doubloon, brings all the characters up once more for systematic review. Chapters C to CXXXII shows all the characters now in rapid movement, introducing some new ones. Every chapter now deepens character and brings the catastrophe nearer. The last three chapters describe the chase. In between Melville periodically introduces a chapter describing a passing ship either to bring in some facet of the outside world, to increase the tension on the Pequod, or to do both. Structurally *Moby-Dick* is one of the most orderly books in the world but orderly in the sociological sense. It is the mark of a man shaped by a civilization where from its foundation the construction and objective classification of material things dominate life and thought to a degree far greater than in any other modern country.

But having once arranged a basic systematic plan, Melville then in his style exhibits all the American exuberance and insatiable grasp at every aspect of life in sight. Ancient and modern history, theology, mythology, philosophy, science, he takes hold of everything and uses it for any purpose he wants. He has in his head the majestic rhythms of the great English prose-writers and he can originate new variations of them. But even within these rhythms he is incurably colloquial and discursive. On occasion some of Ahab's speeches ring slightly hollow. But Melville achieved a harmony between classical English style and the ease of American civilization, which has been managed neither before nor since. He could do whatever he wanted to do, and almost on the same page he could reconcile the most contradictory styles without strain.

And finally he was American, too, not only in structure and in style, but in the deepest content of his great book. No one can really say with any precision what influences shaped a writer's creative imagination. But the period in which Melville wrote was one the most curious in the history of the United States. On the one hand the mass of the nation in the North, disoriented, cut away from old moorings, hungrily seeking a new basis for a sense of community. On the other—some of the most boundlessly egotistical individual personalities the country has ever known. Some of the men of that period, Stanton, the Secretary of War, Thaddeus Stevens, William Lloyd Garrison, were men of a tempestuous force of character such as have no parallel in contemporary life. The lives of the generals, Grant, Sherman, Sheridan, make equally strange reading.

The Civil War put an end to this torment of a nation. The people found themselves in the formation of the Republican Party, and the struggle for the unity of the nation. The great individualists found their energies disciplined or stimulated in the war itself. But it seems clear that in his ruthless probing to the very end of the problem of individual personality and at the same time the search for a new basis of community, Melville was writing about an America that he knew. When with the end of the Civil War normal life returned, Melville was forgotten. But with the return of crisis in 1914, this time on a world scale, he has been rediscovered.

If this essentially American writer now takes on increasingly the status of the most representative writer of modern civilization, one result of it should be to bring more sharply into prominence the period in which he wrote, the period which preceded the Civil War. That period ushered in the world in which we live. For our world, a world of wars, the fact is neglected that the Civil War was the first great war of modern times. The great Americans of the period preceding it knew that something was wrong, something deeper than slavery, but inasmuch as they lived under democracy and the republic, and had no monarchy nor land-owning aristocracy to contend with, their task was difficult. They probed into strange places and what they found they did not often fully understand. There were no precedents. It is only today when democracies and republics once more have to examine their foundations that the work of Poe, Hawthorne, Whitman, Garrison and Phillips, and Melville can be fully understood. Melville today already towers above his countrymen, and such is the hunger of the world for understanding itself, that the time cannot be far distant when men in every country will know him for what he is—a writer in the great tradition of Aeschylus and Shakespeare and the unsurpassed interpreter of the age in which we live, its past, its present and its uncertain future.

Chapter VII

"A NATURAL BUT NECESSARY CONCLUSION"

What the writing of this book has taught the writer is the insepa-rability of great literature and of social life. I read Melville during the great historical events of the last seven years, and without them I would never have been able to show, as I believe I have done, that his work is alive today as never before since it was written. So far, how-ever, the contemporary references I have made have been to events on a world scale. There remains the task of some direct estimate of the relation of this great American to present conditions in the country which produced him.

I had lectured on Melville for three seasons, in many parts of the United States, to audiences of all kinds, putting forward many of the general ideas contained here. What stood out was the readiness of every type of audience to discuss him, and sometimes very heatedly, as if he were a contemporary writer. I had long contemplated a book on Melville, had decided to write it in the summer of 1952, and was busy negotiating with publishers. What form it might have taken had I written it according to my original plans I do not know. But what matters is that I am not an American citizen, and just as I was about to write, I was arrested by the United States Government and sent to Ellis Island to be deported.

My case had been up for nearly five years. It had now reached the courts, and there would be some period before a final decision was ar-rived at. I therefore actually began the writing of this book on the Is-land, some of it was written there, what I did not write there was con-ceived and worked over in my mind there. And in the end I finally came to the conclusion that my experiences there have not only shaped this book, but are the most realistic commentary I could give on the validity of Melville's ideas today.

I shall anticipate in only one particular. Melville built his gigantic structure, a picture of world civilization, using one small vessel, with a crew of thirty-odd men, for the most part isolated from the rest of the world. Here was I, just about to write, suddenly projected onto an island isolated from the rest of society, where American administrators and officials, and American security officers controlled the destinies of perhaps a thousand men, sailors, "isolatoes," renegades and castaways from all parts of the world. It seems now as if destiny had taken a hand to give me a unique opportunity to test my ideas of this great American writer.

I

The first thing that happened was that within an hour of my arrival, I was placed in a special room for political prisoners, the only occupants of which were five Communists. The reader of this book knows what I think of Communists. But this was more serious than my mere thoughts. Though I had expressed radical ideas, and in fact was in trouble because of that, the Communists knew me personally as their open and avowed enemy. I had written or translated books against them, which had been published in England, in France and the United States. They knew me well and knew all about me, or if they didn't, they would soon know. I also knew all about them. I knew their long record of murders of political enemies. In particular I recalled the fate of a friend of mine who had been imprisoned with them in France by the Vichy Government. As soon as the Vichy Government fell, they murdered him.

The Department of Immigration knew my attitude to Communists. Yet here I was placed with them in a single room where we had to live together and sleep together. At the moment I didn't know what to do. I could protest, but if my protest was rejected, the Communists would certainly get to know about it, as they get to know about everything, and I would then have to face them with the antagonism open and declared. I was not so stupid as to think they would murder me. But if they wanted to, they could make my life unbearable. And in any case the reader of this book will not need to be told how deep in me is the revulsion from everything they stand for.

I was conscious of their murderous past, not only against declared and life-long enemies, but against one another, and I was from that moment always aware of the fact that tomorrow I and people like me could be at their mercy in a concentration camp, sentenced by the government which put us there. Very rapidly, as so often happens today, ideas were transformed into life. Within a few days the press and the radio were filled day after day with the self-admitted blunders of the American Government in its treatment of the prisoners on Koje Island. It was at that time that I began to be aware that what was happening to me and the others on Ellis Island was, in miniature, a very sharp and direct expression of what was taking place in the world at large.

I believe that for a day or two the Communists were somewhat uncertain as to what should be their attitude to me. For one thing they seemed to suspect at one time that I might be a stool-pigeon. On the alert, I could see them whispering and consulting together. Finally, however, they seemed to come to the conclusion that they would treat me as a fellow-prisoner. And this they did with that thoroughness and scrupulousness which characterizes them in any line that they are for the moment following. I was continually on my guard, but I had only one really bad moment, on the day when one of them told me that his friend, William Patterson, was coming to see him that afternoon. I knew about this Patterson, a notorious slanderer, Communist hack and misleader of the Negro people, and particularly a slanderer of myself in the old days. But he came and went and nothing happened.

Government officials, and those intellectuals who think they know so much (most of them ridden with fear because of their past association with Communists) may believe or affect to believe that my troubles with Communists do not concern them. I hope that the Koje Island events and the negotiations at Panmunjom which have wracked the nerves of the whole world for so long, have taught them differently.

I did not learn in Melville that Communists were men of purpose. But Melville made me understand how all-embracing was this purpose, its depth, its range, its flexibility, its deep historical roots, the feebleness of all opposition to it which is not animated by feelings as sure and as strong. I thought I now understood all this well, I was mistaken. In the course of the next few weeks, I saw one of these Communists in particular acting with the deepest conviction as the defender and champion of the people on Ellis Island against the cruelties and inhumanity of the

administration. These Communists came militantly to my defense
when I was lying ill in bed, and unable to move a finger to protect myself. One of them in particular, although a prisoner, dominated the
whole floor on which the great mass of prisoners was detained, repeatedly routed the administrative authorities, and finally had the
F.B.I. itself at his feet, soliciting his views on what was wrong with Ellis
Island.

In those four months that I spent in the custody of the authorities
on Ellis Island, I learned more about world Communism and the
struggle against it than in any previous four years of my life. Armed
and fortified as I was, I could see in concentrated form what modern
civilization is up against. I shall leave my own experiences for last.

The political prisoners were isolated from the main body of prisoners in one corner of the building, and opposite this room was another
room where mental prisoners were placed. I saw quite a few men
there. Most of the men put in it were probably not mental cases at all.
They were men who, as far as I could judge, were over-wrought by difficult lives, and the hopelessness of the odds against them in their attempt to enter the United States or to avoid deportation. But the hospital for people on Ellis Island is now the United States Public Health
Service Hospital at Stapleton on Staten Island.

The present infirmary on Ellis Island has neither the staff nor the
equipment to deal with any serious illness. Patients have to be transferred. The authorities at the Island therefore simply dump nervous
cases into this room. If they become obstreperous, they can always be
given some sedative, by mouth or with the needle.

The Communist, I shall call him M, literally took these people
under his protection. He would go and talk to them, and they would
be glad to have someone to talk to. He watched how these unfortunates ate their meals, how they slept, he followed the course of their
illness, and, limited as were his opportunities, always had a word, an
enquiry, or some piece of advice for them after they left the mental
room. On occasions he overrode or won over some sympathetic
guards and would take these men, who had been cooped up for days,
out for a walk on the little patch of grass where we were allowed to
walk. He would walk them up and down, give them a period to sit in
the sun, and then take them back in. I have known him to raise his
voice in anger at the sight of one man who was filthy from days of neglect and carry the man off to the bathroom and himself give him a

bath. Among cases which he told me about, or which I saw myself were the following:

There was a Canadian soldier, a man put in as a mental case, who one Thursday evening threw his dish of spaghetti and meat-sauce on the floor. For the moment he looked dangerous. M, with his usual confidence, went in to see him. He reported that the soldier had lost his wife who was of Italian extraction. Every Thursday she used to cook spaghetti and meat-sauce. The sight of the dish was for the moment too much for him and he had lost control of his already over-strained nerves. What is most remarkable, however, is that he apologized to M for his behavior. He felt some sense of responsibility to him. I doubt if he felt any to anyone else in the building.

Another case was that of an Irishman, whom I knew well because he spent some time in the hospital with me. His was a bad case. He was mentally unstable and his right hand had been badly damaged in an accident. Obviously he had thousands of dollars due to him as compensation. He claimed, however, that he had been reported to the Immigration Authorities as an alien, so that he could be railroaded out of the country before the damages were paid. He was sent to the hospital but could not accommodate himself to the routine there. He was sent back to the Island and found himself in the mental room. M befriended him. The political prisoners were briefly allowed into the big room where the other prisoners passed the day, for such purposes as telephoning or making purchases at the canteen. I have seen M go up to this Irishman, talk to him and maneuver him into the corridor towards some quiet spot. He told me that he could tell from John's general appearance when the fits were coming on, and was on the alert to prevent him collapsing suddenly.

It was not only mental patients. There was an old man of seventy up for deportation. He had no teeth. Somewhere along the administrative road, the proposal that he should have some teeth was rejected. The food he ate was the food he got. The result was terrible bouts of constipation. After some going and coming he was given a suppository. The old man could not use it. He came to M. M somehow maneuvered himself into the old man's quarters and performed the operation.

M interested himself also in the situation of the boys. When boys under age were placed in the same rooms with homosexuals and criminals, M protested violently. If he could not reach officials, he talked to guards. There was one remarkable case he told me about. He befriended a small boy claiming to be an Italian, up for deportation. This boy afterwards turned out to be a frightened American kid from Cleveland who had run away from home, and didn't know what to do with himself. The machinery of the law and the callousness of the authorities, between them, narrowly missed deporting this American citizen.

Sometimes these continually tragic events blundered into the sphere of the comic. M is a Jew, born in Russia. But he came here when he was twelve years old and if ever I saw a man with all the characteristics of the American social type, he has them. The food at the island is tough. In his first weeks there he lost many pounds. After consultation with the authorities it was decided to let him eat in the Jewish kitchen, run by an orthodox Jewish organization for their co-religionists. There the food was a little better. So for the time being M became once more a Jew. Yom Kippur, 1952, approached, and the Jews wanted to hold religious services. But the rule is that to be able to hold a religious service there must be 10 men of that religion. There were nine Jews, and M was the tenth. He said he would go only if they allowed a mental patient, a Jew, and a protege of his, to come too. They tried to remonstrate with him. He was adamant. "If you want me, you must take him too; nothing is wrong with him." Finally M won his point. A guard promised to stand by. So the mental patient was cleaned and polished up, and he and M went to service.

The result of all this can be imagined. Although he could mix but little with the main body of men, in prison people learn to communicate. He had among them a tremendous reputation. Somehow he could give advice to prisoners who did not know what to do. I know at least one case where a man, a perfectly innocent man, was being railroaded out, and M told him what to do in the nick of time and he was saved by minutes. I am sure there were others. I could tell of cases of flagrant injustice which he helped to fight over long periods and lost.

Now a man had to be blind and deaf not to see that whatever were the rights and wrongs of any particular case, here was a powerful demonstration, before a specially selected audience, of the Communist, the man of purpose, in action. But all the authorities could think of was to ask M: what is it to you, why do you interfere in all this? M's reply, as he told me, was always this "I am doing it because I am a human being. My politics have nothing whatever to do with this. But I cannot sit here and see these things going on." M handled his protests with great discretion, for after all he was a prisoner. Sometimes when he was called up or was discussing some business of his own, he would seize the opportunity to raise the case of some poor helpless prisoner. But he was prepared, if need be, to take risks. He knew and had sized up practically every guard and supervisor in the place, and he knew how and when to talk to them.

The climax came just before I was let out of Ellis Island on bail. He had been writing a series of articles in the Communist press, giving case after case of flagrant injustice. They are there for anyone to read. Nobody could challenge them, because he had all the facts, and he wrote with the authority of someone who was actually in the place which he was writing about. He told me that the articles were being translated and reprinted in the Communist press abroad. Americans will ignore such things at their peril. People abroad do not. At any rate, one day I saw M very busy at his typewriter, and some time after he handed me a carbon copy of a report on Ellis Island, written, as he informed me, for the F.B.I. Whether the Department of Justice was feeling the pressure of the repercussion of M's articles in the foreign press, or for whatever reason, a man from the F.B.I. had come to see M and asked him to prepare a report on conditions on the Island. M very cheerfully agreed, prepared his report and sent it off. He also gave a copy of the report to the head of the Detention Department. Finally he asked permission of a supervisor to give a copy of the report to his wife who had come to see him, in order that she might give it to his attorney. What happened was typical of the administration and its relations with M. The supervisor at first refused. M blandly told him: I have sent a report to the F.B.I., on their request; I have given a copy to the Head of Detention; why can't I give a copy to my attorney? The supervisor sputtered, then retreated and M gave his wife the copy. Shortly afterwards I saw the supervisor talking to M. M informed me that he had apologized.

This is the Department of Justice which is leading the struggle against Communism. With all its officers and armed guards, its bolts and its bars, its thick walls and its power, it was morally defeated by one single Communist repeatedly.

The consequences of this were far-reaching. M claimed, and as far as I could see, with truth, that he indulged in no political propaganda on Ellis Island. But he had no need to. He told me that many of the men whom he had helped and others who had seen his actions had told him or passed the word to him that as soon as they reached home they were going to join the Communist Party. His reply was that they should be careful, that joining the Communist Party was not a thing to be done in heat and passion, that they could harm both themselves and the party; such action needed careful consideration. In fact I know that one day a bitter and a rather disreputable South American spat when the American flag was being raised, and M rebuked him sharply.

But perhaps his greatest triumph was among the staff of Ellis Island itself, the guards. These men were of all types (I shall deal with them later). But all whom I saw respected M for the way he conducted himself and his uncompromising stand on elementary human decency. I could see that a great number of them, some Irish Catholics and outspoken anti-Communists, talked to him about their problems and the problems of the Island. Once when a number of them were dismissed, as they believed unjustly, and the whole staff was in an uproar, between those who came to say goodbye and those who came to ask him what he thought of it all, there seemed to be two centers on the Island—the official staff upstairs, and M below, the center of attraction for aggrieved and bewildered men.

Under my very eyes, M had turned the Department of Justice itself into an arena where he struck hard blows for his side in the great struggle now going on for world mastery. He was using the American tradition against those who were supposed to be its guardians. On Ellis Island it was M who stood for what vast millions of Americans still cherish as the principles of what America has stood for since its foundation. You needed a long and well-based experience of Communism and Communists to know that M in reality was a man as mad as Ahab,* in all that he was doing pursuing his own purpose, with the flexibility, assurance and courage that are born of conviction. How many there knew that if it suited his purpose, in fact his purpose would demand that if he were in charge of Ellis Island, he would subject both officers and the men he championed to a tyranny worse than anything they could conceive of? The officials were the

---

*I should say that I do not necessarily believe that all the American Ahabs are in the Communist Party, or will ultimately join it. But that it is a subject that is far beyond the scope of what I am writing at present.

contemporary image of those officers this book describes, who even when competent, morally enfeebled the men they were supposed to lead by their indifference, their lack of any moral principle or conviction. Could anything be more shameful than that they should have to ask this Communist what was wrong on Ellis Island? that he should be able to say that he acted as a human being, and not as a Communist? This is the news that was being taken to every quarter of the globe by the thousands of men who passed through Ellis Island while he was there.

Before I left M told me that they had decided to release him though no country would take him. The phrase the Government used, I was told, was that his release would be "to their mutual advantage."

I have to say a few words about my relationship with M and his fellow Communists. From the time that they, as it seemed to me, decided to accept me, their behavior was not only correct, but genuinely friendly. They did me many kindnesses; if I did something rather stupid, or which could be dangerous to me, they warned me about it. They shared all they had with me. We talked a great deal, by mutual and tacit concern keeping away from certain subjects, but talking very freely on others. M is a remarkable man, they were all in their way men of a calm and indomitable courage, and one or two of them as pleasant fellows as I have met anywhere. It was a long time since I had met any of them at close quarters, and I had never met any of them so intimately and for so continuous a length of time. I observed them closely (as no doubt they observed me). The experience with them became an invaluable part of the study of Melville and the writing of this book. My relation with them raised many serious problems for me, problems which I am sure tens of millions of people in every quarter of the globe have to face every day. I knew them but they were for the time being loyal to me. I finally decided to give them as square a deal as they gave to me. Before I left I asked M if, should I think of writing, I could write freely about him. He said he didn't mind in the least what I wrote.

I did this because of my knowledge built up over the years, that the greatest danger in dealing with Communists is the tremendous pressure that knowledge of their attitudes exercises on you to meet them on their own ground, which is the straight road to your own corruption. But the people really responsible are those who put me in with them, and whose conduct of affairs would have pushed me into their arms, were it not for my knowledge of them. But all that is now over. If I return to Ellis Island, I will have to be dragged with ropes to live in the same room with them, and kept there either bound or all of us under lock and key.

II

I now take up my own personal experience on the Island.

I am 51 years of age, and from the time I was about seven—perhaps before—I have suffered from pains which were finally diagnosed as pains from a duodenal ulcer. For years whenever these pains bothered me I instinctively went on some sort of diet and threw them off; but by 1937, they became worse, I had myself x-rayed and learned exactly what was wrong. In 1938 while I was living in England, I was invited to the United States to lecture. I asked the doctors at the English hospital for their advice. They told me I could go, but they gave me a letter which they said I should carry always with me, and show to a doctor if I ever felt seriously ill; and they said also that I should never be very far from a large and well-equipped hospital. I accepted letter and advice with the best of intentions, but I had not been in the United States three weeks before I lost the letter and forgot the advice. I had attacks periodically, some of them bad ones, but I got over them, until one day in 1942 I collapsed in a movie with a perforated stomach. It is an experience a man does not forget. I had to be carried home, was taken to Lincoln Hospital and operated upon that same evening. I asked that my own doctor be in attendance and this was allowed. I was informed after that the operation was so serious and my condition such that no attempt could be made to remove the ulcer itself. The doctors simply repaired the perforation. Since then I break my diet sometimes, and when I feel well, I am often quite careless, but I am aware of what can happen to me. I am very conscious of some of the stupid things I did between 1938 and 1942, and as soon as an attack is on the way or I have one, I watch myself.

I entered Ellis Island on June 10th, and immediately began to work at this book. I was quite well, and weighed 198 pounds, perhaps a little overweight. My ulcer, for me, means two things: food, and also a good mental condition. It might be thought that the situation I was in meant of necessity a bad mental condition. I had many serious problems to consider, but I had them well under control. On June 17th the judge heard my case and reserved decision. There was time enough for that. All that concerned me was to finish my book. My chief trouble was the food. I do not wish to go into any detailed description of it. I believe that a country like the United States should spend more on the materials and thus relieve the cooks from having such poor meat to work on and such small quantities of it, that, they have to resort to chop sueys, heavily spiced meat loaf, meat-sauces of the same kind, sardines with soya bean oil, etc. It was very difficult for me, particularly because of the way I had been eating since my operation. But Ellis Island is not a pleasure resort. I did not intend to live there permanently, and I knew from long experience that if I wanted to be well, and do my work, I had to avoid two things: worrying about my situation and getting a food complex. I ate with a will. One of my Communist roommates told me that I should be more careful with that food. But I was determined to eat it. The only thing that I asked the doctor for was permission to have some extra milk because of my ulcer. He agreed and told me, as most doctors say, that I probably knew more about my ulcer than he did.

All who can think back to those weeks both inside and outside the Island will remember that I was in very good spirits. I asked and received permission from the Head of Detention to send my manuscript out for typing. He asked me to submit it for examination. I did so. A working relation had been established with the Communists. The fact is that I amazed a few observers by sitting down at a table, working for some twelve hours a day, day after day. I repeat all this because it is an integral part of what I have to say. I never complained about the food at Ellis Island. I never complained about anything. I turned my mind resolutely away from any interference in the things I saw and heard.

But after three weeks, it was too much for me. I had to stop my writing altogether. For one whole week I went to meals and could eat only a mouthful now and then, sometimes I could not eat at all. I struggled with it for a week, hating to get ill, hating to get into any contact with the authorities beyond the usual. I think it was on Friday at mid-day that as I approached the dining-hall, while still some distance from it, I was hit by the scent of the Friday fish, fried in some sort of oil. I sat through lunch without touching the food.

By Friday evening I could hardly move from my bed and the long walk down the corridor and down the steps and round the dining-hall was impossible. If it appeared I was suddenly so ill, it was because I had overstrained myself in the attempt to avoid any friction.

The steward in charge of the wagon from which the people in the infirmary are fed has to pass the room where I was kept. The regular doctor is not on duty on weekends so on Friday evening I went to the temporary doctor and asked that I might be fed the next day from the infirmary wagon. The nurse on duty informed the doctor that it was impossible because I was a "security patient."

Next morning my Communist roommates smuggled in something for me for breakfast. At mid-day the nurse, another nurse, agreed to feed me from the wagon. But that night the nurse of the evening before again refused to feed me. She said now she had no authority. I was pretty hazy at the time, for after all I had been about a week practically without food. But the Communists told me later that they had made a unanimous declaration that if I was not fed they were not going to eat. A supervisor, however, went out of his way to see that I got something to eat, and all of us who knew him knew that he would have done the same, whether the Communists threatened or not.

Any doctor, nurse or ulcer patient knows what is the result of all this excitement, particularly on a physique where both deterioration and recovery from ulcer attacks are often extremely rapid. By this time I was already in a bad way. I knew what was wrong with me. If I could get some ordinarily decent food, I hoped to be able to stave off the attack and pull myself together in a few days. It can be done, I have done it before and I think I could have brought it off, under the strong impulsion to get on with my work. But it cannot be done on milk. You can live on milk for a while but that diet demands that you stay in bed, keep still and have everything done for you. I had no desire to ask for any such thing there. On Monday morning, therefore, I communicated with my attorney and asked him to see if he could make some arrangements about my getting some food to eat. My attorney got into contact with the authorities and was told that I should see the doctor.

Then began a four weeks nightmare. I shall be as brief as possible. The reader will, I hope, be patient with it. I know something of the history of our times. I have read what men have gone through for years in Nazi concentration camps. I know what millions have endured and still endure in the prisons and labor camps behind the Iron Curtain. I have read of the years of torture they have endured and still endure in Russian concentration camps and prisons. Not a word written here implies that Ellis Island is either a Nazi concentration camp or a Russian slave labor camp or anything like them. To the people, unfortunately only too few, who have digested what all this means for modern civilization, it may appear that to write about four weeks is an inflation of a minor personal grievance. But far more is involved. The United States Department of Justice is involved. The attitude to aliens in the United States is involved. I had an attorney, I had friends, I had people to whom I could appeal. Thousands pass through Ellis Island who have none of these. And finally the staff of Ellis Island, the American citizens who work there are also involved.

The doctor, as would any doctor in the whole world, knew exactly what was wrong with me and what should be done with me. However he stated from the beginning that the infirmary had no facilities to deal with a case like mine. He asked me what food I was accustomed to eating under the circumstances. I was at once on my guard. I was not going to put myself in a position where I could be accused of demanding this and that or the other. So after I had made it quite clear that I was replying to a question he asked me about my past, I told him bacon done crisp, lean meat, chopped vegetables. There are countless days on which I have existed on other things beside these. But when you have an ulcer attack, these become as precious as water in the desert. He said he would tell the kitchen. In a day or two he admitted me into the infirmary. But in this infirmary the food is the same as in the dining-room. I did not have to go for it. It was brought to me, but I still could not eat it.

Nobody came from the kitchen. Meanwhile my attorney was pressing the authorities, and my doctor wrote in describing what he knew of my physique and its needs and his deep concern about what was happening to me. I lived on milk and the inside of rolls and scraps of butter which I bought at the canteen when the canteen had them and I could get there in time or someone could get there for me. In a period lasting four weeks, out of twenty-one meals a week, I may have eaten one and some scraps. For hours at a time I had frightful ulcer pains. The doctor ordered pills which I was to ask for when I had pain. But I have a long experience of pills. They relieve you first for about two hours, then after a while for an hour, then less and so on. Sometimes at night about midnight I would take a pill. Twice at nights the night doctors gave me a needle and something to drink and I slept.

After two weeks, my weakness became quite pronounced. I had to eat. I would split a boiled egg and somehow stuff down the yellow. The white I would put away and late at night make a sandwich out of it and a roll. One more word about this eating. Since my operation, I have had a few fits of retching on an empty stomach or a stomach which was empty after I had puked once. The whole business is very terrifying because one has these repeated spasms and nothing comes up. A perforation seems certain. It was not only the sight and scent of the food which by now revolted me. It was this retching that I was chiefly afraid of, for as far as I remembered it came usually after eating things I did not feel inclined to eat.

That is what happened. I have cut it to the bone. My doctor, who heard the details and has known me for many years, corroborated to the administration of Ellis Island what I felt, that if what I was going through continued, my health might be permanently damaged and my life might be in danger. Some may be skeptical. I will merely note that this period came to an end in mid-August. It is now November. I can sit still and do nothing and be well enough, but I have to work for my living, and after any exertion I am immediately conscious of the fact that I am a badly shaken man. My hands have not been very steady for some years. To this day there are times when I cannot lift food from the plate to my mouth.

I have told the illness as a connected story. But it was not connected. I expect if I had been on a desert island after some shipwreck, I would have managed much better. To a man in my condition, there was added not only the sense of unwarranted inhuman persecution but a never-ceasing battle to put an end to it.

My attorney offered to make himself responsible for having some food sent in to me. The Ellis Island authorities replied that it was against regulations, this in a place where not only regulations but law is disregarded at will. My attorney spoke to Mr. Shaughnessy, the District Director of Immigration and Naturalization of the Port of New York. Mr. Shaughnessy's reply was that if I did not like it there, I was not being detained against my will. I could always leave and go to Trinidad, where I was born, and drink my papaya juice.

My attorney explained that I was not trying to get out. Arrangements could be made for me to go to a nursing home to which I would be confined on his recognizance. Mr. Shaughnessy's reply was that he would have to consider that carefully or something of the kind.

Painful beyond measure was the recurring quarrel with the doctor and the nurses. The doctor said that the best he could do for me was to send me to the Marine Hospital at Stapleton. So one evening I was told not to eat anything, not even milk, and to be ready for x-ray examination that day. I went by ferry to the hospital, was examined for five minutes and sent back. I had nothing to eat that day till four o'clock on the ferry when I seized the chance to buy two ham sandwiches which the canteen on the island was not allowed to sell. I gobbled one on the boat and that was all right. But later I tried to eat the other one, could get only halfway and paid bitterly for it.

Some time or other, about halfway through the four weeks, a supervisor called me to his office, told me he heard I was not doing well, and asked me what was wrong, I told him. He said he would do what he could. But all he did was to come ask me the next day; what food did I want? I told him plain, ordinary food, and he went away.

In a day or two, I demanded an x-ray examination from the doctor and wrote to him that in preparation for it I would eat nothing until it was ordered. In half an hour he told me that I would be sent to Stapleton for one the next day. That day I was examined under fluoroscope and x-rayed, but I heard vaguely that the report said that nothing was wrong.

The doctor then told me that on his Saturday off he would go up to Stapleton and speak to the authorities there himself. He did so, with no results.

By this time, however my attorney decided to take the matter to Court. As I shall show later, neither my attorney nor myself had wanted to apply for bail. But by now it looked as if I would continue the way I was going until I fell flat on my face in the corridor. Something had to be done. The matter came up before Judge Knox. Friends of mine in court told me that he was severe with the Government attorney. But a rule in the Second District Court prohibited bail being granted by the Court where a decision was pending. Judge Knox said he could do nothing. But from the bench he counseled my attorney to fly down to Washington and place the whole matter before Attorney-General McGranery who, he said, was a humane man, and had the power to grant bail.

But the day before the case, I was informed in the infirmary that I was to go to Stapleton the next day. So that on the morning of the afternoon the case was tried, I was in Stapleton. When the matter finally reached Mr. McGranery he denied bail, saying that since I was in the hospital there was no need to take the matter further.

I stayed at the hospital for two months. During that time I was guarded twenty-four hours a day by three guards in eight-hour shifts. The guards at night either sat just outside the door or actually in my room. I had committed no crime. The Government itself had admitted that I was of good moral character. Yet this penal regime was imposed upon me. My attorney learned of it in time to protest in the Court. The Department of Justice certainly had the power to relieve me of this imposition which I have always associated with homicidal criminals and dangerous lunatics. If anyone was very obviously not going to try and run off anywhere, it was I. In addition, if I did so, then I would myself have struck a most damaging blow against my own case. But, no, they refused to relieve me.

Once admitted at the hospital I was again back within the boundaries of civilization. During the weeks I stayed there I was treated seriously for my ulcer. When I left the hospital my stomach was in very good shape, and though the guards were there morning, noon and night to remind everyone of my status, neither doctors, nurses nor attendants took any notice of what their presence signified.

What took place during those weeks before I went to the hospital is an unpardonable crime. I can only record it and say what it signifies. I will then have done my part.

1. The United States Department of Immigration is today in its policy-making echelons ridden with national arrogance.

The attitude of Mr. Shaughnessy and his departmental heads on the Island, in my case, as in so many others, showed that for them an alien is not a human being. If a dog snapped at me, and was then run over by a passing car, I would take it up and seek the nearest veterinary surgeon. In war, the men of the medical corps take up the national wounded and the enemy alike. At the Marine Hospital I was treated as a sick man. But at Ellis Island I was an alien, and as such entitled to no consideration whatever. My ulcer was no secret. It had found its place in my hearings. Once when I was staying in Maine and the Immigration Department sent for me, I was ill and could not go. They sent an investigator in a Coast Guard launch to find out if I was malingering and he learned from enquiry in the town that I had been ill with the ulcer and had been attended by the doctor. There was not a single person on the Island who saw me when I came and saw me afterward who could not see how ill I was. Many of them spoke to me about it. But for Mr. Shaugnessy I could have stayed there until I was once more perforated. Then perhaps would have been the time to consider whether maybe I should be sent to the hospital after all. I was an alien. I had no human rights. If I didn't like it, I could leave. How to characterize this otherwise than as inhuman and barbarous? And what is its origin except that overweening national arrogance which is sweeping over the world like some pestilence?

2. The Department of Justice violated the most elementary principles of justice.

Mr. Shaugnessy said that I could leave any time I wanted and go and "drink my papaya juice." I was not being detained, I could leave any time I pleased. The legal theory behind this is that my status in the Courts in a case of this kind is one of grace and not of right.

This is not the first time that learned men have perpetrated learned nonsense which they find to their surprise is used to justify crimes. If there was no court procedure for aliens, if I had been arrested as one, and if under those circumstances the Government had asked me to say what I had to say for myself, then it might be possible to say with some show of legal justification that I had better state my case, and whatever the conditions, accept them. But I ask the average American citizen to consider. The law provides that an alien should have a hearing; then the decision, if unfavorable, can be appealed to the Attorney-General. Then if the appeal is rejected, the matter can be taken to the District Court, then if need be to the Court of Appeals, and finally to the Supreme Court. What theory of law is it which cannot see that such a procedure could have originated only in a country where the traditional role of the immigrant and the tradition of civil liberties, are such as to have created for the alien every possible opportunity to make as good a case for himself as possible? Isn't it obvious that the only interpretation of such a procedure is that it was intended to break down barriers and not set them up, to declare to the alien, and to American citizens, and to the whole world that the United States took upon itself the responsibility of seeing that as far as possible he was treated as a potential citizen? Can that be reconciled with the brutal and arrogant statement: if he does not like what is happening to him, he can go and drink his papaya juice?

Furthermore the law is established. An alien knows this. He lives his life and arranges his affairs with this procedure in mind. And in the midst of it he is informed "We are not keeping you here. You are being granted a privilege. If you do not like it on Ellis Island, leave. In any case, even the most elementary facts are against this vicious violation of the law. I never at any time said that I did not like it on Ellis Island. I never complained of procedures there. I strove to avoid any contact beyond the formal as I have explained. All I said was: I am a sick man with an illness known to you; I require a certain amount of medical attention. The speed with which they seized upon this to inform me that if I didn't like it I could always leave, shows what was involved. By making it as difficult for me as possible even to exist, my spirit might be broken and I might throw up the whole case. Is this the way the people of the United States expect their Department of Justice to behave; to set itself up in opposition to an alien as if the two of them are a pair of gangsters contending over some piece of territory?

3. The whole procedure to which I was subjected was a classical piece of bureaucratic stupidity.

First, if there was any excuse for it, it was that I was pretending to be ill, in order to bluff my way out of the Island.

But I did not want any bail. After the first application for bail was rejected and my case went to the judge, my attorney carefully instructed me. I am, he said, challenging the whole basis of the case against you; in my opinion it would be better if you did not apply for any bail. Furthermore, he added, however long the judge will take, leave him alone—it is always better to do so. So make up your mind to spend some long weeks there, and occupy yourself with your book. I accepted his opinion and settled down to my own business. The illness was for me a grievous personal setback. It was only in the last days, with great reluctance, when it seemed to me that I was up against an impenetrable wall of cruelty and stupidity, that my attorney decided to ask for bail.

I say bureaucratic stupidity. Here is the final proof. While I was being guarded night and day in the hospital, there was in the same room with me another alien, a man who had served over three years in prison for burglary with violence. He did not give any details of his case, but he told me that when arrested originally bail had been set at $15,000, so the matter must have been serious. He suffered from ulcers and when he reported this in prison, he was immediately given a light job in the laundry which was near the kitchen. In this way he could get some food more suitable to his ulcer.

He was not guarded. One night he simply walked out of the hospital and went his way. For all I know he is still at liberty.

Still more. He escaped from the hospital with another alien from Ellis Island who had complained of, if you please, a stomach ulcer. He had been deported from the United States a few months before. He had returned and been caught. His ulcer complaints got him into Stapleton. I am informed that while in the hospital he had $3,000 and gave it to the hospital authorities to keep. One afternoon he drew it out and that evening he escaped, in company it seems with the ex-burglar. He was caught soon and I saw him in the kitchen a few days after, as lively and active as I had always seen him in the hospital. If this is not bureaucratic stupidity, what is?

During these days, I asked myself persistently, and I have asked myself the question often enough since: in what way were the ends of justice served by this? The answer is obvious. In no way whatever. What was the motive? The only reasonable one I can think of is that if they could have beaten me down, then I would have left and that would have been the end of my case. There may have been other reasons. But it is idle to speculate on this. What really matters is: what are the objective causes and what are the objective results?

In my opinion the cause is simple enough. The whole system of law and the legal procedures that have been developed in the United States were an expression of a deep faith in civil liberties and were designed and intended to help the alien. But the Department of Justice as a whole is now engaged on a policy whose main aim can be described as the extermination of the alien as a malignant pest.* When they attempt to carry out this policy, they are met at every turn by all the legal safeguards and procedures which aim at exactly the contrary. Hence on Ellis Island, in particular, the arbitrariness, the capriciousness, the brutality and savagery where they think they can get away with it, the rapid retreats when they suspect that they may have gone too far, the complete absence of any principle except to achieve a particular aim by the most convenient means to hand. When I returned to Ellis Island from the hospital for two or three days before I was released on bail, some attempt was made to help me out with the diet

* The authorities on Ellis Island insist on the word "detainees" instead of prisoners. After my own experiences and what I have seen, it would be a mockery for me to assist them in still more deceiving the American people. Under that administration the people on the Island are prisoners.

prescribed by the dietician at the hospital. For some reason or other, it had been decided in my case to change the previous policy.

This I believe to be the root cause of the administrative disorder that now exists on the Island. And as I shall show later, not at all only on the Island. Either the traditional legal procedures will have to be changed, or the present policy will have to be changed. The McCarran Act is an attempt to change the laws to correspond to the administrative policy. The attempt may succeed. It may. But if and when the complete success has been achieved, there will also have been achieved the complete demoralization of the staff of the Department of Justice and large sections of the American people. It is a comparatively simple thing to mobilize majorities in Congress to pass laws, and for judges and administrators to set out to apply them. But you cannot reverse the whole historical past and traditions of a people by packaged legislation and loud propaganda. Certain policies demand total destruction of a legal system, its replacement by a new one, totalitarian indoctrination of the population in the new doctrines, and stormtroopers or G.P.U. men to enforce them. Try to carry them out by grafting them onto a traditionally democratic system, and the result is complete chaos. I saw precisely that happen step by step to a whole nation 1934 and 1939.

III

I believe my total experience should be told.

Three men examined me in the preliminary hearings which began in 1948. The first one took a general statement of my political ideas. I believe he was a lawyer. He and a colleague had previously walked into my apartment one morning at 7:30 and sought to get me to speak. I refused to say anything without my attorney being present. This time he examined me closely enough. But he was neither impolite, hostile, nor mean. The second examiner took up my whole case, acting as both presiding officer and examiner. I remember that my attorney very often raised objections and he invariably overruled them. But points of law apart, no one could possibly have made any complaint. In a long examination of what you have been doing over ten years, there are times when your memory fails you, you get confused. Furthermore, you have a political past which is a weight around your neck. You answer questions. You want to answer precisely what you are asked, and at the same time not make any observations which may help to make your case worse than is necessary. My examiner did his job but he never sought to embarrass me, nor to catch me by any cheap tricks, or to press me like a prosecuting attorney trying to convict a murderer. I made some mistakes. He noted them but gave me an opportunity to try and correct them.

Later, Congress passed a law which prohibited the same person acting as prosecutor and presiding officer. In the last examination another officer presided. He was a singularly urbane person and I had the satisfaction of seeing some of my attorney's objections sustained. But my old examiner who was now still acting as prosecutor took it equably. My wife was examined and was not for a single moment pushed around. The decision was against me. I thought and still think that the decision is wrong. But there was no venom in it. Far from being vicious it seemed to me even sympathetic in its statement of the points, those points which were in my favor. The British Civil Service in Britain has a great reputation for the scrupulous fairness and politeness with which they handle such maters. Certainly these men did not fall in any way below that standard.

My examinations ended in 1950, I went to the Island in June 1952. I did not and do not have the long experience of the Island that my fellow-prisoners in the political room had. Some of them had been in and out, and in again. But I know that in his report to the F.B.I., M stated that the most unfortunate result of the whole unprincipled regime on the Island was the demoralization of the staff itself from top to bottom.

M has been in the United Stated for some 35 years. He grew up here from childhood. I did not. I have learned much about the United States, but I have learned, a great deal unconsciously no doubt but as much as I can, consciously and deliberately.

Within a few hours on the Island you realize that in the hundred and more security officers there, you have a cross section of the American lower middle classes, placed in a position of authority over hundreds of aliens, mariners, renegades and castaways. Struggling to penetrate into the full significance of Melville's audacious isolation of American officers and the nondescript people of the world upon the Pequod, the conflict over the McCarran Immigration Act actually going on at the time, the United States entangled as no modern nation has ever been in ever-growing relations with the vast masses of the world. I was sensitized to see at firsthand as in a scientific experiment where exactly a very representative section of the American people stood. I can testify without reservations. In them the old traditions of the United States still live. And despite the unceasing agitation about aliens and the hostile legislation, which must hit these above all others in the country with especial force, they bring to their work a sense of responsibility unsurpassed by anything I have seen in the United States for the fourteen years I have lived here.

Consider the situation of these men, bombarded night and day by anti-alien propaganda. They have to supervise and keep order among sometimes a thousand men, of nationalities from all parts of the world, men most of them in a highly nervous condition owing to the situation they are in; many of them men who have lived lives in difficult circumstances, some of them men with long criminal records. For the greater part of the day they have nothing to do. Prisoners are always breaking regulations. An officer has continually to decide how far he will let it go, with whom he can be more indulgent than with others; he has to listen to all sorts of stories, the lies of obvious criminals, men who want advice that he cannot give; even some who are burning to tell their life story. Callousness, brutality and above all national arrogance could easily have been permanent, if even repressed, elements in the situation. Yet with all their variety of individual background, temperament and personality, as a body of men they maintained constant self-control, patience and humanity. I saw in them that consideration for and interest in the individual human being as a personality, which is the distinguishing characteristic of American social life. They were not formal as a similar body of Englishmen would have been; they often shouted and sometimes showed their irritation. But these things passed as quickly as they came. I saw them repeatedly going out of their way to assist and smooth the way for all sorts of prisoners, it was done for me many times.

The deafening thunder in the world outside against aliens, and against Communist aliens in particular, would have led you to expect some reflection of it in this typical body of Americans. Here and there in individual security officers you could see it, in others you could sense it or to be quite accurate, think you did. But, as a body of men, their attitude to the alien politicals was impeccable.

I want to be quite specific.

I was in the hospital for two months. And there was a guard on duty every hour. I was not to be out of his sight at any time. This was, as I have explained, in itself a cruel burden for any man to carry, both internally and externally, particularly in a public place. It could have been unbearable. From this the security officers saved me. I had in all some eight different guards, of all types and ages. Their business was to watch me and they did, scrupulously, when I went to weigh, when I went to ask the nurse a question, when I went for blood tests, when I went to telephone, if I strolled down the corridor to talk to anyone. But I could see them always, never failing to avoid anything which might unnecessarily embarrass me, and repeatedly going out of their way to avoid intruding their role upon me, upon the hospital staff or any of my visitors. Eight weeks of never-ceasing forced association of that intimate kind is a very long time. They never slipped once. Obviously I was not one to give any trouble. But I had in my room at various times, the Irish epileptic, the ex-burglar, and a little stowaway from Bogota, Colombia. The guards were not specifically responsible for them, but a guard always is responsible whenever there are prisoners from Ellis Island around. They showed no marked difference in their attitude to the others.

Naturally we talked, they talked to one another, or sometimes to people in the same ward. Certain attitudes recur. One of them was a pensive mood on the part of one guard, an extremely alert and observant man, whenever he saw or heard of some stupidity or lack of character on the part of a prisoner. Always he would say half to himself, "You try to give them a break, and look at what they do." Another that recurred was the dilemma into which guards were frequently thrown, when on the day before deportation, a prisoner was taken to his home for his clothes and other effects. The family generally prepared a big dinner. They and their friends were assembled. They might never see each other again. Yet the instructions of the guard usually are never to let the alien out of his sight, to see that what has to be collected is collected promptly and to leave on a schedule. I am not speaking here of the justice or injustice of the regulation. What matters is that after so many years of this work, this would come up so often as a part of their duties which bothered them.

These men are as much victims of the anti-alien policy of the Department of Justice and the disorder in the administration as the unfortunate aliens themselves.

I shall again be specific, confining myself mainly to my own experiences.

Why was I so senselessly persecuted? Why, when I returned to the Island from the hospital for two days before I came out on bail was the persecution stopped? What had happened in between? Had someone from Washington intervened to put a stop to it? And if so, why? Whatever the reason Mr. Shaughnessy and his department heads had been flagrantly exposed before their own staff as cruel and inhuman. There must have been at least a dozen security officers who at different times showed me quite clearly that they thought what was happening to me during my illness was a scandal and a disgrace. They showed it in the way they inquired after my health, asked with emphasis when I was going to the hospital, in lonely stretches of corridor would inquire and shrug their shoulders as if to say: "I can't do anything," in a number of ways, not least of all, when I returned in the warm and friendly greeting "Hello. Glad to see you are looking better, but I thought you were going out." They, none of them, knew me. I was only an occasion. They work at the Island. Prisoners, far more security officers, begin to feel a sort of responsibility for the place where they spend their days. Without that sense of responsibility they could never have maintained the consistently temperate and considerate attitude.

My relation with the doctor and the nurses on the Island are among the most painful I have ever had with any group of people. Except for that nurse who refused to feed me, a notoriously unpleasant person in any case, no nurse was guilty of any unprofessional or even hostile act against me. The doctor was doing all he could. That I knew. But he was the man I had to complain to. At the beginning we even had little snatches of conversation about this or that topic. But before long he and I and the regular nurse quarreled, shouting at one another, once I remember over whether some carrots were fit to eat. After one sharp altercation I remember both of them coming in later and speaking in a very different tone, while I myself mumbled some apology which I felt was necessary. How often the administration puts them into similar situations I don't know.

The officers who guarded me had nothing to do. I heard even a supervisor joking with some of them about the hard work they had to do in watching me. Yet many of them were bored stiff with the uselessness of it all and I could see them turning and twisting and counting the minutes until their session would be over. Remember this lasted eight weeks.

When the ex-burglar in my room escaped, the irony of the situation was obvious to all in the hospital. They were not responsible but they did not feel too happy about it.

When it appeared in the press that the American Legion passed a resolution demanding the prosecution of a millionaire, an alien who had gone to jail for two years for draft-dodging but who was, according to rumor, still enjoying himself in resorts and nightclubs, there was further embarrassment. The officers did not like it. But the only thing to do was to shrug their shoulders.

Their very embarrassment and confusion showed an instinctive recognition of the fact that the work they were doing was not ordinary work. "I am only doing a job here." I heard it, heard about it from other prisoners, and repeatedly saw the attitude which both betrayed the consciousness that this was not just another job, and at the same time their determination to make it clear that they were not to be held responsible for the general policy.

Morale was sapped in another way. There was always some talk of spies and F.B.I. agents introduced among the men and unknown to the officers. These things I cannot speak of for certain. But I know that the general attitude of an individual officer is that he trusts no one. To whatever extent these spies and agents wander around, the officers are at least as much concerned with them as the prisoners are. For the average prisoner is doing nothing seriously wrong and your really tough criminal type among the prisoners does not really care what anyone finds out about him, he is going to be deported anyway.

Perhaps I can sum up the whole business by bringing up once more the visit of the F.B.I. representatives to M to find out his views as to what was wrong on the Island. M wrote what was in its way an excellent report. But except as an exposure of grievances and maladministration, I have as little use for it as I have for any recommendations which may come from it. The people who know what is taking place on Ellis Island, what is wrong and how it is corrected are first of all, the ordinary prisoners, and the security officers. These officers deal with the fundamental problem every day. I have noted among them men of conspicuous ability. (I had little to do with the supervisors immediately in charge of the security officers, but in that little they did not seem very different from the average security officer.)

They were a body of men in a difficult spot. Brutality would have been easy. Still easier, callousness if not hatred and a venomous arrogance. Yet they remained, not as individuals but as a body of men, not only human but humane.

What did they need? Nobody expected Ellis Island to be transformed into Utopia. But any shred of national pride, any consciousness of the role that America now plays and must forever play in the visible future of society, any sense of the past history of the century, what it claims, and, also, what it is being tested by in the eyes of hundreds of millions all over the world, would have dictated that the security officers be given, on the very lowest conceivable level, some sense of direction, some elementary consciousness, however primitive, that a Department of Justice stands for justice. That is precisely what gave M his astonishing influence, intangible but none the less real. He stood for something, stood for it like a rock. None of the men who knew him will ever forget him. But instead of direction, of some principle, the security officers received from the men who directed policy nothing but blows.

If the security officers could not defend themselves, M could. He usually took charge of these things, and here again, he protested, retreated, wrote to Washington, compromised or refused to give in in a manner which continually threw his jailers, with all their locks and bars and keys and power, into the utmost confusion. They did not know the full significance of this. But I, who have spent many years studying Communism, knew very well what it symbolized.

Finally, when I returned to the Island from the hospital, I learned a little of what had happened among the political prisoners while I was away.

One of them, a Turkish student, was gone. One afternoon a guard had come in and told him to get ready to move his things to another room. He was unshaven, in slacks and slippers. He gathered his things together, only to find out that he was really being deported that day. Guards taking the ferry to go to work saw him on it as they came to ask what had happened. M's explanation was that they had done this to prevent him having time to call a lawyer to seek a writ of *habeas corpus*. But, as happens so repeatedly, this man wanted no writ of *habeas corpus*. He had been detained for months, and he had decided to go home.

Another example, for me personally a very sad one. Among the Communists was a German worker, a man of nearly 60. He was a devoted Communist, but in a way that I cannot explain here, he was very different from the others. He did me many personal kindnesses. He was a great man for sports and he and I talked about soccer and track by the hour. He loved to play soccer with the men in the field, but he was, as a political, prevented from playing with them. But he persisted in going out whenever he got the chance. He was reported, he was warned not to play, he went back to play, and when I left for the hospital he had been threatened with some punishment. He had always insisted that he played because he had to have exercise, while we on the other hand believed that he just loved to play. But he was right. When I returned he hadn't been playing and I was startled at the change in him. He had put on weight, his hearing, never good, was worse, his sight was, I thought also, not as good as it was. He was an old bachelor, a bit crotchety, but a man of character. He had been there many weary months, nowhere to go. What the American Government keeps him there for is something that no one can ever determine.

One final example. M told me that one day the political prisoners were suddenly told that they were not to walk as usual in the grass enclosure. To a prisoner this walk is a very important part of his life. M protested. There was the usual wrangle. A ditch was being dug on the patch of grass and the prohibition, they were informed, was to prevent them falling into the ditch. Any reader of comic strips would know what happened. The guard fell into the ditch.

The Department of Justice and its policies, not the aliens, are the chief source of the demoralizing regime on Ellis Island. It cannot even organize and give some sense of direction to its own American security officers. Its misunderstanding of the aliens themselves is absolute.

The whole of the world is represented on Ellis Island. Many sailors, but not only sailors; Germans, Italians, Latvians, Swedes, Filipinos, Malays, Chinese, Hindus, Pakistanis, West Indians, Englishmen, Australians, Danes, Yugoslavs, Greeks, Canadians, representatives of every Latin-American country. As I write each word, I see someone whom I knew. To the administration on Ellis island and I presume, at 70 Columbus Avenue, these are just a body of isolated individuals who are in reality seeking charity, or a home in the United States which is a better place to live in than their backward or poverty-stricken countries. Of all the blunders I encountered on Ellis Island this is undoubtedly the most colossal.

These men, taken as a whole, know the contemporary world and know it better than many world-famous foreign correspondents. They discuss among themselves their attitudes to the United States, their attitudes to World War III, to Russia, to totalitarianism, to democracy, to national independence. I have never heard or read in any newspaper such coldly realistic discussions as to the possibilities of war, and weighing of which side offered the greater advantages. They pass to one another political articles in the popular press, and they discuss and fill in from personal knowledge. With a devastating simplicity they sum up regimes. I have heard a man say in five minutes all that needed to be said about one of the most controversial regimes in the world today. He ended, "I know. I have lived and worked there." Their consistently recurring view of the United States is worth recording. "America is all right if you have money."

Some are ready to support Russia in a war which they accept as absolutely inevitable. But they are for the most part, as far as I could judge, the most militant enemies of tyranny in the world. I am in difficulties here, as I have been in difficulties elsewhere in this account. I do not want to say anything which could involve men who may be still on the Island and who could be traced. With this in mind I shall choose only a few examples.

One is of a young Latin American sailor. His ship was in harbor in Santo Domingo which is ruled by Trujillo, a byword among them for tyranny and savage brutality. A man he knew came to him and told him he had hidden in his house two men wanted by the government. Their lives were at stake. Could he help to stow them on board his ship? I only wish that those vociferous defenders of democracy who nevertheless spend nights of torture wondering whether it would be safe to sign an alien petition. I wish they could have seen the simplicity and naturalness with which this young sailor said that he agreed. He risked his life as easily and spontaneously as Tashtego or Daggoo. It was obvious that not to agree was something outside his comprehension. The men were safely smuggled on board and escaped. On his next visit to Santo Domingo, he had no sooner landed than he was arrested by the police and imprisoned. They had somehow been informed of how the two men had escaped. His ship left without him. He was tried and sentenced to three months in prison, but he said that those three months could mean three years or thirty. Much depended on his sending news outside of where he was. He managed to give an urgent message to a fellow-prisoner who was about to leave the prison. The message was faithfully delivered, a thing involving no small risk. His captain also, it seemed, had been privy to the original stowing away, and guessed what had happened. The plan of the Trujillo government was based on the hope that the sailor would be reported as missing. Then they would be able to do what they wanted with him. But this plan was foiled. His whereabouts were made known and his consul intervened. Whereupon the Trujillo Government told him to leave. He refused. He said he had been sentenced to three months, he had served only six weeks, and three months it would be. This young man memorized all details he could gather, noted all conditions and took messages during the remaining six weeks. When he finally left and got home, he went to a liberal journalist whom he knew, gave him all the information and the Trujillo regime was blasted in an authentic series of articles.

At any moment, a man in the same ward in the infirmary can tell you of events of similar range and scope. And it means nothing to them. That is how they live. I have never seen such hatred as I saw on the Island for the Peron regime. One article describing its barbarities would pass from hand to hand, and evoke astonishing tales of corroboration. It is from these sailors that one can hear biographies of Eva Peron, personally vouched for.

Indo-China, the Malay States, Pakistan, Franco Spain, Yugoslavia, Europe yesterday, today and tomorrow, Asia today, Germany, East and West, I picked up, sometimes at second-hand, sometimes confused, sometimes contradictory but always authentic views. There was a Scandinavian who had traveled all over the world, spoke many languages and knew Europe and Europeans to his fingertips. I spent some days in his company. He spent his time alternately declaring with great emphasis that he didn't care a damn about anything any more, not a damn thing—it was too much for him—he was tired of it. And then he would immediately launch into such descriptions, reminiscences, analyses and forecasts of the European situation as I had never heard before. He wanted to, but he could not leave it alone.

This is my final impression. The meanest mariners, renegades and castaways of Melville's day were objectively a new world. But they knew nothing. These know everything. The symbolic mariners and renegades of Melville's book were isolatoes, federated by one keel, but only because they had been assembled by penetrating genius. These were federated by nothing. But they were looking for federation. I have heard a boy, a young oriental, say that he would fight in the war on either side—it didn't matter to him. What he wanted was a good peace, no half-peace. This peace, however, he added almost as an afterthought, should include complete independence for his own little country.

This then is the crowning irony of the little cross-section of the whole world that is Ellis Island. That while the United States Department of Justice is grimly pursuing a venomous anti-alien policy, and in the course of so doing disrupting and demoralizing its own employees desperately trying to live up to their principles, the despised aliens, however fiercely nationalistic, are profoundly conscious of themselves as citizens of the world.

IV

It is beyond the scope of what I am writing to go outside of what I experienced, what I saw or such information as I sought to clarify my own experiences. It is in this manner that I have dealt with the United States Department of Justice on Ellis Island. I shall now relate in the same way my other experiences with other sections of the Department of Justice. This time it is a question of the alien and civil liberties.

Briefly the facts are as follows. I went to Great Britain from the West Indies in 1932, with good prospects as a writer. But I had not been in Europe two years before I came to the conclusion that European civilization as it then existed was doomed, an opinion which I have never changed and am not likely to change, among other reasons because many very profound, or very learned, or very highly placed or highly respectable people now either say the same thing or have a very hard time preventing themselves from saying it. But by reading and instinct, I never for one single moment was anything but an enemy of the Communist Party and the Stalinist regime. I was attracted instead to the ideas of Trotsky. I once caught a glimpse in a United States Immigration Office of a file of papers two or three inches thick dealing with my activities in England. The ways of governments are past all understanding. The Trotskyist group I was associated with never at any time exceeded 35 people. It quite often was less than half that number. I was then as I am now, essentially a writer. I earned my living by speaking and writing, I worked on newspapers and published books, one of them a large history of the Communist International. I came to the United States in 1938, intending to stay for only six months, and then had my visa extended for another six months. But I fell ill and then came the war. I received my papers for military service and had my first examination, when it was decided that men over 38 were not required. During this time I associated with the Trotskyites here and I wrote in their papers. All this I have admitted to the Immigration authorities. I did not go into any more detail than was required, and I do not intend to here, except as I shall hereafter make clear. But from 1941 I became known in Trotskyite circles here and abroad chiefly as a biter opponent of Trotsky's theory that Russia, despite Stalinist crimes was a workers' state. Instead I denounced Russia as the greatest example of barbarism that history has ever known.

In 1948 my hearings with the Immigration began. In 1950 a decision was rendered against me, and my attorney appealed to Washington. Looking back now I can see that the rejection that came from Washington was the first in a series of events which have finally forced me to this public protest.

The writer of the rejection propounded doctrines which need to be publicly known. He noted that I had written *World Revolution, The Rise and Fall of the Communist International;* a *History of Negro Revolt, The Black Jacobins,* had translated the life of *Stalin,* and was now engaged in translating from the French a history of the French Revolution. He considered that all this looked very suspicious. My attorney had claimed that I was a writer. The founders of revolutionary movements, he said, had been writers.

I ask every teacher of history, every columnist, every radio commentator, what is it he has been dealing with more than anything else during the last forty years but revolutions, the causes of revolutions, the effect of revolutions, the fear of revolutions. I believe that more people have experienced revolutions or felt the effect of revolutions in the forty years since 1914 than in all the previous centuries of the Christian era. These books were not pamphlets published by some revolutionary organization. They were considered worthy of acceptance by hard-headed publishers who discussed them with me before they were written and paid me money for them. Some have been reviewed at length in the *Manchester Guardian,* the *Literary Supplement of the*

London Times, and *New Statesman and Nation, Time Magazine,* the New York *Times,* the New York *Herald Tribune, Saturday Review of Literature,* and various French newspapers, I quote from some of the reviews: On *The Black Jacobins,* a study of the French Revolution in San Domingo:

> "Mr. James is not afraid to touch his pen with the flame of ardent personal feeling, a sense of justice, love of freedom, admiration of heroism, hatred for tyranny, and his detailed richly documented and dramatically written book holds a deep and lasting interest."
>
> —*New York Times Book Review,* December 11, 1938

> "'The Black Jacobins' is not a simple account of this epic revolt in the West Indies. Nor could it be simple. But for the first time the scene is viewed with complete perspective and the theme recorded with understanding. It is not only one of the most sharply defined stories of the period to be published in our time, it is told in terms which have contemporary significance. 'To the African robbed of his land and segregated, what does it matter whether the robbers are fascists or democrats?' It may prove to be the text of tomorrow's events in Africa."
>
> —*Saturday Review of Literature,* January 7, 1939

On *World Revolution:*

> "Mr. James is always a lively critic. . . . Though fiercely partisan and inspired by all the fury of a doctrinaire misunderstood, his book is thorough and well documented. It cannot be easily dismissed."
>
> —*Manchester Guardian,* June 1, 1937

> "This most competently written book deserves some serious attention from anyone who is honestly trying to understand present Russian events. For it is no mere pamphlet thrown out in the face of the Moscow Trials but a close historical study of the theoretical differences within Marxist doctrine and the bitter struggle to which they have given rise within the organization and policies of the Soviet Union. It is based too largely upon the

writings of one of the chief protagonists; nevertheless it does
cast some light into a dark situation."

—*New Republic*, August 27, 1937

On some of these books I have spent years of study and labor,
working for money as a journalist and lecturer in order to be able to
keep myself going while I did the preliminary work. Scholars in Haiti
(formerly French San Domingo) say that my book on the San Domingo revolution is the best they have ever read written by a foreigner.
My publisher advertised my book on Negro revolt as the first ever
written on that subject. In the same series appeared books by, among
other people, Ernest Hemingway and George Lansbury, at one time a
Minister of the British Crown. My account of the *Rise and Fall of the
Communist International*, biased and seriously mistaken as it was in many
places, was greeted in England and in America also as the first comprehensive study of the subject that had ever been made.

It now appears that such work, serious work and some of it pioneer
work, on some of the burning problems of the day, have unfitted me
to become a citizen of the United States.

This can mean only one thing: that the Department of Justice now
assumes the right to say what a citizen or would-be citizen should
study. Or if he does choose for himself, it warns in advance that it
must approve the conclusions he should come to. Would I have been
more eligible for citizenship if I had written the history of the persecution of the Waldensians, or studies of the massacre of St. Bartholo-
mew, or the crushing of the Russian peasants in the Pugachev Rebel-
lion, or the defeat of the Indian Mutiny? Should I have deplored the
freeing of the slaves in San Domingo, or marshalled arguments to show
how the Bourbons and the landed aristocrats should have triumphed
over the great revolution in France? Would I have been more welcome
as a citizen? Unfortunately that would compel me also to denounce
George Washington, Thomas Jefferson and Benjamin Franklin. Or
should I have judiciously mixed both, taking care that studies of the
victorious counter-revolution should prevail? Or should the would-be
citizen understand that books on gardening and other such non-
controversial subjects are henceforth to be his sole scientific sphere?

I have been associated with revolutionaries, I have taken part in
their papers, etc. but the governments of Great Britain and the
United States can gather every inch and ounce of my activity from

1935 to the present day, multiply it by one hundred, and they could not transform me into a clear and present danger to the people of the United States. It is my books that the writer who rejected my appeal dwelt upon.

Conscious that something was wrong, the writer of the rejection sought to cover it by his astounding argument that though I might be only a writer, the great revolutionary organizations had been founded by writers. Is this the kind of argument that aliens will have to deal with henceforth? I cannot unfortunately recommend my book on this subject, for it is a bad book, and I now do not want to be held responsible for what is in it. But any elementary textbook will show that Lenin and Marx were organizers of masses of workers, leading them in great strikes, demonstrations and revolutionary actions. True they wrote, but to smuggle me in with them under the title of "writers," this is something new in jurisprudence.

This is my chief offense, that I have written books of the kind I have written. And I protest against it as a violation of the rights of every citizen of the United States. The very highest executive officers and politicians in the United States, the very highest, have assured the American people and the listening world that the drive against Communists is not directed against freedom of intellectual investigation, it is not directed against freedom of speech, it is not directed against differences of opinion. Over and over again it is repeated that the drive is directed against an international conspiracy, aimed at destroying the freedoms and liberties of the American people and establishing by any and every means a totalitarian government.

If this is true, then any charges against me, any decisions against me, can be based only upon the view that I am a person who, directly or indirectly, aims at accomplishing, assisting or encouraging these monstrous abominations.

The American Government can imprison me, it can deport me, it has the power to do so. But the imputation that I have at any time in my life proposed or advocated or encouraged or sought ways and means of establishing a totalitarian government, here or anywhere else, that is as serious a charge as can be made against any man in the world in which we live, I denounce it, whether made directly or indirectly, as an infamous slander, and I defy any Government attorney to stand up in any court and say so. Let them send squads of F.B.I. agents digging into my life and fishing up this or that article which I have written; or speech which I have made, let them put all of these through a microscope, they will never be able to pin the label of totalitarianism upon me. I shall not easily forget June 17th when my case came up before a Judge in the District Court of Southern New York. The attorney for the Government had little to say. He uttered a few perfunctory words and then played his ace. He handed a copy of my book on the Communist International to the Judge. This for him settled it.

Since that day I cannot get the picture out of my mind. The attorney in question is a little man, and I see him always standing on tiptoe, hand outstretched, delivering to the Judge the final, the crowning, the undefeatable argument—a book I had written in 1937.

I landed in the United States in October, 1938. The British and the European educational systems pay little attention to the United States, and I knew more about France and Russia and Ancient Greece and Rome that I did about this country. I remember my first journey from Chicago to Los Angeles, by train—the apparently endless miles, hour after hour, all day and all night and the next morning the same again, until the evening. I experienced a sense of expansion which has permanently altered my attitude to the world.

From that beginning, stage by stage I have spared no pains to understand the United States and become a part of the American people. I remember that for years I pertinaciously read comic strips, unable to see what Americans saw in them. I persisted until at last today I will walk blocks to get my comics. In Europe and when I first came here I went to see movies of international reputation. Now I am a neighborhood man, and I prefer to see B gangster pictures than the latest examples of cinema art. I know the tension of American life and the underlying tension which give American movies, however superficial, the permanent attraction that they have.

I am familiar enough with what the European intellectuals call culture, which they claim they must preserve against American vulgarity. I know how rotten it is today, a poison that destroys. And I know the petty imitators of things European in literature and politics, as far removed from the lives of people of the United States as the Left Bank in Paris. I have seen and have heard over and over again American intellectuals apologizing for their "Coca-Cola civilization." Though their ancestry may go back for three hundred years, they are greater enemies of the American people than I am.

Every American citizen, ignorant of so many things that his European counterpart knows, is conscious of himself as a distinct personality, in his own opinion and the opinion of his fellows, as entitled to special consideration of his ideas, his feelings, his likes and dislikes as the most aristocratic heroine of a European novel. And at the same time he is consumed by the need of intimate communion with his fellows. This is the crisis of the modern world and because of the material conditions and the history of the United States, that crisis is here, in every personality, in every social institution, permeating every aspect and every phase of life. I watch it every hour of the day, I have spent countless hours studying American history and American literature, relating the present to the past, and estimating the American future. I am profoundly conscious of the deficiencies of American civilization. But they are as nothing to the fact that America is unburdened by the weight of the past which hangs so heavily on Europe, that as a result there is here not culture but a need for human relations of a size and scope which will in the end triumph over all deficiencies.

Year by year I have sought to probe more deeply into the great achievements of Europe, not for personal culture, but to examine and test and weigh and speculate on the future of the United States and by that means to understand Europe and try to explain it to the American people. This book is evidence enough. For three years, I have lectured in New York, in Detroit, in Pittsburgh, in Philadelphia, in San Francisco and Los Angeles, to all types of audiences, workers, intellectuals, church members, whites and Negroes, students, hundreds at a time. Foreigner as I am, it was from me that many of them gained their first enthusiasm and interest in Melville. We argued often but never quarreled. We understood one another. They learned from me and I from them, because my ultimate aim, and my book on Melville is merely a preparation for it, is to write a study of American civilization. I have friends all over the country in very different walks of life.

Fourteen years. Yet the Government attorney stood on tip-toe and handed up a book to the Judge. This, he said, I had written in 1937. This settled it. I was of good moral character; I had no police record of any kind neither here nor anywhere else. I can support myself and my family. But I had written a book in 1937. Here it was. The scene remains in my mind. But there are fortunately in my mind many other scenes, beginning from 1620 and stretching to the present day. This was not what had made the United States. If this had been the mentality of its citizens in the centuries that have passed, the continent would have been a wilderness to this day.

But, I am told, you forget the law, there is the law. Very well, then, let us take the law.

The attorney for my case filed two briefs on June 17th. One of the briefs incorporated the legal points of the American Civil Liberties Union and was signed jointly by my attorney and by the attorney for the A.C.L.U., as friend of the court.

What I am putting down here, the explanations I shall give, will be in layman's language. I am not able to expound the intricacies of the law; I would not wish to even if I could. What I shall show is what the Department of Justice is doing to the alien under the name of law.

The brief my attorney filed demanded my unconditional release on two points:

1. That my association with Trotskyites was not of such a nature as to debar me from citizenship.

2. I had been examined under the Act of 1918 and my examination was concluded on August 16, 1950. The Internal Security (McCarran) Act was passed September 23, 1950, and the Attorney General's decision was handed down October 31, 1950. But my appeal was rejected under the McCarran Act. I had therefore been denied due process of law; the McCarran Act had been applied—he claimed erroneously since I am not a Communist and the Act specifically refers to Communists—in the decision, but could not have figured in the hearings.

After a number of months, June 17th to August 28th, the Judge rendered a decision which upheld my attorney's position on due process. In his decision he instructed the Department of Immigration to hold additional hearings so that I could answer questions posed specifically by the McCarran Act. This was to be done within 60 days. If not, he would sustain the writ of *habeas corpus* and he would order my release.

A business associate and close friend of mine accompanied my attorney to court whenever it was possible. I learned from him that when the Government attorney in charge of my case heard of this decision, he reacted as if the court buildings had themselves collapsed over his head. *The Judge cannot do this,* or *How could he do such a thing?* It was, as will be seen, not a phrase.

The Judge had taken from June 17, 1952 to August 28, 1952 to come to his decision. He obviously thought that he could do what he did, and that it was right to do so. My friends and I believed that it was a

great victory. But some few people experienced in Immigration matters were more sober. Their opinion was: The Immigration Department will never allow the Judge to get away with that. One forecast
was startling enough. The Department could, I was informed, refuse
to give me hearings. The Judge would let me go. I would be rearrested
within a few hours, and then the Department by ways and means of
its own would force the case so fast through the courts that unless the
Supreme Court intervened, this apparently favorable decision would
be for me a catastrophe.

Of all this I naturally understood nothing, knew nothing. But that
men practised in the law could believe that such a thing was possible,
meant to me, layman though I may be, that the Immigration Department was in effect both prosecutor and judge. And not the most
learned lawyer in the world could ever convince anyone that either the
Constitution of the United States or Congress or the law ever intended any such relation. I was further warned that in all probability
there were many cases dealing with Communists to which the same
ruling might apply. And the department would move heaven and
earth to prevent any such precedent being established. The Department did not have to move heaven and earth. The Government attorney applied for a rehearing, and after a number of weeks the Judge reversed himself. The revised opinion, "on reconsideration" was handed
down September 25, 1952.

On October 7th, twelve days afterwards, I was granted bail and
since that time I have felt it a public duty to find out what I could about
the legal prospects of aliens in the District Court at the present time.
This is what I have learned, and it is borne out by what I have heard,
sometimes at first hand during my stay on Ellis Island. In regard to the
treatment and disposition of aliens, the Immigration Department acts
as if it is a master of the Southern District Court. The starting point is,
on the surface, the drive against Communism. In reality it embraces
all aliens. The Immigration Department as good as dictates to the
Judges who shall have bail and who shall not have. Worse that that, I
have heard in Ellis Island of cases where the Judge has said: either deport this man or let him go free within so many days. And the Immigration Department has ignored the Judge's decision. My experiences
on Ellis Island now assumed an importance far greater than appeared
to me at the time. What was taking place behind those walls was taking
place openly in the courts in the light of day.

The President of the United States had appointed a Special Commission to investigate the situation in regard to Immigration. During the campaign he attacked the now President-elect with unusual venom on this issue; and the speed and the manner of the reply showed how sensitive the electors are on this whole issue. I have, however, scrupulously avoided making general charges. Here are specific ones. Let these be investigated.

I am informed that things being as they are, I am a singularly fortunate person to be out on bail at all. The legal skill, adroitness and persistence of my attorney played an important role. Once the Assistant District Attorney had the law interpreted as he wanted it, he not only did not stand in my way, he was courteous and helpful. He could have piled up obstructions. He did not. The same Judge granted bail within the State of New York. My case has been appealed to the Court of Appeals where it will come up in due course. Only a rigorous investigation will establish how many unfortunates there are who have in the past suffered, and who, destitute of any opportunity to defend themselves, will in the future suffer unwarranted penalties.

The second point in my case, presented jointly by my attorney and the American Civil Liberties Union, is as follows. It attacked the constitutionality of the proceedings against me as being violations of the First and Fifth Amendments. As I understand it, the Constitution of the United States forbids the limitation of the free speech and free expression of opinion of any person in the United States. It specifically does not say citizen: it says person, meaning anybody. As I have always understood it, if an individual, citizen or alien, commits some action, breaks the law, then a Government is entitled to proceed against him, but not for what he says. That is what I have always understood by freedom of speech. I shall not change my opinion.

I have now to add further experiences which have been as startling to me as those I have related.

Though I know a certain number of working people, I, being what I am, my acquaintances in the United States have been chiefly among radical intellectuals and liberals. I met or heard of many of these people in 1938. Fourteen years have passed. It is as if they have been stricken by the plague. They are today, as a body, the loudest shouters for the war against Communism in defense of democracy. I can now testify that many of them no more believe in democracy than the Communists do. The Communists have immeasurably exposed themselves by being openly and brazenly opposed to civil liberties for people of other political persuasions than their own. As a body, these ex-radicals are exactly the same. Naturally in a case like mine you seek assistance. There has been a response, on the whole a very heart-warming response. But the sad truth is that where it does not come from personal friends, it comes chiefly from old-fashioned American liberals. Some of them are men who can guess at my past, or know it, merely from the list of the books I have written. Some are scholars interested in my ideas. Many are deeply concerned about the United States, its past traditions, and the appearance it makes to a stranger and to the world.

But the ex-radicals behave exactly like the Communists. Some of them are sympathetic but do not wish to be involved. Others wish to set up a little G.P.U. or Gestapo of their own. One man wanted to examine me personally. I gathered what his questions were to be: What did I think of this? Did I still believe in that? What was my attitude to the other? If my answers were satisfactory, then he would exert himself on my behalf.

It is an unspeakable degradation, in which I shall not play even the humble role assigned to me. Above the correspondence in the *Herald-Tribune* is printed Voltaire's famous statement: "I wholly disapprove of what you say and I shall defend to the death your right to say it." In years past I have smiled indulgently at the grandiloquent statements and illusions of these old liberals. But recently in the light of modern events I have been re-reading some of them and the conditions against which they struggled to establish the principles by which only a few years ago we thought we lived. Today it is not their limitations I am conscious of, but rather the enormous service they did to civilization, as decade after decade they struggled for the right of *habeas corpus*, freedom of assembly, freedom of speech, went to jail for them, died for them.

I say here and now that as soon as the opportunity presents itself, whether I am still on trial, in detention or out on bail, out of the United States, in the United States, with first papers, second papers or what not, I shall write my views of American civilization. I shall also give an accurate and detailed account of my political ideas, what they were, how and when they changed, and what they are today. I shall give also an account of my political activities, in detail, what I see in the future, what if I can I shall do in the future. The Immigration

Department and the F.B.I. will have their copies as soon as possible after publication. I believe the time has come for me to do so. But never shall I submit myself to any inquisition and grovel in the dirt, as the price for bail or for assistance or for citizenship, or for anything at all. That would be to make freedom of speech and freedom of opinion a mockery. I will have no part in it and will live in the desert first.

Judge Learned Hand, as recently as Oct. 24, declared in public,

> "I believe that that community is already in the process of dissolution where each man begins to eye his neighbor as a possible enemy, where nonconformity with the accepted creed, political as well as religious, is a mark of disaffection; where denunciation, without specification or backing, takes the place of evidence; where orthodoxy chokes freedom of dissent; where faith in the eventual supremacy of reason has become so timid that we dare not enter our convictions in the open lists to win or lose."

He went on to say that the fears which he had cited were "a solvent which can eat out the cement that binds the stones together" and that they might in the end "subject us to a despotism as evil as any that we dread."

> "The mutual confidence on which all else depends can be maintained only by an open mind and a brave reliance upon free discussion. I do not say that these will suffice; who knows but we may be on a slope which leads down to aboriginal slavery. But of this I am sure; if we are to escape, we must not yield a foot upon demanding a fair field, and an honest race, to all ideas."

These are eloquent words, and I am informed that the distinguished jurist has demonstrated in the past that for him they are no mere words.

But the Judge went on to say that "the powers of the courts are too limited to reach the more controversial questions that arise under them."

With all due respect I have to say that I believe I have given sufficient evidence here to show the grave injustices which are being perpetrated in the name of the law, and that it is inconceivable to me, and, I am positive, to the great majority of American citizens, that the laws of the United States prevent the judiciary from putting an end to them.

I have only a few more things to say.

First. It is my good fortune that I am not a displaced person. I wish to be a citizen of the United States. The Immigration Department itself has agreed that my citizen wife and citizen child will suffer grave economic hardship if I am deported. But I am not begging for charity. It would appear that in the eyes of some only two types of persons are today suitable for citizenship: millionaires and others who come on their knees thanking God and all in sight that they have been fortunate enough to be admitted to a place where bombs may not fall and meat is not rationed. I belong to neither class. I esteem citizenship as a privilege. But I also esteem myself as a person fit and proper to be a citizen and a citizen who would be of some value to his fellow-citizens.

Finally, I have to make here some public acknowledgements. First to my attorney. I am profoundly grateful for the labor and ability he has given to my case. The money that I was able to pay him was quite inadequate for the services he has rendered. But the slightest reflection will show that I could not consult him on the publication of this protest. It was done and had to be done, without his knowledge. When I went into Ellis Island, such a publication as this never crossed my mind. I was busy negotiating with publishers for normal publication. Even when I felt I had to prepare myself for the worst and had letters written abroad to influential friends in Africa, in London, in France and in the West Indies, I stipulated that it was only information so that they could be ready to act if I were driven to the last extremity. But by degrees I came to the conclusion that I would never be able to recover from the shame and disgrace if I let all this pass without saying a word, or waited until my case was decided before speaking. Some time or other someone had to speak and not some philanthropist, but someone who was involved. I publish the protest with the book on Melville because as I have shown, the book as written is a part of my experience. It is also a claim before the American people, the best claim I can put forward, that my desire to be a citizen is not a selfish nor a frivolous one.

I am informed that the Court of Appeals is a very powerful court and interprets the law as it sees it, irrespective of any Immigration Department. I am equally informed by experts that between the Immigration Department and the F.B.I., I shall now be ground to pieces. There is also the infinite capacity of the Communist Party for relentless and totally unscrupulous persecution of its enemies. Things will take their course. What has happened or may happen to me has happened before and to others who have far greater claim to public consideration than I have. I rest my case with the public. An appeal has been sent out for funds to help my case in the courts. It was specifically stated that this appeal would be closed on December 31st. Not a penny collected by that means goes to the publication of this book, the money for which has been advanced by people who respect all humans beings, citizens or aliens, who are proud of their country's great traditions and are ready to make great sacrifices to maintain them. All that is asked is that those who feel the same should buy copies of the book at a dollar a copy. They can get them singly or in any number that they wish by writing to C. L. R. James, 1186 Broadway, New York 1, New York. I hope by this means to repay the money spent on publication, to meet the perils of the future, and at the same time to advance both the understanding of literature and the cause of freedom. Whatever the outcome, I shall always look upon this as having been not a burden but a privilege.

Notes

In case any non-literary reader of this book should wish to make a study of Melville instead of merely reading him. I would recommend two books:

Herman Melville, by Leon Howard, University of California Press, 1952;

Melville Log, by Jay Leyda, Harcourt, Brace & Co., 1951.

These books are works of solid scholarship, worthy of the author they deal with.

A very interesting book which explains a great deal that is confusing and obscure in Melville is *Melville's Quarrel with God* by Lawrance R. Thompson, Princeton University Press, 1952.

The best edition of *Moby-Dick* and of *Pierre* is published by Hendricks House.

APPENDIX

Dedication to the 1978 edition

FOR MY SON NOB.

"There is something in the contemplation of the mode in which America has been settled, that, in a noble breast, should forever extinguish the prejudices of national dislikes.

"Settled by the people of all nations, all nations may claim her for their own. You can not spill a drop of American blood without spilling the blood of the whole world. Be he Englishman, Frenchman, German, Dane, or Scot; the European who scoffs at an American, calls his own brother *Raca,* and stands in danger of the judgment. We are not a narrow tribe of men. . . . No: our blood is as the flood of the Amazon, made up of a thousand noble currents all pouring into one. We are not a nation, so much as a world. . . .

—MELVILLE, in *Redburn*

"Those whom books will hurt will not be proof against events. Events, not books, should be forbid."

—MELVILLE, in *Las Encantadas*

Afterword to the 1978 edition

AFTERWORD

Mariners, Renegades and Castaways was published in 1953. It is now a quarter of a century that I saw the importance, as a modern historical type, of Captain Ahab in Melville's *Moby Dick* and the attendant personalities. The world in 1978 cannot be what it was in 1953. During the last 25 years, what I have learned is what De Tocqueville saw before the Civil War and the Emancipation of the Serfs, that the irreparable conflict in the coming world was between America and Russia. Now since 1953 the European artists, critics, and social thinkers (I mention two—Sir Isaiah Berlin, V. S. Pritchett) all have concentrated on Turgenev as the decisive figure in Russian literature. What is important to them about Turgenev is that between the revolution and counter-revolution, both apparently inescapable, he held to the middle of the road, the road to which the European intellectuals of today are holding on by teeth and nails. Yet in those 25 years two things have become increasingly clear. Beginning with Pushkin, the Russian men of talent and genius, excluded from the dominant Tsarism, landowners and clergy, have been far and away the most farseeing interpreters of the road that all Russia was going to take, and not only Russia but the whole world.

The highest pitch that they reached from 1789 (which educated Pushkin, the greatest of them all) was Lenin in 1917. But by the 20th Party Congress in 1956 they had glimpsed a depth far lower than Ahab. They had attempted to repudiate Stalinism (20 million souls) and by now Stalinism has received a literary embodiment, which, beyond conception in past ages, is at present unsurpassable: *The Gulag Archipelago* of Solzhenitsyn.

The outstanding fact, however, of the 19th century is that Melville in *Moby Dick* saw more clearly than even Dostoevsky in *The Possessed* what the future of capitalism was going to be. But what Dostoevsky did not see was the creative power of the popular mass which Melville saw and portrayed in *Moby Dick* (see pages [17–20] above).

In my view, it is as idle to keep on preaching of the virtues of Turgenev as it is to point out the religious fantasies of Solzhenitsyn. In 1978 we can point to the artistic vision of the future in Melville's *Moby Dick* (page [89] above) and its actual reality in Solzhenitsyn, *The Gulag Archipelago*. I, for one, after the last quarter of a century, look forward with confidence to the next quarter of a century and the year 2000. Today at least we *know*.

May 1978   C. L. R. JAMES

Dedication, Introduction, and Preface
to the 1985 edition

FOR MY SON NOB

In all recorded history men have exploited, persecuted, ignored and mistreated the women in their society. Somewhere in his early writings Marx stated, and truly, that women are the most exploited section of society: which is evidence enough, since he spent his lifetime exposing the exploitation and degradation of the proletariat.

That is why, in anticipation of what I hope to write and publish, I here record the following names—

Juanita
Gloria
Constance
Martina
Wilma
Judy
Renée

—who showed me the immense possibilities that American civilization has created in friendship, affections, the race question, family and all aspects of life and relationships in that huge society.

This is not an apology. I merely state my regrets—the result of my ignorance and public miseducation. I hope to have left that behind for the future.

INTRODUCTION

The miracle of Herman Melville is this: that a hundred years ago in two novels, *Moby Dick* and *Pierre,* and two or three stories, he painted a picture of the world in which we live, which is to this day unsurpassed.

The totalitarian madness which swept the world first as Nazism and now as Soviet Communism; the great mass labour movements and colonial revolts, intellectuals drowning in the incestuous dreams of psychoanalysis—this is the world the masses of men strive to make sense of. This is what Melville coordinates—but not as industry, science, politics, economics or psychology, but as a world of human personalities, living as the vast majority of human beings live, not by ideas but by their emotions, seeking to avoid pain and misery and struggling for happiness.

In the course of lecturing upon Melville in many parts of the United States, I have discovered that, once the veil of bookishness is torn away, his characters are instantly recognizable by us who have lived through the last twenty years and particularly the last ten.

I have written all that I wanted to write. Yet the book has been written in such a way that a reader can read it from beginning to end and understand it without having read a single page of Melville's books. I believe that this is the spirit of what Melville had to say.

A great part of this book was written on Ellis Island while I was being detained by the Department of Immigration. The Island, like Melville's *Pequod,* is a miniature of all the nations of the world and all sections of society. My experience of it and the circumstances attending my stay there have so deepened my understanding of Melville, and so profoundly influenced the form the book has taken, that an account of this has seemed to me not only a natural but necessary conclusion. This is to be found in Chapter VII.

28 November 1952   C. L. R. J.

PREFACE

Our greatest artists record the world in which people live—the Greek tragedians; Moses; Michelangelo, Leonardo da Vinci and Raphael ("The Transfiguration"); Shakespeare and Puskin; Dostoevsky and Tolstoy. Their gloom is never total. Small or large, areas of light are authentic. In those areas I do not stumble; my darkness is always en-lightened. Except in the case of Melville.

After many years of silence, Melville wrote a brief novel, *Billy Budd* (1924). Billy is a Jesus—he suffers and turns cheeks for future blows. He is absent from this study not because he is forgotten but because he is rejected. It is many years since I found myself unable to fit an author's gleams of light into his prevailing gloom. *Billy Budd* has not helped that deficiency and I remain unable to incorporate it into the lush pastures made by Melville in the arid prairies of the United States.

1984   C. L. R. J.